I0820142

STORM
AT THE
CAPITOL

STORM AT THE CAPITOL

AN ORAL HISTORY OF JANUARY 6TH

MARY CLARE JALONICK

NEW YORK

PublicAffairs
Hachette Book Group
1290 Avenue of the Americas, New York, NY 10104
www.publicaffairsbooks.com
@Public_Affairs

Printed in Canada

First Edition: January 2026

Published by PublicAffairs, an imprint of Hachette Book Group, Inc. The PublicAffairs name and logo is a registered trademark of the Hachette Book Group.

Library of Congress Cataloging-in-Publication Data

Names: Jalonick, Mary Clare author
Title: Storm at the Capitol : an oral history of January 6th / Mary Clare Jalonick.
Description: First edition. | New York : PublicAffairs, 2026. | Includes bibliographical references and index.
Identifiers: LCCN 2025020477 (print) | LCCN 2025020478 (ebook) | ISBN 9781541705982 hardcover | ISBN 9781541706002 ebook
Subjects: LCSH: Capitol Riot, Washington, D.C., 2021 | Presidents—United States—Election—2020 | Political violence—Washington (D.C.) | Domestic terrorism—Washington (D.C.) | Democracy—United States
Classification: LCC E915 .J35 2026 (print) | LCC E915 (ebook)
LC record available at https://lccn.loc.gov/2025020477
LC ebook record available at https://lccn.loc.gov/2025020478

ISBNs: 9781541705982 (hardcover), 9781541706002 (ebook)

MRQ-T

10 9 8 7 6 5 4 3 2 1

To my family, and to the police
who protected us on January 6, 2021

Nothing will stop us. . . . They can try and try and try but the storm is here and it is descending upon DC in less than 24 hours . . . dark to light!

—January 5, 2021, Twitter post on the account of Ashli Babbitt,
a California pool company owner and QAnon follower headed to
Washington to protest President Donald Trump's election loss

CONTENTS

JANUARY 7, 2021

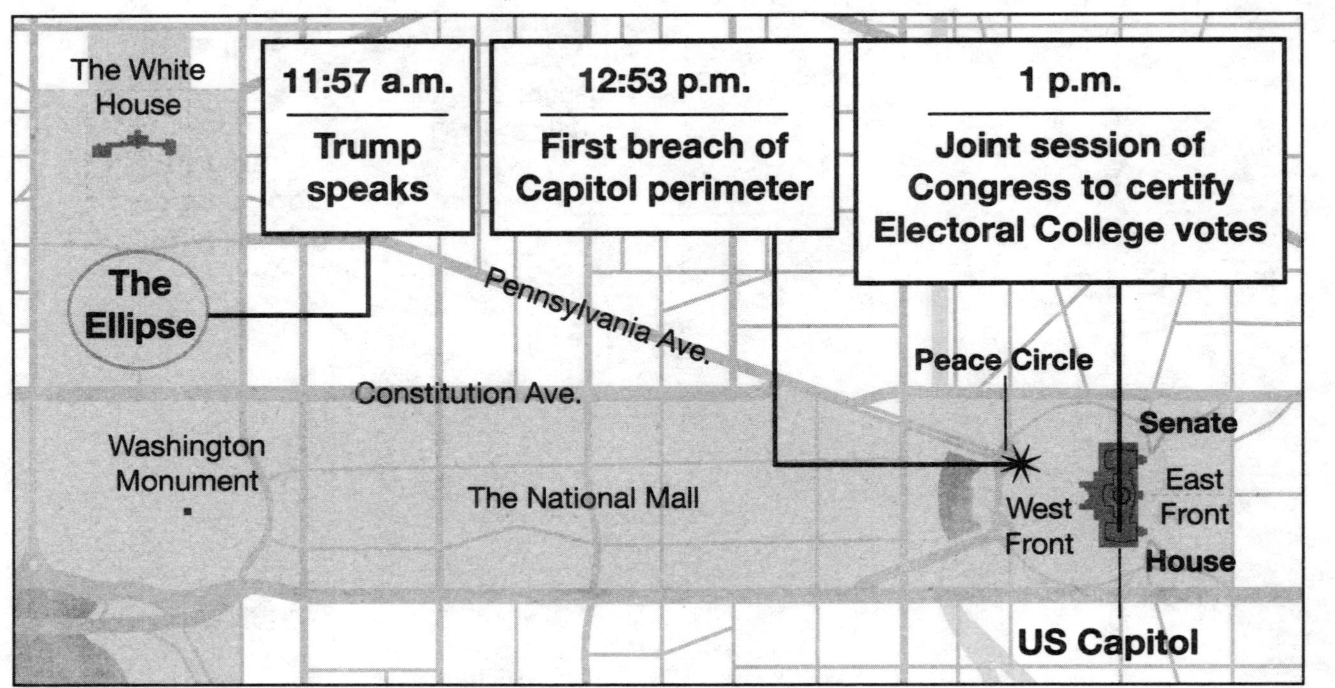

SOURCE: Associated Press

CREDIT: CLO Communications LLC

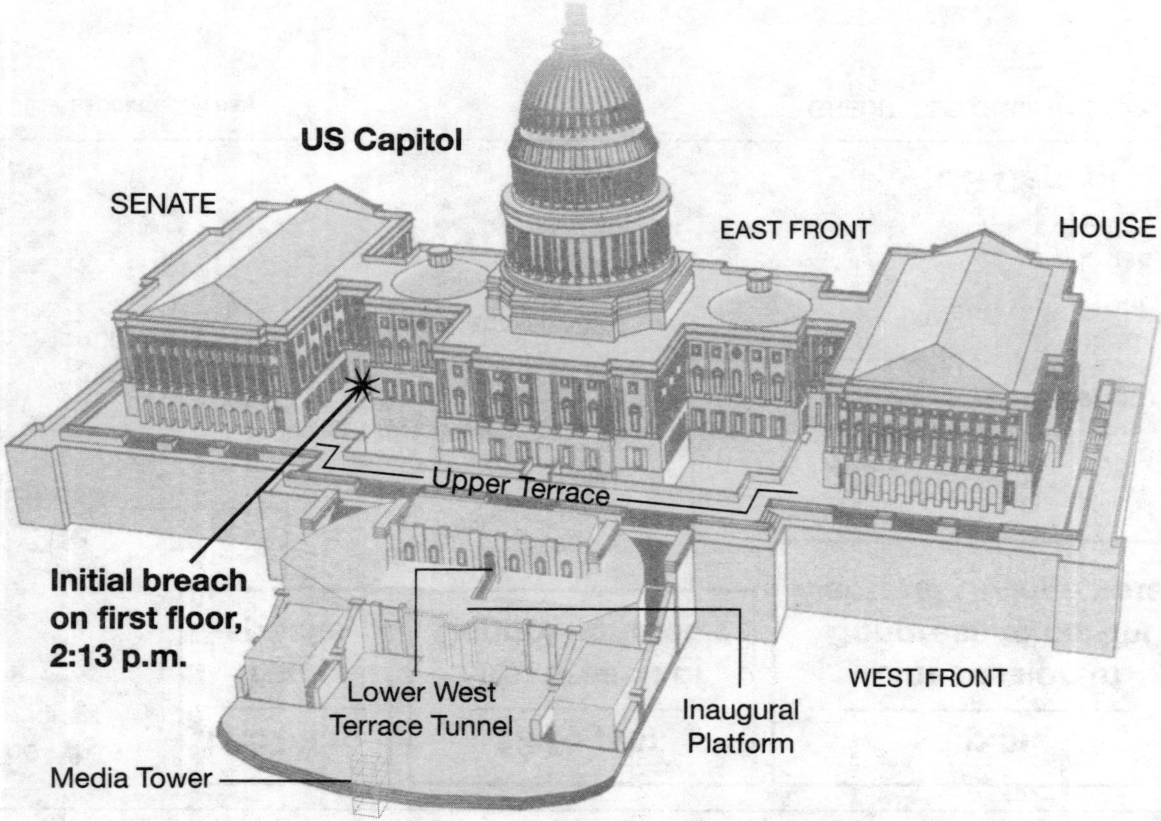

US Capitol

SENATE

EAST FRONT

HOUSE

Upper Terrace

Initial breach on first floor, 2:13 p.m.

Lower West Terrace Tunnel

Inaugural Platform

WEST FRONT

Media Tower

SOURCE: Associated Press

CREDIT: CLO Communications LLC

Interior of US Capitol

2ND FLOOR

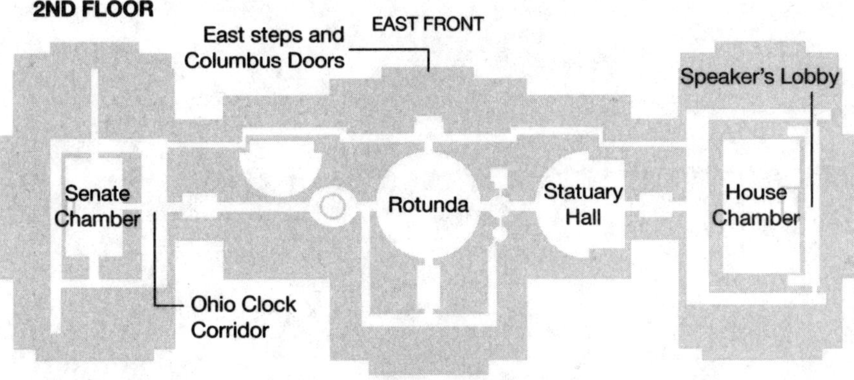

1ST FLOOR

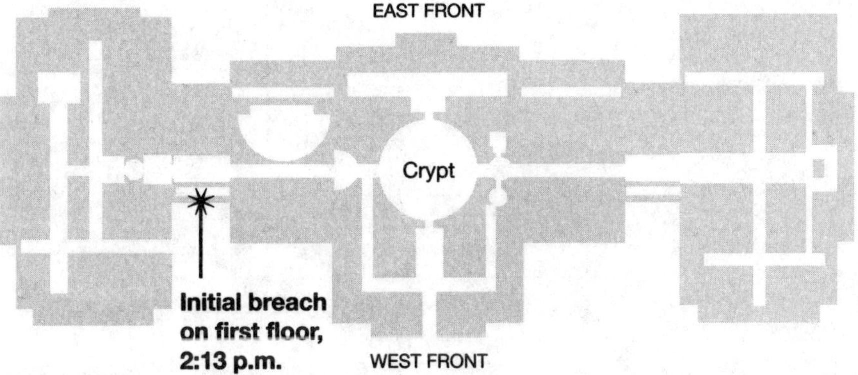

SOURCES: Associated Press; US Government Publishing Office

CREDIT: CLO Communications LLC

TIMELINE

JANUARY 6, 2021

8:17 a.m.

On Twitter, President Donald Trump urges Vice President Mike Pence to try to overturn his presidential defeat when he presides over the congressional session to count electoral votes later that day: "Do it Mike, this is a time for extreme courage!"

11:57 a.m.

Trump begins his speech to thousands of assembled supporters on the Ellipse in front of the White House. He encourages the crowd to walk to the Capitol and says he will go with them.

12:30 p.m.

As Trump is still speaking, US Capitol Police track a "very large group" headed down Pennsylvania Avenue, seven blocks from the Capitol.

12:36 p.m.

Vice President Mike Pence arrives at the Capitol to preside over the joint session of Congress.

12:45 p.m.

A Metropolitan Police Department camera captures a "wall of people" one block from the Capitol.

12:45 p.m.

Pence releases a statement making clear that he will not follow Trump's wishes and challenge the electoral count.

12:53 p.m.

Protesters arrive at the Capitol and quickly breach weak police barricades at the West Front.

12:56 p.m.

US Senate, including Pence, begins to walk across the Capitol for the 1 p.m. joint session to count electoral votes and certify Democrat Joe Biden's presidency.

12:58 p.m.

Capitol Police Chief Steven Sund requests assistance from the Metropolitan Police Department as protesters overwhelm Capitol Police and quickly advance toward the building.

12:59 p.m.

Senators reach the doors of the House and enter the joint session.

1:00 p.m.

Pence gavels in the joint session.

1:06 p.m.

Capitol Police Civil Disturbance Unit is directed to deploy chemical munitions against protesters.

1:10 p.m.

Trump finishes his speech, and a new wave of protesters heads toward the Capitol.

1:10 p.m.

Metropolitan Police Department officers arrive at the West Front of the Capitol.

1:12 p.m.

Rep. Paul Gosar, R-AZ, and Sen. Ted Cruz, R-TX, object to Arizona's electoral votes, triggering votes in both chambers. Senators walk back across the Capitol for up to two hours of debate.

1:45 p.m.

Protesters breach barricades on the plaza of the East Front of the Capitol.

1:48 p.m.

Protesters breach the upper terrace on the West Front immediately adjacent to the Capitol building.

1:49 p.m.

The Metropolitan Police Department declares a riot at the US Capitol.

2:00 p.m.

Assistant Capitol Police Chief Yogananda Pittman orders a lockdown of the Capitol building.

2:11 p.m.

US Secret Service removes Vice President Mike Pence from the Senate floor.

2:13 p.m.

The Capitol building is breached when rioters break in on the first floor of the Senate.

2:13 p.m.

Senate President Pro Tempore Chuck Grassley, R-IA, recesses the Senate. Grassley, third in line to the presidency, is evacuated.

2:15 p.m.

House Speaker Nancy Pelosi, second in line to the presidency, is pulled off the House rostrum and evacuated.

2:15 p.m.

Rioters reach the second floor of the Senate side of the Capitol, immediately outside the chamber. Senators are still inside.

2:18 p.m.

The House pauses debate on Arizona's electoral votes.

2:24 p.m.

Rioters break through the Columbus doorway on the east side of the Capitol.

2:24 p.m.

Trump tweets that Mike Pence did not have the "courage" to try to send electoral votes back to the states.

2:26 p.m.

US Secret Service evacuates Pence from a room off the Senate chamber to a secure location.

2:26 p.m.

Capitol Police Chief Steven Sund, Metropolitan Police Chief Robert Contee, and others plead for National Guard support in a conference call with the Pentagon. Pentagon officials do not immediately agree to send help.

2:26 p.m.

The House gavels back into session and restarts debate over Arizona's electoral votes.

2:28 p.m.

Rioters break through another line of Capitol Police and Metropolitan Police Department officers on the West Front, allowing them to take over the inauguration stage.

2:28 p.m.

The Senate chamber is evacuated. Senators are led to a secure location within the Capitol complex.

2:29 p.m.

A live pool camera shows people streaming through Statuary Hall and heading toward the House chamber. Rioters begin to gather outside the main House doorway and push past a small line of police trying to protect the members inside.

2:29 p.m.

The House recesses again.

2:31 p.m.

District of Columbia Mayor Muriel Bowser issues a citywide curfew for 6 p.m.

2:37 p.m.

Rioters surround the House chamber in multiple hallways and are now beating on the main doors. Lawmakers and police use furniture to barricade the door from the inside.

2:38 p.m.

Trump tweets, "Please support our Capitol Police and Law Enforcement. They are truly on the side of our Country. Stay peaceful!" He does not ask the rioters to leave.

2:39 p.m.

The House floor is evacuated, and a majority of members are led to a secure location. Several dozen members, staff, and reporters are still trapped in the third-floor gallery.

2:41 p.m.

Outside on the West Plaza, rioters surge toward the inaugural tunnel on the Lower West Terrace after police officers retreat inside.

2:44 p.m.

Ashli Babbitt, a pool company owner from California, is fatally shot by a Capitol Police lieutenant as she tries to enter an area immediately outside the House chamber.

2:48 p.m.

Members, staff, and reporters remain trapped in the upper gallery as rioters have breached the third-floor hallway just outside the locked doors.

2:50 p.m.

Rioters breach the empty Senate chamber.

2:51 p.m.

Rioters jammed in the Lower West Terrace Tunnel engage in a brutal fight with the police officers guarding the door. The brawl will last for more than two hours.

2:57 p.m.

The House upper gallery is fully evacuated after police detain rioters and hold them down at gunpoint in the hallway just outside.

3:13 p.m.

Trump tweets, "I am asking for everyone at the U.S. Capitol to remain peaceful. No violence! Remember, WE are the Party of Law & Order—respect the Law and our great men and women in Blue. Thank you!" He does not ask the rioters to leave.

3:32 p.m.

Police clear rioters from the Senate floor, Rotunda, and most of the House side of the Capitol.

3:44 p.m.

Congressional leaders in a secure location hold a call with the Secretary of the Army, again pleading for National Guard support.

4:08 p.m.

Vice President Pence calls the Pentagon and orders military officials to "Clear the Capitol!"

4:17 p.m.

Trump posts a video asking his supporters to leave the Capitol for the first time.

4:52 p.m.

Acting Defense Secretary Christopher Miller issues a statement that the National Guard is "fully activated" to assist at the Capitol.

4:59 p.m.

Police sweep rioters off the East Front stairway and away from the building.

5:04 p.m.

Police deploy smoke bombs and rioters begin to retreat from the Lower West Terrace Tunnel.

5:20 p.m.

The National Guard arrives to assist with clearing the Capitol complex.

6:01 p.m.

Trump tweets that "these are the things and events that happen" when an election "is so unceremoniously & viciously stripped away from great patriots who have been badly & unfairly treated for so long." He tells the rioters to go home and "remember this day forever."

6:28 p.m.

House Speaker Nancy Pelosi announces that the joint session will resume.

8:06 p.m.

The Senate returns to session.

8:31 p.m.

After having swept the entire West Front, the Capitol Police declare it clear.

9:02 p.m.

The House returns to session.

10:12 p.m.

The Senate rejects the objection to Arizona's electoral ballots, 93–6.

11:08 p.m.

The House rejects the objection to Arizona's electoral votes, 303–121.

11:35 p.m.

The Senate returns to the House to resume the joint session. The counting of electoral votes continues.

JANUARY 7, 2021

12:14 a.m.

Sen. Josh Hawley, R-MO, joins House members in objecting to Pennsylvania's electoral votes, triggering debate and votes in each chamber for a second time. Senators agree to skip debate and immediately vote. House Republicans insist on holding debate.

12:44 a.m.

The Senate rejects the objection to Pennsylvania's electoral votes, 92–7.

3:11 a.m.

The House rejects the Pennsylvania objection, 282–138.

3:48 a.m.

The joint session adjourns after Pence announces that they have counted the electoral votes and Democrats Joe Biden and Kamala Harris have won the election.

AUTHOR'S NOTE

I began reporting this oral history in the moments just after the January 6, 2021, attack on the Capitol began. I conducted my first interviews while I was evacuating from the gallery of the House after crouching on the floor for safety, with rioters just outside the doors. "We've known for four years that our democracy was in peril, and this is hopefully the worst and final moment of it," Connecticut Rep. Jim Himes, a Democrat, told me as we rushed through a basement hallway to a secure location.

In the years since, as a congressional reporter for The Associated Press, I have collected stories from lawmakers, police, reporters, and staff. When I am interviewing someone in the Capitol, no matter the topic, I often ask about their January 6th experience. Many lawmakers, especially Republicans who have backed President Donald Trump, will not go on the record, though some have. But they all have a story, and once they start talking, it is often hard for them to stop. It was a traumatic event for everyone involved, whether they acknowledge it publicly or not.

Of course, January 6th was especially traumatic for the hundreds of officers who defended the building and narrowly held off a much worse outcome. Around 140 were injured, but as one officer noted in an interview, the real number of injuries was likely much higher than that, and many of them simply returned to work without complaint. Others were so seriously injured that they never returned to work at all.

I have collected the stories of some of the rioters as well, from court transcripts, FBI interviews that have been made public, official testimony, and personal interviews. Their stories sometimes defy stereotypes, and several of them have discussed falling down the social media rabbit hole of lies about a stolen election. Others have argued, in court and elsewhere, that the violence against law enforcement was justified or portrayed themselves as the victims of police brutality. Some regret their actions and some do not. Some walked into the building and left, while others destroyed property and beat police officers with American flags. Almost all of them were pardoned by Trump when he returned to office on January 20, 2025.

Quotes in the book have been edited and condensed for clarity, and the titles used for the speakers are as they were on January 6, 2021—Nancy Pelosi is identified as the House speaker, for example, even though she left that job in 2023.

Some of the protesters and rioters have voiced falsehoods regarding the 2020 election, and their perspective at the time is an important part of understanding what happened that day. I am letting their comments stand as part of the narrative. But throughout the book, I present the facts. And to be very clear, the facts are these: The election was not stolen. It was certified by election officials from both parties in all fifty states. Courts ruled against Trump or dismissed dozens of lawsuits brought by his campaign challenging the results. Trump's own attorney general, William Barr, said there was no evidence of widespread voter fraud that could have altered the results in the states that Biden narrowly won, or in any state. Joe Biden won the 2020 election, just as Trump won in 2016 and 2024.

As with any oral history, the recollections in this book are personal memories, which can occasionally be imprecise. With this story in particular, perspectives may have shifted—some of the rioters have altered their stories over time, either expressing insincere regret in court or eventually realizing that what they did was wrong. Others may have been emboldened by their pardons.

In many cases, multiple people will describe the same situation differently—one rioter describes "picnics" outside the Capitol that afternoon, for example, while others describe a violent scene. Those discrepancies illustrate the ways in which the recollections of the attack have been warped and whitewashed over time.

And while almost every lawmaker condemned the violence and shared their experiences immediately after the attack, a number of those same people are now downplaying it or falsely portraying it as peaceful. For full transparency, I have included the dates of the interviews and testimony in the endnotes.

Some stories are missing from these pages. Many first responders have been reluctant to speak out about their January 6th experiences, partly because of the many threats directed toward those who have. Workers and police officers who are still employed in the Capitol are discouraged, and in most cases prevented, from speaking publicly about that day by their supervisors, who have to answer to Republican leaders loyal to Donald Trump. Luckily, many Capitol Police officers have testified in court or shared their stories after leaving the department.

In the last five years, the significance of January 6th has been fiercely debated, but that does not change the facts of what happened or the real experiences of people who were there. The aim of putting these voices down on paper is to tell the story in the words of the people who lived it. The accounts here are slices of the day that, taken together, capture a dark moment in American history.

My own personal story on January 6th is not extraordinary compared to the stories of the first responders who risked their lives to defend the building, the lawmakers who were determined to return to the Capitol to certify the vote, or even the rioters whose lives were upended by their decisions to join the mob. But it has stuck with me nonetheless and become a major part of my work life as I have covered the aftermath for the last five years. There isn't a day that goes by in the Capitol that I don't look around and remember some detail.

My first indication that January 6, 2021, would not be a normal day was on my commute to work, driving down Independence Avenue along the National Mall. The streets had been empty for months because of the pandemic, but on this gray winter morning they were packed with Trump supporters headed toward the Ellipse, a park in front of the White House where the president would later be speaking. I was taken aback by how many people there were—some who appeared to be normal protesters, others wearing fatigues, many with signs—and I snapped photos of them out my car window. It was peaceful, but the massive crowds were the first sign that I had not fully grasped what this day might have in store.

We had heard about the possibility of violence, and a House aide had forwarded me a warning from security officials to take precautions. But protests, threats, and warnings are routine on Capitol Hill, and we were used to ignoring them because they rarely came to fruition. The Capitol Police had always kept us safe.

Plus, I wanted to be at the joint session. I had covered it in previous years, but we all knew this one would be different. However the drama played out, it would be historic. In an effort to overturn his defeat, Trump had been publicly urging Vice President Mike Pence to somehow object to or delay the congressional certification of Joe Biden's victory—even though Pence had only a ceremonial role and no legal pathway to do so. No one knew what Pence would decide, and all of Washington was on edge.

I realize now that I'd had a false sense of security for years. In the summer of 2004, just three years after 9/11, I was a young reporter working in a Senate press gallery when alarms started to blare. I marveled at how quickly the Capitol Police emptied the building, yelling at us to take off our shoes and run. "There is a plane headed for the Capitol! You have two minutes!" they yelled as we rushed out the doors. As I ran down the east steps of the Senate, I was shoved aside by security officials hauling then–Majority Leader Bill Frist out of the building. It was, of course, a false alarm, triggered by a plane that had accidentally traveled out of its airspace. Since then, though, I'd had faith that similar security procedures would always be in place.

On January 6, 2021, I parked in my regular spot outside the Capitol and met my husband, George, who was at the time a congressional reporter for E&E News, an environmental news service owned by Politico. He was also covering the joint session, and we were both planning to be in the House press gallery that day. He had driven separately, but we walked into the building together, passing hundreds more protesters who were already there, hours ahead of the 1 p.m. joint session. They held signs that said, "Stop the Steal" and "Make the Bastards Pay." A flag read, "Fuck Joe Biden." I took more photos, typed up a quick news feed to send to my colleagues about the scene outside, and walked into the building.

Hours later, just before the insurgents started to make enough noise that we could hear them through the thick Capitol walls, my mother would send me a text: "Stay safe." I would text her back that I was inside the House chamber. "Probably the safest place in Washington right now," I wrote.

PROLOGUE

"Congress Itself Is the Target"

At 7:37 p.m. on January 5, 2021, the day before Congress was to convene a joint session to certify Joe Biden's presidency, an intelligence analyst with the FBI's Washington field office sent an email to law enforcement partners in the area, including the Capitol Police, Metropolitan Police Department, and US Park Police. The innocuity of the message belied the explosive content of the attachment, reading only "Please see the attached SIR released this evening by Norfolk for awareness."[1]

If any of the intended recipients had read the so-called situational information report (SIR) for the joint session of Congress the next day—and many of them had not—they would have seen an ominous excerpt from an unidentified online discussion that the Norfolk, Virginia, field office had considered of great enough concern to escalate:

> Be ready to fight. Congress needs to hear glass breaking, doors being kicked in, and blood from their [Black Lives Matter] and Pantifa slave soldiers being spilled. Get violent. Stop calling this a march, or rally, or a protest. Go there ready for war. We get our President or we die. NOTHING else will achieve this goal.[2]

A Capitol Police analyst who opened the email forwarded it to his supervisor, or maybe to the force's Intelligence Operations Section—accounts afterward differed. But one thing was certain: It never reached Capitol Police Chief Steven Sund.[3]

The warning of "war" from supporters of President Donald Trump was far from the only indication of possible violence surrounding the January 6th certification. Trump had been signaling throughout 2020 that he wouldn't accept the election results if he were defeated. "The only way they're going to win is by a rigged election," he said of Democrats at a rally in August. He made similar remarks many more times leading up to November and then predictably challenged the results when he lost.[4]

On December 14, the day of the Electoral College vote, Oath Keepers founder Stewart Rhodes published an open letter to Trump on the organization's website, encouraging him to invoke the Insurrection Act and call up the military to block Biden's presidency. "If you fail to act while you are still in office, we, the people, will have to fight a bloody Civil War and revolution against these two illegitimate communist China puppets and their illegitimate regime," Rhodes wrote of Biden and Vice President–elect Kamala Harris.[5]

Five days later, in a December 19 tweet, Trump predicted that the day of the certification "will be wild!" and called on his supporters to attend a rally in front of the White House on the 6th.[6] Many of Trump's backers, including some in far-right extremist groups, saw the tweet as a call to action. Online forums of devotees to Trump were overflowing with plans to travel to the nation's capital at the behest of the president, full of bombastic language and threats against lawmakers. A week before January 6th, the Capitol Police received an email pointing to "countless tweets from Trump supporters saying they will be armed on January 6th" and "tweets from people organizing to 'storm the Capitol.'"[7]

By calling his supporters to Washington, Trump and his allies were making one final attempt in a stunning monthslong effort to overturn his November defeat. Courts had rejected dozens of his lawsuits, Republican state legislatures had declined to invalidate results despite pressure, and top Department of Justice officials, including Attorney General William Barr, had pushed back against Trump's demands for intervention.[8] Bipartisan election officials in all fifty states had approved their state results, and the Electoral College had officially confirmed Biden the winner on December 14.[9] Republicans in Congress had talked vaguely of "concerns" and "questions" about the vote, but none had contested their own election on the same ballots.

In the final push, Trump's aides and lawyers were now strategizing with a small group of House Republicans on how they might use congressional procedure to try to thwart Biden's victory on the House floor during the January 6th certification, the final election ritual of the season when Congress rubber-stamps the November election results.[10]

The certification of the presidential election is a routine and often celebratory affair. Under federal law, Congress meets in a joint session and opens sealed certificates containing the electoral votes from each state on the sixth day of January after a presidential election. The sitting vice president presides, and a bipartisan group of four lawmakers—"tellers"—announces each state's votes. Members of Congress have an opportunity to object, and a signed objection to a state's results from one House member and one senator triggers up to two hours of debate and a vote in each chamber. (Congress has since changed the law, and one-fifth of each chamber must now object to prompt votes.) If a majority of the House and a majority of the Senate each votes to support the objection, then the votes from that state are not counted. No objection to a state's electors has been sustained by both chambers since the Electoral Count Act was enacted in 1887.[11]

House Republicans loyal to Trump had already promised to formally object to the results in several swing states where Biden had narrowly won, including Arizona, Georgia, Michigan, Nevada, Pennsylvania, and Wisconsin. Democrats had made similar objections after the 2004[12] and 2016[13] elections, but this was a much more coordinated effort, and if House Republicans were able to find a senator to join them for each of the six states, then the process could take days to complete. Still, it would be only symbolic, as Republicans wouldn't have enough votes to sustain any of the objections. The House had a Democratic majority, and only a handful of Republican senators had shown any willingness to support Trump's extraordinary campaign to stay in office.[14]

With few options left, Trump and his allies had been lobbying Vice President Mike Pence to make an unprecedented move—to somehow reject or delay the electoral count for certain states, even though the vice president's role is only ceremonial.[15] As part of the plot, Trump's allies had recruited slates of fake electors in battleground states to sign alternative certificates that could be presented by Trump allies during the certification and used as justification for Pence to delay the proceedings.[16]

Privately, Pence and his advisers had decided there was no legal standing or precedent for such a move, and Pence had communicated as much to an increasingly frustrated Trump.[17] But Pence had not commented publicly, and Trump's supporters held out hope that he would somehow block the count.

As Trump and his allies convinced themselves of the potential success of this last-ditch plan, the Capitol Police's intelligence had indicated the potential for unrest. But their "Special Event Assessments," which were widely disseminated security updates for Capitol Police staff and law enforcement partners, did not reflect that intelligence. The first of those threat assessments, issued December 16, said violence could not be ruled out but that there were "NO social media indications for specific threats or concerning comments directed at the Joint Session of Congress."[18]

By December 21, though, the Capitol Police's intelligence division had issued a separate report to a small group of the department's leadership describing concerning posts on a blog called thedonald.win. Those posts referenced the Capitol's underground tunnel system and included a map. Comments on the posts discussed whether people should infiltrate the tunnels on January 6th or stand outside the Capitol building and try to get in. "Forget the tunnels. Get into Capitol Building, stand outside congress. Be in the room next to them. They wont have time [to] run if they play dumb," read one.

Another called for people to surround every building in the complex: "They better dig a tunnel all the way to China if they want to escape."[19]

Other comments urged taking up arms:

> If a million patriots [show] up bristling with AR's, just how brave do you think they'll be when it comes to enforcing their unconstitutional laws? Don't cuck out. This is do or die. Bring your guns.[20]

Despite that intelligence, the Capitol Police's December 23 and December 30 threat assessments for wider audiences echoed the earlier analysis—"no information regarding specific disruptions or acts of civil disobedience targeting this function."[21]

A January 3 threat assessment contained a new, starker warning buried in the middle of the document:

> Due to the tense political environment following the 2020 election, the threat of disruptive actions or violence cannot be ruled out. Supporters of the current president see January 6, 2021, as the last opportunity to overturn the results of the presidential election. This sense of desperation and disappointment may lead to more of an incentive to become violent. Unlike previous post-election protests, the targets of the pro-Trump supporters are not necessarily the counter-protesters as they were previously, but rather Congress itself is the target on the 6th. As outlined above, there has been a worrisome call for protesters to come to these events armed and there is the possibility that protesters may be inclined to become violent.

The warning concluded by noting that the protests could attract "white supremacists, militia members, and others who actively promote violence" and could lead to a "significantly dangerous situation for law enforcement and the general public alike."[22]

The report's summary, however, repeated language similar to that used in the previous assessments, directly contradicting the blunt warning contained within the document's pages. The events of January 6th were expected to be similar to two previous Trump protests that had occurred in the District of Columbia in November and December, it said, and protesters were expected to remain in their designated areas.[23]

After the January 3 assessment, the Capitol Police put out daily assessments on January 4, 5, and 6. None contained the dire warnings found in the January 3 document. In fact, each predicted that civil disobedience was "remote" to "improbable."[24]

Still, Chief Sund decided to ask for National Guard support in the days before January 6th. Instead of submitting a formal request, he discussed the matter informally with two of the three members of the Capitol Police Board, an arcane panel in charge of Capitol complex security. Neither of the security officials he talked to—House Sergeant at Arms Paul Irving and Senate Sergeant at Arms Michael Stenger—thought there was an urgent need for the National Guard, based on the intelligence reports they had seen. Accounts of those conversations differ, but guard support was not officially approved.[25]

At the same time, Irving sent out an email security alert to "all members of Congress and staff" on Monday, January 4, that said they should "expect demonstration activity" at the Capitol for the joint session that Wednesday. The missive said that members and staff were "strongly encouraged to arrive as early as possible on January 6" and suggested that they use underground access from garages instead of walking outdoors.[26]

On the evening of January 5, as thousands of his supporters headed to Washington, Trump praised them and egged them on. "Washington is being inundated with people who don't want to see an election victory stolen by emboldened Radical Left Democrats," he tweeted. "Our Country has had enough, they won't take it anymore! We hear you (and love you) from the Oval Office. MAKE AMERICA GREAT AGAIN!"[27]

At the same time, police officers across the city readied for what many figured could be a long, potentially disruptive day. One of them was Capitol Police Officer Brian Sicknick, who texted his brother Ken at 6 p.m. that there were a lot of Trump flags out on the streets, and he expected more the next day.[28]

Three hours later, Sicknick sent his older brother a second, more ominous text: "I think hell may break loose tomorrow," he wrote.

January 6, 2021

Early Morning

Barry Black, Chaplain of the US Senate: I'd had some foreboding about the potential for the cataclysmic on January 6. I had been awakened in the middle of the night, and I had a sense that this was probably going to be a day like no other day we had ever experienced.

Sen. Mike Rounds, R-SD: I had been approached by a couple of our constituents who I knew who said they were coming to DC for the big rally. And I told them, "Look, I assume it's going to be crowded. If you're coming in, be prepared to get your food someplace else. And don't stay downtown. Get outside of the area." If you're going to come in to the rally, great. But I'm hoping that's all it is.

Rep. Ronny Jackson, R-TX: There was this big rally downtown; the president was going to speak. I'm from a pretty pro-Trump district, the Thirteenth Congressional District—lots and lots of support for President Trump and for the Make America Great Again agenda. So I had people reaching out to me from Wichita Falls and Amarillo and places in my district saying, "Hey, we're going to be in DC for the rally, are you going to be down there?"

House Speaker Nancy Pelosi, D-CA: Security had told us there were going to be crowds. We're used to the First Amendment being honored with people speaking out, and that's nothing we disrespect. But that doesn't mean a violent protest. So when we saw people coming to the Capitol, it was, well—that's what they do. They come to the Capitol. We didn't anticipate it was going to be with weapons.

Rep. Rodney Davis, R-IL, the top Republican on the House Administration Committee, which oversees Capitol Police: On January 5, I had security briefings from the Capitol Police. Those briefings didn't give me any indication of what the Capitol would see and what the nation would see the next day.

John Bresnahan, congressional reporter and cofounder, Punchbowl News: On January 5, there was a rally on the east side of the Capitol, so I went outside. They weren't talking about raiding the Capitol, but they were talking about civil war, and they were talking about violence. I was stunned just to listen to it. It was right out there in the open. I've been coming to the Capitol since 1992, a long time, and I had never heard anything like that.

Sen. Mark Warner, D-VA, the top Democrat on the Senate Intelligence Committee: We'd been following press, law enforcement, and other reports about what was going to happen. We all knew there was going to be something on January 6. I'm not sure any of us really knew exactly what it would be, how many people were going to show up. I had called the FBI director, and then one of the deputy directors got back to me Tuesday evening. And he said, "I think we're okay." I kept saying, "Are you sure?"

Sen. Roy Blunt, R-MO, chairman of the Senate Rules Committee, which oversees Capitol Police: I had checked a couple of times the previous week with the chief of the Capitol Police. His view was that they were in good shape. I think what they were anticipating—there had been two previous times since the election when there were Trump supporters in Washington, and in both of those cases, it turned out to be more about managing the confrontation between them and the counterprotesters who were there.

Igor Bobic, senior politics reporter, HuffPost: We all have this—at least had—a sense that the Capitol is super-secure, and that Capitol Police are there every day making sure everything's fine. It always felt like the safest place you could be.

Senate Democratic Leader Chuck Schumer, D-NY: At 4 a.m. in the morning, I learned that our two Democratic senators had won in the Georgia runoff and we would gain the majority. At 4 a.m., it became clear. I tried to get some sleep, but I couldn't. I got in my car and drove to Washington.

Sen. Chris Murphy, D-CT: I drove in by myself that day. And I remember there being a really eerie feeling in the Capitol that morning. I remember watching people walking through the city on their way to the protests. And the city was kind of empty. And there's just a real sort of weird, dangerous vibe to the city that morning as I was coming in. So I remember feeling pretty unsettled early on.

Rep. Colin Allred, D-TX: I remember that morning speaking to my wife before I left. She was at home with our not-yet-two-year-old, and she was, I think, eight months pregnant. And saying goodbye to her and knowing that it was going to be a long day—because at that point, we expected maybe six states to be challenged with two hours of debate for each state. And knowing that I probably would not be home for a long time. So we just had kind of an extra goodbye, also expecting that there might be some difficulty that day. Obviously not anticipating anything like what happened.

Manu Raju, anchor and chief congressional correspondent, CNN: I remember my wife telling me, "Be careful going into the Capitol." And I was like, this is just any day for me. So I was not even slightly concerned about our safety or about what could happen next.

Rep. Rodney Davis, R-IL: I woke up and came to the Capitol, and you could just see—it just was an eerie day. I was not looking forward to it because I knew that it was going to be a long day. There were going to be objections, we're going to have to debate those objections. And I thought it was absurd that we would have to do that. But give everybody their voice—come in, take a vote, and then certify the election. It was as simple as that.

Sen. Richard Burr, R-NC: I think it was a typical day where you're going to spend hours on the Senate floor that you dreaded. I mean, it's almost like impeachment. You're going to be sitting there and you're going to go through this laborious process and it's going to take a long time. So I'm not sure that there was anybody that was excited about doing it. There was a great sense of let's get it over with.

Rep. Brian Fitzpatrick, R-PA: Not many people were in the chamber that day in 2017 for the electoral count, because it was pretty much procedural. But there was a lot of focus on it this year. So I wanted to be there.

Rep. Pramila Jayapal, D-WA: I did know that it was a contentious day, and I just assumed that we were going to have plenty of security and that the safest place to be would be in the Capitol. And so I wanted to be there because I felt like this was one of the most important duties that we had, to certify the election.

Emily Cochrane, congressional reporter, *The New York Times*: I lived on Capitol Hill, so I had my routine. I would mobile-order at my Starbucks on Pennsylvania Avenue and pick up my coffee and my little sausage-egg-and-cheese sandwich. And I remember, as I picked it up that morning, thinking, wow, there's a lot of people. And it was a lot of people in red hats and patriotic attire. You knew why they were there. And I remember just kind of quietly navigating around them to get into the building and thinking, okay, yes, it's going to take me a while to leave tonight and walk home.

Rep. Lisa Blunt Rochester, D-DE: That morning, coming towards the Capitol, I felt something different. There was a truck in front of me, and someone had taken their fingers or some instrument to write in the dust on the back of the truck, "Stop the steal."

Sen. Bob Casey, D-PA: I didn't think about it too much until after I left my apartment that morning. We'd all heard and read that there was going to be some kind of demonstration. I remember getting into my car and thinking, what if something happens today where there are people on the streets? And will it be confrontational? But never if I had imagined the worst possible scenario could I have come up with what happened on that day. But it's strange, because in the morning, I had just a feeling that something could happen. And how would we handle that?

Joe Novotny, US House reading clerk: I live in the neighborhood, and so typically I would either Metro or walk. And they told us, don't go up to the Capitol, come in through one of the House office buildings and then go through the tunnels. So that's what I did. And what I found very odd was how little [police] presence there was.

Rep. Stephanie Murphy, D-FL: I knew it could be a tough day. I had my staff drop a "go bag" in my office that had two changes of clothes and a blanket in case I was sleeping in my office overnight. I had planned my entry that morning through the garages, because they are a few blocks off. I didn't want anybody here, so I was by myself.

Jen Daulby, Republican staff director, House Administration Committee: My worst-case scenario was that we were going to be stuck in the building—that there were going to be so many people, and it was going to get out of control, and that they weren't going to be able to get us out and we were going to be surrounded. I brought a change of clothes. I brought a pillow and a blanket. And I'm a Midwesterner, and I had tons of food and snacks, and I literally had a spread for everyone.

Chad Pergram, senior congressional correspondent, Fox News: I had brought hoards of food because I thought we might be there for like thirty hours or more.

Sen. Mike Rounds, R-SD: When I came in that morning, I did not see anything that was unusual. But I remember getting a call from my chief [in South Dakota] saying, "Is everything okay there?" And he said that the word out there was that something bad is going to happen.

Sen. Patty Murray, D-WA: I texted my family and said, "I'm on my way. I will let you know when I get safely to the Capitol." And I did. I texted them. And I said, "I'm in my office. I'm safe."

Jason Dolan, former marine, Oath Keepers, Florida: It didn't seem possible that he was going to lose.

Annie Howell, Pennsylvania: Even before we had the final results, I believed that the election was going to be stolen.

Robert Schornack, business development manager, Michigan: The night of the election, it seemed like Trump had won and that, you know, that was it. And then we wake up in the morning to find out that they're still counting, you know, all these ballots, and all these ballots are still coming in, and that is not how elections normally go. So it was—it wasn't that hard to believe that the election was stolen because of all these different individual instances where people could point to and say, "Well, look at this and look at that," you know. Maybe Trump's right.

Doug Jensen, construction worker, Des Moines, Iowa: I voted both terms for Obama, and during the presidency, I thought he was a great president. The health thing. The health thing didn't benefit me and my family because I had union health insurance. So I got no benefits from it, but I was happy that all those people got insurance, you know? And so I was happy with him. And then I was going to vote for Hillary because I've been a Democrat my whole life.

Lewis "Easton" Cantwell, North Carolina: I'm pretty much independent. I lean more conservative, but I have a ton of different values that I share on all sides of the political scheme, so I'm not really biased. Like, I voted for Obama.

Doug Jensen, construction worker, Des Moines, Iowa: It all started with all the crap I found out about Hillary Clinton, John Podesta, you know, all of that stuff, and then so right before I was going to vote for

Hillary, I was like, whoa, we've got to vote Trump in because we can't have Hillary.

Dustin Thompson, former exterminator, Columbus, Ohio: It was hard at first, like, I mean, I've always had a job. And then with like the pandemic and everything, it just—I couldn't go anywhere, couldn't do anything, no one was hiring, so just kind of stuck at home. And I kind of got involved in conspiracy theories and going down the rabbit hole on the Internet.

Doug Jensen, construction worker, Des Moines, Iowa: And it all started from that WikiLeaks drop, you know, four years ago. And then Q came along. And there was things that happened in the beginning that Q said that came true. And everything he always said happened real shortly after, like certain things.

Dustin Thompson, former exterminator, Columbus, Ohio: It just seemed like everyone was against [Trump] and that he needed someone to stand up for him.

Doug Jensen, construction worker, Des Moines, Iowa: Q always told us that when [Trump] says "My fellow Americans, the storm is here," that's when we're supposed to go. That's when we're supposed to do anything. Well, [Trump] started off that speech a couple weeks ago with "my fellow Americans." That's all he had to do.

Stephen Ayres, cabinet company employee, Ohio: I was pretty hardcore into the social media, Facebook, Twitter, Instagram. I followed President Trump on all the websites. He basically put out, come to the Stop the Steal rally. And I felt like I needed to be down [there].

Alondra Propes, former parole and probation officer, Oath Keepers, Florida: I wanted to go to the largest Trump rally ever.

Christopher Grider, winery owner, Texas: It is kind of akin to having your favorite band on the final concert tour.

Pamela Hemphill, retired drug and alcohol counselor, Idaho: We might be screaming and holding signs, but you go there just thinking it's going to be a protest, no big deal.

Jason Riddle, former correctional officer and mail carrier, New Hampshire: I didn't believe in the lie. I more or less felt like I was going to see Trump one last time as president.

Annie Howell, Pennsylvania: There was still, like, maybe a 10 percent part of me that believed something could happen, you know, in terms of overturning the results.

Shawna Martin, missionary, Arizona: I have church at my house, and I know it was brought up there. I said, if God would have me go, I would go. And God opened the doors and off I went in support.

Doug Jensen, construction worker, Des Moines, Iowa: I worked that whole day [before] until 4 p.m., rushed home, took a shower and got my Q stuff on, and hopped in my car, and I went.

Jason Riddle, former correctional officer and mail carrier, New Hampshire: It was more or less kind of a routine at that point. I was just driving around to Trump rallies all the time, and we considered it a rally we were going to. We stayed outside of DC in a hotel the night before, and we took a train to DC, and then we Ubered.

Annie Howell, Pennsylvania: We all woke up super-early and got in line. So I want to say, we woke up at like 3:30, 4:00 in the morning.

Jessica Watkins, US Army veteran and bar owner, Oath Keepers, Ohio: I woke up at like, 4:30 in the morning. We wanted to get to the Ellipse super-early before there was a line and before it's going to be a problem.

Jason Riddle, former correctional officer and mail carrier, New Hampshire: As we were passing the Washington Monument, the Uber driver said, "I think you guys want to get out here."

Jason Dolan, former marine, Oath Keepers, Florida: I was asked to bring my firearms up there. They were going to be used, if we had to use them, for several different reasons. There was a lot of discussion initially about antifa. So there was a fear of some type of attack by antifa or other—other groups that were like them against us.

Doug Jensen, construction worker, Des Moines, Iowa: I took a backpack with food and water, you know, in case chaos broke out, I needed food and water. You know? So I had my wife pack my bag with water and a couple cans of pop, some ramen noodles, some pears, you know, just canned good stuff.

Daniel Rodriguez, California: I don't fly because I have issues with flying. But there was an idea that if anybody needed to take anything, like, weed maybe, knife, pepper spray, that stuff's not going to be able to get on the plane.

Shawna Martin, missionary, Arizona: I had heard that antifa would be showing up dressed as patriots and might cause some issues. I came as a medic. I had canteens, a medipack, and a gas mask in case antifa showed up.

Matthew Greene, former US Army National Guard, Proud Boys, New York: We, as the Proud Boys, viewed ourselves almost as the foot soldiers of the right where antifa was the foot soldiers of the left.

Annie Howell, Pennsylvania: [Trump social media director Dan] Scavino was going on social media daily saying, "Wait for the storm, the storm is coming," and kind of, like, preluding to something big that was going to happen, making us all believe that something was going to happen or something big was going to develop or, you know, somebody was going to prove something.

Alondra Propes, former parole and probation officer, Oath Keepers, Florida: I believe that there are a group of people whose hate for Donald Trump is much greater than their love for this country and that they would do anything it took at all costs to make sure that he did not win the election, specifically, people on the left that were against Donald Trump.

Janet Buhler, music teacher and college fashion instructor, Utah: I wanted Congress to understand how many people were there that were concerned about the election. I just wanted to be part of that, like, visibility of how many people.

Robert Schornack, business development manager, Michigan: One of my buddies, or family friend, he said something I'll never forget. He said, "Trump has only asked me for two things: He asked me for my vote and he asked me to come on January 6th." So I wanted to be there to support him, as well as defend other people because we had heard that antifa or other counter protesters were going to be there to try and attack Trump supporters.

Annie Howell, Pennsylvania: I thought that a presence or a large presence of people would influence a decision or the outcome of that day.

Robert Schornack, business development manager, Michigan: And then with all the things that they kept saying were going to be exposed and were going to come out in court and elsewhere, you know, and we wanted to believe it.

Matthew Greene, former US Army National Guard, Proud Boys, New York: We were openly expecting a civil war at that point.

Lewis "Easton" Cantwell, North Carolina: All I heard was it was supposed to be, like, a million-person rally.

Daniel Rodriguez, California: Trump called us. Trump called us to DC.

Matthew Greene, former US Army National Guard, Proud Boys, New York: The one that really stood out was, be there, "be wild."

Annie Howell, Pennsylvania: The only violence that we expected was from like a clashing group, like antifa, or possibly BLM.

Jason Dolan, former marine, Oath Keepers, Florida: A lot of us were prepared—I was prepared to stop the certification process one way or the other.

Officer Adam Eveland, Metropolitan Police Department, Civil Disturbance Unit: We had heard that there would probably be a march towards the Capitol that day and that it was going to be a very big protest. And when you have a very large protest, you never really know how it's going to go.

Officer Jesse Leasure, Metropolitan Police Department, Civil Disturbance Unit: In the weeks beforehand, I was not on full duty status because I had injured my wrist. A couple days before, I was recertified to go back into full duty. I was texting with my mother, and she was asking if I was cleared for work, and I said, "Back tomorrow." It was January 5th. And my mom was just telling me, basically, to do what I needed to do to be careful. She said she believed most people tomorrow are going to be in favor of the cops.

Officer Adam Eveland, Metropolitan Police Department, Civil Disturbance Unit: Right-wing protesters operate a little differently than left-wing protesters do. That's not to say that both can't get violent. They just get violent in different ways.

Officer Jesse Leasure, Metropolitan Police Department, Civil Disturbance Unit: I tell people all the time that when I deal with the MAGA people being far, far right is that when they fight you, they will fight you face-to-face. And if you spray them with pepper spray, they'll spit it right back at you.

Officer Adam Eveland, Metropolitan Police Department: Most right-wing protesters are very friendly to law enforcement, to your face, and they only get upset when you have to intervene, because, quote, you're supposed to be on their side. But we're not on anybody's side. We're supposed to be neutral.

Officer Jesse Leasure, Metropolitan Police Department: The average antifa rioter is wearing all black. And whenever they fight you, they only will do like, hit-and-run tactics.

Officer Adam Eveland, Metropolitan Police Department: [Antifa rioters] would throw bricks at you, throw bottles of urine at you or something like that. And then they would want to capture the police response to that so that they could publish it and put it on social media and say, "Look how brutal the police are." But the right-wing people—these are people who will fight you.

Captain Carneysha C. Mendoza, field force commander of the Civil Disturbance Unit, US Capitol Police: In my career, I have been activated to work demonstrations with various controversial groups. I've been called some of the worst names so many times that I'm pretty numb to it now. As an agency, we have trained for and handled numerous demonstrations. It's something we do on a regular basis, and it's something I have always felt we've excelled at.

Officer Adam Eveland, Metropolitan Police Department: Previously, when we had dealt with the Proud Boys and the Oath Keepers and all those right-wing groups, you had to be very careful, because a lot of these people were militarily trained, ex–police officers, current police officers, current military, combat experience, firemen. So they operated differently. Basically, the vast majority of them would do their march, while fractions of them would splinter off, find people that they identified as BLM or left wing, and beat them up.

Officer Caroline Edwards, US Capitol Police, First Responder Unit: Usually, 99.9 percent of the time, we're just using verbal judo to calm people down, deescalate, move people along, making sure that nothing happens.

Officer Adam Eveland, Metropolitan Police Department: The majority of the protests you work are mostly peaceful. There's always some bad actors or whatever. But the thing about a protest that's large, that's dangerous, is that if you have bad actors in a large protest, mob mentality can take over, and it doesn't matter if they're left or right wing. So that's the danger in it. It's a hive-mind kind of mentality.

Officer Winston Pingeon, US Capitol Police, Civil Disturbance Unit: I had worked the protests that happened the weekend after the election in November and then a month later, both of which had felt a little bit like a powder keg, in the sense that there was something else coming.

Captain Carneysha C. Mendoza, US Capitol Police: During the Million MAGA March, multiple white-supremacist groups, to include the Proud Boys and others, converged at the Supreme Court along with counter groups. The Civil Disturbance Unit fought hard that day, physically breaking up fights and separating the various groups. I literally woke up the next day unable to move without being in pain. On January 6th, we anticipated an event similar to the Million MAGA March on November 14th.

Officer Caroline Edwards, US Capitol Police, First Responder Unit: The briefings were mostly that this was going to be a peaceful march. They weren't expecting too much disturbance, except for the possibility that there might be scuffles between protesters and counterprotesters, which was what we were supposed to look out for—was potentially, you know, antifa or anyone like that, who would be stirring up dissent among the protesters.

Lieutenant Tia Summers, US Capitol Police, shift commander, Communications Section: This is not the first time I've worked on a day when we had to certify electoral votes. I came to work thinking I was going to come in, it was going to go on. Once the event was over, I would go home. That would be it.

Officer Harry Dunn, US Capitol Police: I reported for duty at the Capitol, as usual, early on the morning of January 6. We understood that the vote to certify President Biden's election would be taking place that day and that protests might occur outside the Capitol, but we expected any demonstrations to be peaceful expressions of First Amendment freedoms, just like the scores of demonstrations we had observed for many years.

Officer Eugene Goodman, US Capitol Police: I think start time that day was maybe 6 a.m. It was really, really early. I got there an hour early. When I first parked, I set my clock because I had plenty of time before I was to go in the building. There were individuals who I presumed were coming from Union Station, and they were walking down the mall. And some were even at that point yelling things. And they had Trump paraphernalia, hats, flags.

Officer Daniel Hodges, Metropolitan Police Department: We started that day at 7:30 a.m., and our assignment was to maintain high visibility along Constitution Avenue, namely, the blocks leading up to President's Park, where Trump was holding his gathering. My particular station was in front of 1111 Constitution Avenue, where I stood on foot as the crowd poured down the street and into the park.

Chief Robert Contee, Metropolitan Police Department: We started seeing, you know, thousands of people—I mean, they were gathering very, very, very early in the morning.

Chief Steven Sund, US Capitol Police: At approximately 7:15 a.m., as I was driving in to work, I called [Metropolitan Police Department] Inspector Robert Glover to inquire about the crowds he was seeing for the event, which was beginning at the Ellipse. Inspector Glover stated that there were already lines to get into the event, but that the crowd was compliant and he did not observe any concerning issues.

Inspector Robert Glover, Metropolitan Police Department: The crowd just kept getting bigger and bigger and bigger and bigger through the morning.

Officer Winston Pingeon, US Capitol Police: At our roll call that morning, my lieutenant basically said we think there's a group probably coming to the Capitol today, and so have your riot gear on standby.

Officer Harry Dunn, US Capitol Police: After roll call, I took my overwatch post on the East Front of the Capitol, standing on the steps that lead to the Senate chamber. As the morning progressed, I did not see or hear anything that gave me cause for alarm.

Chief Steven Sund, US Capitol Police: I arrived at the Command Center, where I remained to monitor the activity on the National Mall and the Ellipse. I sat at the center console with Assistant Chiefs Pittman and Thomas nearby.

Yogananda Pittman, assistant chief, US Capitol Police, Protective and Intelligence Operations: As we are taking in information, we're pushing out that information to our officers. I had countersurveillance teams out and deployed.

Officer Daniel Hodges, Metropolitan Police Department: There were a significant number of men dressed in tactical gear attending the [rally]. Wearing ballistic vests, helmets, goggles, military face masks, backpacks, and without identifiable, visible law enforcement or military patches, they appeared to be prepared for much more than listening to politicians speak in a park.

Inspector Robert Glover, Metropolitan Police Department: We were prepared to do crowd separation if we had to. But we did not see any antifa in that crowd. This was all pro-Trump, Make America Great Again, Oath Keepers, Proud Boys.

Officer Daniel Hodges, Metropolitan Police Department: One of [the protesters] asked my colleagues something to the effect of "Is this all the manpower you have? Do you really think you're going to be able to stop all these people?" Dumbfounded, my colleagues simply expressed that they didn't understand what the speaker meant, and the group continued on.

Captain Carneysha C. Mendoza, US Capitol Police: I've received various awards from the army and the Capitol Police, including an award for recovery efforts during the Pentagon attack. Unfortunately, I didn't save any lives or anything, but there are certain lessons that always stuck with me after 9/11. One of those lessons is knowing the unthinkable is always possible. So be ready.

9:00 a.m.

House Speaker Nancy Pelosi arrived at the Capitol a little after 9 a.m., sat down at a laptop in her conference room, and logged on to a virtual meeting. Members and staff were going over their plans for the floor debate one last time. "You're in the game; this is it," Pelosi told them.[1]

Feeling increasingly uneasy during the final weeks of 2020 that Trump would focus on the January 6th certification as an opportunity to overturn the results of the election, Pelosi had gathered some of her most loyal legal minds on the House Judiciary Committee and asked them to figure out how they would respond if Pence tried to block the certification. They included Rep. Adam Schiff, the Californian who had earned Trump's wrath as the lead prosecutor in the president's first impeachment trial; Rep. Zoe Lofgren, another fellow Californian and a seasoned legislator who had been a young Hill staffer during Watergate; Maryland Rep. Jamie Raskin, the energetic former constitutional law professor; and Colorado Rep. Joe Neguse, a rising leader on the committee who had just been elected in 2018.[2]

House Speaker Nancy Pelosi: I made one requirement of them—that this isn't about Donald Trump. This is about the votes, the law, and who won. It's not about "he said," or "it must have been this." No hearsay, no nothing.

Because they controlled the House, it was the Democrats' view that a House majority vote could stop Pence if he tried somehow to overturn the election or object to a state's legitimate results. But they also knew that the Constitution and the Electoral Count Act that govern elections were vague, and there was no precedent for such a move. The group consulted with the new House parliamentarian, Jason Smith, and his predecessor, Thomas Wickham, a twenty-five-year veteran of the parliamentarian's office who had retired in 2020 but stayed on as an adviser. As they worked through different possibilities, they quickly understood that they had no perfect solution.

Rep. Adam Schiff, D-CA: We didn't know for sure, until the very end, what Pence would do. And so in our preparation for January 6, we talked through the different scenarios—if they did send an alternate slate of electors or if the vice president did refuse to do his duty, and who would object and how an objection would work and how to make sure that was resolved without having to go to a court. And with some of those questions, there really weren't good, clear answers because there was no precedent for them.

Rep. Jamie Raskin, D-MD: We had a series of parliamentary maneuvers worked out. First, appealing to the parliamentarian to reject what the vice president was doing. And then to ask for a vote of the assembled Congress in the joint session, which we would have won. So that would have been our first choice. The second choice would have been a move to adjourn, to then try to work it out politically with them to back off. And there were several other conceivable options, but the truth was that it would have been a great leap into the unknown had Pence followed orders.

Keith Stern, House director of floor operations: [Pence] was the one who was going to have all the control here, and we had no idea what he was going to do. There were conversations like "Will he walk in with fake envelopes, and as the envelopes get passed to him, swap them out and put the wrong one in?"

Thomas Wickham, former House parliamentarian and senior adviser to the parliamentarian: We in the parliamentarian community knew the statute was flawed, and also because it's only used once every four years, there's just not a lot written about it and not a lot of clear understanding of what it does.

Rep. Zoe Lofgren, D-CA: We had gamed out different things that might happen. The truth is, if you violate the law, which is basically what was being promoted by some, it's very difficult to manage that assault on democracy.

On the conference call, Pelosi said they would try to hold any necessary votes quickly to speed the process. The Catholic speaker then said a prayer, connecting the January 6th certification to the other traditional January 6th celebration, the Christian holiday of Epiphany. She hoped there would be "an epiphany for the American people" as they saw Congress respecting the democratic process.[3]

Raskin, who was on the call, had lost his twenty-five-year-old son, Tommy, to suicide only a week earlier, on New Year's Eve. Tommy's funeral had been the day before. But Raskin was determined to carry on as they had planned.

Rep. Jamie Raskin, D-MD: It was a gloomy, dark day. There were just all kinds of signs of foreboding everywhere you looked. But of course, like most other members of Congress, I assumed that if there was going to be ugliness and violence, it would be kept at bay.

House Speaker Nancy Pelosi, D-CA: We anticipated mischief in terms of process. We never expected violence.

Democrats were in charge of the House floor, but at least one House Republican was gaming possible scenarios as well. Wyoming Rep. Liz Cheney, the chairwoman of the House Republican Conference and number three in GOP leadership, had been outspoken since November about the election results, calling on

Trump to respect the sanctity of the transfer of power if the courts did not rule in his favor. In Wyoming, though, she found that many of her constituents truly believed the election had been stolen.

Rep. Liz Cheney, R-WY: What you had was a lot of people who had heard the false claims from Trump and some in his campaign. And so I was saying, "No, the president had the chance, his campaign had the chance to put forth the evidence. They didn't because there was no evidence."

The White House had responded by disinviting her to a holiday party, but somehow the Trump campaign had left her on an email advertising a January 4 call to plan for the joint session. She dialed into the call and heard Trump aides discussing the plan for Pence to reject electoral votes. She immediately went to see Smith, the parliamentarian, and Wickham, the former parliamentarian.

Rep. Liz Cheney, R-WY: It was a very concerning discussion, because I realized there's just not that much you can do. When you're in the joint session, it's not the parliamentary procedures and rules of the House that apply.

Cheney didn't call House Republican Leader Kevin McCarthy—she suspected he could be working with Trump—but she did talk to Senate Majority Leader Mitch McConnell, who seemed to be aware of the situation, and to the Senate parliamentarian's office in case the Senate would need to help shut down a rogue move by Pence.

Rep. Liz Cheney, R-WY: I have a very clear memory of driving home, leaving the Capitol that night and just feeling nauseous, like physically nauseous. And the realization of—oh my God, if Mike Pence decides he's going to reject these votes, we were going to be in uncharted territory.

Unbeknownst to the others, Mike Pence had also consulted the House parliamentarian's office, along with the Senate parliamentarian, about the rules of the session and the limits of his ceremonial role.[4]

Greg Jacob, counsel to Vice President Pence: The vice president's first instinct when questions came up about authorities that he might or might not have was that there was just no way that the framers of the Constitution would have entrusted that kind of authority to one person.

Thomas Wickham, former House parliamentarian and senior adviser to the parliamentarian: The interpretations that were occurring at that time caused the pressure to increase that somehow, that during the proceedings of January 6, the election results could be changed—in that Vice President Pence had more of a say in the outcome than I think his advisers, which included me, were comfortable with.

Trump's top allies in the House had also been preparing. Led by Alabama Rep. Mo Brooks and Ohio Rep. Jim Jordan, a group of around a dozen House Republicans had gone to the White House before Christmas to discuss challenging the results on January 6th. One meeting was supposed to last an hour but stretched to three, with Trump participating in much of it along with his lawyer, former New York Mayor Rudy Giuliani. Bolstered by Trump, the Republicans had raised questions about how states had conducted elections during the pandemic, with some having changed procedures and shifted to more mail-in ballots. The group was focused on those issues only in the states that Biden had narrowly won, however, and none questioned their own elections on the same ballots.[5]

Across the Capitol that morning, Majority Leader Mitch McConnell, R-KY, had gotten his second shot of the new coronavirus vaccine in the Capitol ahead of the 1 p.m. joint session. His aides had been briefed on building security in the days before, but he was focused on the debate.[6] *He would tell his colleagues later that day that this would be the most important vote of his thirty-six years in the Senate.*

McConnell had been trying to head off any votes at all, quietly working for weeks to convince members of his conference not to object to any states' electoral counts. The two chambers would vote only if one House member and one senator objected to a particular state's results, and McConnell had told his conference that opposing the results would be a "terrible" vote. McConnell himself had waited to say that Biden was the winner of the election until mid-December, when all of Trump's court cases were exhausted and the Electoral College had voted.[7]

Missouri Sen. Roy Blunt, the even-keeled Republican chairman of the Senate Rules Committee and one of McConnell's top allies, was also working behind the scenes to try to convince his colleagues to stand down.

Sen. Roy Blunt, R-MO: It was my view and most of the other senators' view that the thirty-day protest after the election is where you make that case or not. There had been a lot of court cases, and they'd all uniformly reached the same conclusion.

Blunt was particularly focused on his Missouri colleague, Republican Sen. Josh Hawley, a Trump loyalist who was being coy about whether he might object. Blunt and South Dakota Sen. John Thune, the number-two Senate Republican, spoke with Hawley privately to try to convince him not to move forward with an objection. Thune had told reporters in December that he expected Trump's efforts to overturn the election to "go down like a shot dog" in the Senate.[8]

Sen. Roy Blunt, R-MO: It looked for a while as if none of our members would protest. Thune and I had specifically talked to my colleague Josh about this, and he said he was still thinking about it.

The pleas were unsuccessful. Hawley announced on December 30 that he would object to the results from Pennsylvania, noting that Democrats had objected to results in the past. "At the very least, Congress should investigate allegations of voter fraud and adopt measures to secure the integrity of our elections," Hawley said. "But Congress has so far failed to act."[9]

After Hawley made his announcement, Texas Sen. Ted Cruz soon joined in, releasing a statement a few days later with six of his Republican colleagues and four Republican senators-elect.[10] *They called on Congress to pause the count and conduct an audit of the election, an idea based on a commission appointed by Congress in 1877 after the disputed 1876 election between Republican Rutherford B. Hayes and Democrat Samuel Tilden. The senators called for a ten-day election audit before the inauguration in certain states—all of which happened to be the swing states that Biden had narrowly won. A release from Cruz's office said that if Congress did not form such a commission, then the group of senators would vote to reject the electors.*[11]

Sen. Ted Cruz, R-TX: I suggested that we could object to certifying electors only in states where there were significant claims of fraud. We would not object based on conspiracy theories or the many baseless claims that were floating around the Internet.

Instead of attempting to throw out the results and simply install our preferred candidate, we would call specifically for the appointment of an election commission modeled after the commission of 1877. Thus, no matter what the results ended up being, we could be sure that the American people could have confidence that the right man was in office.

Signing on to Cruz's statement were Republican Sens. Ron Johnson of Wisconsin, Steve Daines of Montana, John Kennedy of Louisiana, Marsha Blackburn of Tennessee, Mike Braun of Indiana, and James Lankford of Oklahoma. Senators-elect Cynthia Lummis of Wyoming, Roger Marshall of Kansas, Bill Hagerty of Tennessee, and Tommy Tuberville of Alabama also put their names on the release, as they would be sworn in on January 3rd and able to vote and object, if they wanted to, by January 6th. Several of the senators said that they were doing so because of concerns they were hearing from their constituents—concerns first voiced by Trump and his allies and amplified on social media.

Sen. James Lankford, R-OK: We were attempting to make a point, which is what the Congress is all about, is to be able to bring the voices of people, including the thousands and thousands of Oklahomans that have come to me to say "I have questions," to be able to honor their questions and to be able to say, "How do we get answers to these things?"

Sen. Ted Cruz, R-TX: On January 5, later in the evening before we were set to carry out our plan, I got another call from President Trump. He had heard what the eleven of us were planning to do, and he was elated. But he wanted more. Over a call that lasted about thirty minutes, President Trump urged me and my colleagues to object to all seven of the contested states, not just one or two. I told him that although I understood his frustration, it was really important that we keep our coalition of eleven senators together.

Senate Rules Committee Chairman Roy Blunt, R-MO: I was surprised at the totally unworkable idea that somehow you could revert to the 1877 commission. I was surprised not only that Senator Cruz proposed that but that at least half-a-dozen other senators thought, "That's what we're for. We're for this unworkable commission." It just could not possibly—it didn't work in 1877 and wasn't going to work then. But it was suddenly—it's kind of like grabbing hold of something that is at least something to hold on to.

Sen. Angus King, I-ME: [Cruz] knows better. He's a really smart guy. I think it's interesting that he and Hawley are probably in the top 10 percent of IQs in the US Senate, and that makes it less excusable what they did. Because they knew damn well that what they were doing was wrong.

Sen. Ted Cruz, R-TX: I would object to Arizona, and then I would support Senator Hawley's objection to Pennsylvania. The eleven of us would force the debate, and we would try with all our might to win on the merits.

11:00 a.m.

Christopher Alberts, a handyman and former National Guardsman who lived in Maryland, had met with others from his county at a bus stop earlier that morning. He didn't have $50 for the bus ticket, so he drove his Jeep Wrangler behind the buses and parked at the first garage he saw once he got to Washington. It was far from the Ellipse—a thirty- to forty-minute walk—but there were other people there who were headed to the rally.[1]

Christopher Alberts, handyman and former National Guardsman, Maryland: I got out of my vehicle, grabbed the gas mask, draped it on my leg. Saw a few other people parking. Said, "Hey, you know, where are you guys from?" One was from Montana. The other was from Wyoming. I said, "Where are you guys heading to?" And they're like, "We're going to the Ellipse."

In addition to the gas mask, Alberts was wearing body armor. He was carrying what he called his "three-day" backpack full of supplies, including ready-to-eat meals. And he had his sidearm—a Taurus G2C 9-millimeter with the magazine in the pistol.

Doug Jensen and his friend Anthony were also headed toward Washington, nearing the end of an all-night drive from Des Moines. Anthony wasn't into politics, but he had agreed to come along for the ride. The rally was supposed to start at 11 a.m., and Jensen's GPS showed that he was cutting it close. He pulled into the driveway of his hotel in downtown Washington just before Trump was scheduled to speak.[2]

Doug Jensen, Iowa: We made it only because Trump was late. I paid to check in early, but I never went to my room. I just did the valet to turn my car in. And then we walked to the rally.

The crowd on the National Mall was huge—around fifty-three thousand people spread out from the Ellipse, where Trump would take the stage, to the Washington Monument across the street.[3]

Pamela Hemphill, retired drug and alcohol counselor, Idaho: I walked around, and it was peaceful. Everybody's just—it's like a love-in. Flags, selling T-shirts, music going on, people talking, groups of people. It was very pleasant.

Annie Howell, Pennsylvania: I met up with contacts from Facebook and various other people that we had been talking to throughout our time there. We got in line. We were taking pictures. There was a point in time that I left the line to go look at some of the landmarks.

Rep. Ronny Jackson, R-TX: I wasn't planning on going. Then I was with a couple of folks in my office, my scheduler in particular, and she was kind of waiting to go down there. And so I looked at the clock and I said, "Well, look, we don't have to be on the floor until around noon."

Alondra Propes, former parole and probation officer, Oath Keepers, Florida: It was really full of energy. I mean, people were freezing. Normally there is nothing that would make me go stand out in the cold.

Rep. Ronny Jackson, R-TX: We couldn't stay very long because it took us a while to get down there. So I thought, well, we'll just stay for thirty minutes, see if we can find some of my constituents down there, say hi to them, and get back. Of course, there were way too many people for that to happen.

Rep. Peter Welch, D-VT: I remember it was a really beautiful day. I took a walk around the mall to Lincoln Memorial and back, and I was by the Ellipse where folks were waiting for the president. And it was a feverish pitch there.

Rep. Ronny Jackson, R-TX: I looked, and there's just thousands and thousands of people between the Ellipse where the stage was set up and the Washington Monument, and then both to the east and the west. There's a huge, huge sea of people, you know, all red, white, and blue. Trump hats and flags and everything. It was super-peaceful. People had their kids down there, and it was pretty festive.

Alondra Propes, former parole and probation officer, Oath Keepers, Florida: People were singing. People were chanting.

Rep. Peter Welch, D-VT: What I found so alarming about it was that there was this raw anger that was being expressed. And there was a chant people were yelling—really alarming. It was "F those people, F those people."

US Park Police officers reported seeing "numerous individuals" with firearms, pepper spray, pipes, and other possible weapons. Others were wearing body armor and riot gear, carrying radio equipment, and wearing "military-grade" backpacks. Among those who were screened, the Secret Service had confiscated hundreds of prohibited items—knives, pepper spray, brass knuckles, gas masks, Tasers, body armor, and batons.[4]

Police identified members of extremist groups in the crowd, some of them wearing tactical gear or signature clothing. A large group of Proud Boys wore orange hats. Many of the protesters carried flags with "Trump" emblazoned on them or symbols adopted by the far right, including the bright yellow Revolutionary War–era Gadsden flag with its rattlesnake and the words "Don't Tread on Me." One man who would later walk to the Capitol was wearing a "Camp Auschwitz" T-shirt. Another man had climbed a tree and was waving a Confederate flag.

Chief Robert Contee, Metropolitan Police Department: We were getting reports of some individuals armed.

Inspector Robert Glover, Metropolitan Police Department: I saw the veteran groups showing up in their helmets and their vests, the armored-plate carriers and things like that. Started to see a lot of people with the Gadsden flag showing up. Saw a group with orange hats show up and kind of stay together.

Julio Cortez, photographer, The Associated Press: We were trying to wade through the crowds. They couldn't really see our cameras because they were down, but they could see we were wearing masks. And that alone made people really hostile to us.

John Minchillo, photographer, The Associated Press: We understood that this situation was rapidly degenerating even before POTUS came to speak, because the warm-up acts were particularly aggressive.

Trump had not yet taken the stage, but many of his allies were giving raucous speeches.[5] *Giuliani, the former New York mayor and Trump's lawyer, was repeating conspiracy theories about voting machines and suggested "trial by combat." Republican Rep. Mo Brooks of Alabama encouraged the crowd to take his message to the Capitol. "Today is the day that American patriots start taking down names and kicking ass!" he said. Brooks continued,*

> Our ancestors sacrificed their blood, their sweat, their tears, their fortunes, and sometimes their lives, to give us, their descendants, an America that is the greatest nation in world history. So I have a question for you: Are you willing to do the same? My answer is yes. Louder! Are you willing to do what it takes to fight for America? Louder! Will you fight for America?

Annie Howell, Pennsylvania: I think people were overall happy, like I said, hopeful. But once the speakers came out, for me at least, I felt like—I don't know, I felt like people were getting angry because of the way that the speakers were talking. They were very abrasive. They were very combative. They were very accusatory.

Chief Robert Contee, Metropolitan Police Department: Emotionally, I mean, there were a lot of people that were just kind of charged up. And I mean, you can tell when—I mean, some people who may have never been in a fight before, they might not even understand what I'm talking about. But when you see people that are, like, tensed up, kind of amped up, I mean, that feels different from, you know, everybody just, you know, here having a lovefest, expressing their First Amendment rights. This was different. It was altogether different from anything else that I've ever experienced.

John Minchillo, photographer, The Associated Press: There were television screens up, and it very much had the feeling of a concert. It had a circus-like quality to it. In the photograph that I made, that really sticks with me. They zoomed into a close-up of [Trump's] eyes [in a photo on one of the screens], and the color grading is really aggressive, very high contrast. So the darks are really dark and the lights are really light and the color is really saturated. It almost seems like a movie trailer for a Michael Bay movie, like *Transformers*, you know, something like *Rambo*. There was really intense music, and it was very militaristic.

Julio Cortez, photographer, The Associated Press: There was a guy walking around with a megaphone saying, "As soon as Trump is done speaking, we're going into the Capitol!"

Cortez and Minchillo worked together often, and they were familiar with volatile protests. The two men had spent weeks together the previous summer documenting the riots that erupted after the murder of George Floyd, and the work had at times been dangerous as they photographed fires and violence in the streets of Minneapolis. So they knew to stick together, and they knew the signs of a peaceful demonstration that is about to turn into something else.

John Minchillo, photographer, The Associated Press: I grabbed Julio and said, "We need to get to the Capitol now. If we don't get there now, we're going to be behind it." It was just a vibe; it was a feeling. You just knew it was going to happen the moment you heard them speaking.

12:00 p.m.

A few minutes before noon, an hour late, Trump strode onto the stage and spoke for more than an hour. As the enormous crowd roared, he falsely declared that the states wanted to "recertify" and that Pence could hand him the win:

> States want to revote. The states got defrauded, They were given false information. They voted on it. Now they want to recertify. They want it back. All Vice President Pence has to do is send it back to the states to recertify and we become president and you are the happiest people.[1]

He told the massive crowd to "peacefully and patriotically make your voices heard." But then he delivered a different and powerful directive:

> And we fight. We fight like hell. And if you don't fight like hell, you're not going to have a country anymore. Our exciting adventures and boldest endeavors have not yet begun. My fellow Americans, for our movement, for our children, and for our beloved country. And I say this despite all that's happened. The best is yet to come. So we're going to, we're going to walk down Pennsylvania

> Avenue. I love Pennsylvania Avenue. And we're going to the Capitol, and we're going to try and give—the Democrats are hopeless, they never vote for anything. Not even one vote. But we're going to try and give our Republicans—the weak ones because the strong ones don't need any of our help. We're going to try and give them the kind of pride and boldness that they need to take back our country. So let's walk down Pennsylvania Avenue. I want to thank you all. God bless you and God bless America.

Jason Riddle, former correctional officer and mail carrier, New Hampshire: It was really surreal. You felt like you were in a movie, because his voice is echoing everywhere. These flags waving, you just hear people chanting here and there.

Annie Howell, Pennsylvania: I remember leaving a couple minutes early when Trump was speaking, probably about twenty minutes early just because of the size of the crowd.

Pamela Hemphill, retired drug and alcohol counselor, Idaho: I was by myself. And so I said to a couple people, "Is there like, a brochure? Is anything else going to happen today?" And they said, "No, but we heard that Trump's going to the Capitol."

Janet Buhler, music teacher and college fashion instructor, Utah: Some people started saying, "They're about to vote." And then I feel like then you could see who was concerned about that, because people started just, like, leaving.

Julio Cortez, photographer, The Associated Press: Most people were walking and listening to the speech on their phones with speakers.

Jason Riddle, former correctional officer and mail carrier, New Hampshire: My friend Paul kept pointing out that someone had a pitchfork. He kept going, "Why does he have a trident?"

At 12 p.m., as Trump was speaking, the House gaveled in for the day.[2] *Chaplain Margaret Kibben, on her third day on the job, opened with a prayer:*

> We, who have pledged to defend our Constitution against all enemies, we pray your hedge of protection around this nation. Defend us from those adversaries, both foreign and domestic, outside these walls and perhaps within these chambers, who sow seeds of acrimony to divide colleagues and conspire to undermine trust in your divine authority over all things.

A half hour later, the Senate opened with a prayer from Chaplain Barry Black, who had his own divine request:[3]

> Almighty God, have compassion on us with your unfailing love. As our lawmakers prepare to formally certify the votes cast by the electoral college, be present with them. Guide our legislators with your wisdom and truth as they seek to meet the requirements of the U.S. Constitution. Lord, inspire them to seize this opportunity to demonstrate to the nation and world how the democratic process can be done properly and in an orderly manner. Help them to remember that history is a faithful stenographer, and so are you. We pray in your sovereign name. Amen.

Senate Chaplain Barry Black: I was awakened early in the morning and given a heads-up that this is going to be a different day. Without that experience, I would not have ended the prayer by saying, "remind our lawmakers that history is a faithful stenographer, and so are you." In other words, what they do here today will be etched in stone going forward.

As the Senate opened, Mike Pence was traveling by motorcade to the Capitol with his chief of staff, Marc Short, and his counsel, Greg Jacob.

Pence had been working for days, if not weeks, on a three-page letter to send out just before the 1 p.m. session began. It came after Trump had aggressively pressured him—as recently as that morning in a contentious phone call—to thwart the Constitution and try to delay the count. In the letter, Pence had written that while "I share the concerns of millions of Americans about the integrity of this election," he would not challenge the results.

> As a student of history who loves the Constitution and reveres its Framers, I do not believe that the Founders of our country intended to invest the Vice President with unilateral authority to decide which electoral votes should be counted during the Joint Session of Congress, and no Vice President in American history has ever asserted such authority. Instead, Vice Presidents presiding over Joint Sessions have uniformly followed the Electoral Count Act, conducting the proceedings in an orderly manner even where the count resulted in the defeat of their party or their own candidacy. . . .
>
> . . . Four years ago, surrounded by my family, I took an oath to support and defend the Constitution, which ended with the words, "So help me God." Today I want to assure the American people that I will keep the oath I made to them and I will keep the oath I made to Almighty God. When the Joint Session of Congress convenes today, I will do my duty to see to it that we open the certificates of the Electors of the several states, we hear objections raised by Senators and Representatives, and we count the votes of the Electoral College for President and Vice President in a manner consistent with our Constitution, laws, and history. So Help Me God.[4]

Greg Jacob, counsel to Vice President Pence: The whole trip up [to the Capitol], I was proofing and proofing the statement to make sure that there were no periods or commas in the wrong places, that it was formatted correctly. And then I think just as we were pulling up to the Capitol, I sent it off to our communications director, Devin O'Malley, so that he could then make sure that it got distributed properly. So I didn't get to pay as much attention to who was lining or not lining the streets or anything like that.

Marc Short, chief of staff, Vice President Pence: We felt like it was important that this get out before 1:00 and we couldn't wait for [Trump] to finish. And so, roughly at about 12:40, 12:45, it was distributed.

Chris Hodgson, director of legislative affairs, Vice President Pence: I think our decision, based on the logistics, was to have it go out simultaneously with the start of the joint session. It wasn't relevant to the president's comments.

As Pence arrived in the Capitol, senators were gathering on the Senate floor to walk to the House for the 1 p.m. session. He had a brief conversation with Chaplain Barry Black, a longtime friend.

Senate Chaplain Barry Black: It was an opportunity for me to share with him what I felt God was saying to me early in the morning, and that this was going to be—I think my opening line was "Mr. Vice President, this will be a day like no other day you could possibly anticipate."

Nancy Pelosi was in her office preparing for the 1 p.m. session with her top aides and her daughter Alexandra, who was filming her mother for an upcoming documentary. Alexandra's son, accompanying his mother, was looking out the window down the National Mall when he alerted the room to a crowd marching down Pennsylvania Avenue and toward the Capitol. But Pelosi wasn't immediately worried. In her many years as speaker, she had seen a lot of protests out her windows.

House Speaker Nancy Pelosi, D-CA: As speaker, how many times outside the window had we had pro-life, pro-choice, pro-war—whatever it happens to be, it's the vitality of a democracy.

Trump was still speaking down the street, and he told the crowd he was going to the Capitol.

Alisa La, special assistant to House Speaker Nancy Pelosi: Our staff were scrambling to get the rules of the House and the sergeant at arms to try to find out if POTUS could come to the House floor uninvited.

Terri McCullough, chief of staff, House Speaker Nancy Pelosi: I got a call from the House sergeant at arms making me aware that he had been in contact with the Secret Service and that there had been some talk that Trump was going to come from the rally down with the rallygoers at that moment to the Capitol. But the Secret Service was dissuading him. I let the speaker know, and her response was one for the ages.

"I hope he comes; I'm going to punch him out," Pelosi said with a flash of anger captured in Alexandra's video. "This is my moment." She added, "I'm going to go to jail, and I'm going to be happy."[5]

House Speaker Nancy Pelosi, D-CA: I wasn't joking. It was self-defense.

Trump would sit in his car for a while after the rally, and it wasn't clear initially whether he might head down Pennsylvania Avenue. But his security team pushed back, and he stayed at the White House.[6]

House Speaker Nancy Pelosi, D-CA: He didn't have the courage to come to the Capitol. We knew that.

Down the hall, Rep. Liz Cheney, R-WY, was in the Republican cloakroom just off the House floor. She had gotten there ahead of the session's 1 p.m. start to work on the remarks she was planning to give during the debate over state electors. She would be one of a handful in her party speaking out against the objections. Trump was still speaking down the street, and he mentioned Cheney's name as he riled up the huge crowd:

> We've got to get rid of the weak Congress people, the ones that aren't any good, the Liz Cheneys of the world. We got to get rid of them.

Soon after that, Cheney's phone rang. It was her father, former Vice President Dick Cheney.

Rep. Liz Cheney, R-WY: He said to me, "You're in danger." He knew I was getting ready to speak, and he said, "We need to think about the fact that you're about to speak because the president has put a target on you." And then we had this conversation where—he was very worried and angry as a dad, and he was very sad, I'd say heartbroken, about what was happening to the country at that moment. But we both knew I couldn't not speak.

Capitol Police and the Metropolitan Police Department were closely watching the crowd at the Ellipse as Trump's speech wore on. But they suddenly had an even more urgent concern—a pipe bomb discovered in an alleyway behind the Republican National Committee headquarters, a block from the Capitol complex.[7]

Chief Robert Contee, Metropolitan Police Department: At about 12:45 p.m., the first of two pipe bombs were found.

Chief Steven Sund, US Capitol Police: We responded immediately to coordinate and send resources to the scene, including a number of officers, officials, and a bomb squad. We also dispatched resources to look for other explosive devices, suspects, and vehicles.

Chief Robert Contee, Metropolitan Police Department: The second pipe bomb was found about thirty minutes later, at the Democratic National Committee headquarters. MPD [Metropolitan Police Department] responded to the scenes for the pipe bombs to assist the Capitol Police. Additional officers were on standby.

Assistant Chief Yogananda Pittman, US Capitol Police: USCP officers facilitated the evacuation of House office buildings located near the pipe bombs and, with the assistance of law enforcement partners, also evacuated residents and businesses in the area. Once the evacuations were complete, the USCP and its law enforcement partners securely detonated the two bombs.

Chief Steven Sund, US Capitol Police: At almost the exact same time, we observed a large group of individuals approaching the West Front of the Capitol.

With Trump's speech going long, many of his supporters hadn't waited for him to finish before heading to the Capitol. The department's resources had been diverted to manage the recently discovered bombs, temporarily distracting Capitol Police from the incoming protests.

Inspector Robert Glover, Metropolitan Police Department: I could look further north and saw a group, a large group that caught my attention moving east down Constitution Avenue. I didn't know their destination, but it was unplanned, and it wasn't something that we were expecting.

Lieutenant Tia Summers, US Capitol Police: We started observing the crowds on the news. We had some of the cameras in place to look down the avenues and down the mall. We were also getting reports over the radio of a large crowd on its way to the Capitol.

Before long, the police cameras would capture what looked like a "wall of people" headed down Pennsylvania Avenue.[8]

Officer Winston Pingeon, US Capitol Police: At least one other officer in my squad was watching live on his phone what Trump was saying. But I don't think I was paying much attention to that. I was just hoping this was just going to be another day.

Capitol Police Inspector Thomas Loyd, who supervised around 350 officers, was waiting in the Senate to escort Vice President Pence across the Capitol just before the 1 p.m. joint session. But around 12:45, Loyd got a call from Assistant Capitol Police Chief Chad Thomas. Loyd had known Thomas for twenty-five years, and it was the first time he'd ever heard such an urgent tone in his voice. Thomas was panicked.

Inspector Thomas Loyd, US Capitol Police: He told me that there were a lot of people coming my way. I was a bit confused about that statement because we knew a lot of people were coming on the outside of the building on that particular day, and that's what I told him. But he ended the conversation by saying, "Tom, you have a lot of people coming your way."

The Proud Boys, who enthusiastically described themselves as a "pro-Western fraternal organization" of men who "refuse to apologize for creating the modern world,"[9] *had received a shot of energy the previous fall when President Trump had told them to "stand back and stand by" at a debate with Joe Biden.*[10] *The group had been building momentum since then, exchanging hundreds of messages in the weeks since Trump had lost that predicted a revolution. "The media constantly accuses us of wanting to start a civil war," Proud Boys Leader Enrique Tarrio wrote in one message. "Careful what the fuck you ask for we don't want to start one . . . but we will sure as fuck finish one."*[11]

Tarrio had been arrested at the airport when he'd arrived in Washington two days earlier, the charges stemming from a protest in December when he'd burned a "Black Lives Matter" banner that had been taken down from a historic Black church. He had been released, but he wasn't there when his crew approached the Capitol that afternoon.[12]

One of Tarrio's top allies, Joseph Biggs of Ormond Beach, Florida, was now standing in a group of people at the northwest edge of the Capitol lawn, staring down a thin line of Capitol Police officers guarding a sidewalk leading up to the building. It was fifteen minutes before the joint session of Congress was about to start.[13]

US Capitol Police Officer Caroline Edwards, stationed at the West Front of the Capitol: They came up chanting "F-U-C-K antifa."

Caroline Edwards had started training to become a Capitol Police officer a few days after Trump had been inaugurated in 2017. She'd joined the First Responder Unit, which guards the outside of the building, and the Civil Disturbance Unit—partly to prove that her small size and gender didn't prevent her from doing some of the toughest jobs that often went to "big burly guys." She had worked maybe three hundred protests by January 6th, and based on those experiences, she did not expect the day to be exceedingly violent.[14]

Officer Caroline Edwards, US Capitol Police: So there was our bike rack, and then at the bottom of the Pennsylvania Avenue walkway right by Peace Circle there was another bike rack. And so the crowd had kind of gathered there.

Edwards and just a few other officers in the Capitol Police First Responder Unit were posted at the front of the west lawn, on the Senate side of the building almost at the road, defending a flimsy line of waist-height bike racks set up as barricades when the first protesters approached from Pennsylvania Avenue. Edwards and the handful of officers alongside her were supposed to be the "hard" line of defense, as security officials had decided against the more fortified perimeter that would have been in place for the president's State of the Union speech and other major events. Still, Edwards was wearing only her regular uniform, and her hard gear was in a bus a block away. Her supervisors had not given them any instructions about what to do if they suddenly needed that gear.[15]

The group of Proud Boys, along with other protesters who had left Trump's speech early, stood on Peace Circle, just across from her. Biggs had been using a megaphone to lead chants for a large crowd: "We love Trump! We love Trump!"[16] *As Edwards tried to look strong behind the bike racks, the group approached the line.*

Officer Caroline Edwards, US Capitol Police: Joseph Biggs' rhetoric turned to the Capitol Police. He started asking us questions like you've—you didn't miss a paycheck during the pandemic. Mentioning stuff about our pay scale. And, you know, started turning the tables on us.

Nick Quested, documentarian following the Proud Boys: I was surprised at the size of the group, the anger, and the profanity.

Officer Caroline Edwards, US Capitol Police: We heard, "Animal"; we heard, "You're Nancy Pelosi's dogs. Bark for us."

As the group of protesters confronted them, Edwards and the other officers grabbed the bike racks. From there, the push was quick. "USA! USA! USA!" the crowd roared as several dozen men tried to rip down the barricade in front of her. Edwards held two racks together at chest level and pushed toward the men, most of whom were much bigger than she was.

Officer Caroline Edwards, US Capitol Police: I wasn't under any pretense that I could hold it for very long. But I just wanted to make sure that we could get more people down and get our [Civil Defense Units] time to answer the call. So we started grappling over the bike racks. I felt the bike rack come on top of my head and I was pushed backwards and my foot caught the stair behind me and my chin hit the handrail. At that point I had blacked out. The back of my head clipped the concrete stairs behind me.

While Edwards lay on the ground, temporarily knocked out, a handful of officers still tried to beat back the crowd, using their hands and fists to try to push people back. But they were vastly outnumbered. Edwards came to, and she and the other officers ran back toward the Capitol as the crowd climbed over the racks and chased them.[17]

The first section of the Capitol perimeter had been breached. It was 12:53, seven minutes before the start of the joint session. The Proud Boys and the rest of the crowd pushed into the northwest lawn and started to fill the lower terrace in front of the building.

Chief Robert Contee, Metropolitan Police Department: At 12:58 p.m., Chief Sund asked for MPD's assistance to address the growing violent mob at the Capitol. Officers were immediately authorized to deploy to the West Front of the Capitol and arrived within minutes.[18]

Detective Phuson Nguyen, Metropolitan Police Department: Our incident commander went over the radio and stated that the Capitol Police needed our help.

Michael Fanone, plainclothes officer, Metropolitan Police Department: Like many other officers, I could not ignore the numerous calls for help coming from the Capitol complex. For the first time in nearly a decade, I put on my uniform.

Assistant Chief Yogananda Pittman, US Capitol Police: We have phone lines blowing up, radios blowing up, hundreds of officers starting to engage, and that was well before the president's speech ended.

Chief Steven Sund, US Capitol Police: As soon as they came to the West Front, the fighting was on. I've never seen anything like it.

Officer Harry Dunn, US Capitol Police: We were not prepared.

As the violence escalated on the West Front of the Capitol, the crowd was growing on the East Front as well. That side of the building was also protected by a thin line of officers and the same short, moveable bike racks, but the protesters were so far compliant and had not tried to break through. Francis Chung, a photographer for Politico's environmental news outlet E&E News, mingled with the crowd, hoping to get some good shots of the protests.

Francis Chung, staff photographer, E&E News: The speech over by the White House was still going on, but some people had apparently gone straight to the Capitol, and they had the bike racks set up. It was just bike-rack fences, and there were a few cops out there watching. It was kind of dead, actually. There were a few sporadic chants, but the energy was low. I remember thinking that my shots were boring. Up until the Josh Hawley moment.

As the joint session was about to start, Republican Sen. Josh Hawley of Missouri, one of two Republican senators planning to object to the election results, appeared on the plaza.

Francis Chung, staff photographer, E&E News: Josh Hawley was the first and only lawmaker I did see that day. I just suddenly noticed him, and he was walking from the Senate side of the plaza over towards the House side, where the joint session was going to happen. I was pretty far away from him, so I ran over. It took me a little bit of time to catch up to him. He was like, waving and fist pumping. That's not even registering in the moment. I'm just trying to get a picture of him and whatever he's doing.

Sen. Josh Hawley, R-MO: I was pumping my fist at demonstrators who were gathered peacefully. So there were barricades set up. And there were a bunch of demonstrators there with American flags and whatnot, standing behind the barricades. I was going into the House chamber. This was before we started the count process. I was on my way in and I waved at them and some of them called out to me and so I waved and pumped my fist and said hello.

Francis Chung, staff photographer, E&E News: The frame I filed was the fist pump because it was the best frame.

Chung sent the photo in, and his editor tweeted it out, and the photo immediately went viral. Whatever Hawley meant with the gesture, many saw it—symbolically or otherwise—as a link between the Republican lawmakers' challenges and the day's violence outside.

Sen. Josh Hawley, R-MO: People who want to demonstrate and who want to express their views and do it peacefully, which is what those folks were doing, that's the First Amendment, and I will absolutely defend that every time.

1:00 p.m.

The Senate arrived at the doors of the House one minute before the joint session was scheduled to start. Oblivious to the chaos outside, senators had paraded across the Capitol, as per tradition, following young aides who carried the three mahogany boxes holding the certificates of electoral votes sent by every state. Vice President Mike Pence, who served as the president of the Senate, walked immediately behind the boxes and in front of the senators.

Greg Jacob, counsel to Vice President Pence: The whole Senate needed to process across the Capitol to the House chamber for the count. And we got up there relatively shortly before the count, so we had to pretty quickly move into that. And I think the vice president was asking, even as he headed into the House chamber on the other side, "Have you got the statement out? Is it out?" He wanted to make sure that was out before they started.

Chris Hodgson, director of legislative affairs, Vice President Pence: I brought hard copies as well to be distributed for anybody who didn't receive it via email or hadn't seen it yet, so they could read it on the floor if they wanted to. And I gave it to both floor staff of the Republicans and Democrats to put down on the tables in the front in the House chamber.

Rep. Jamie Raskin, D-MD: It was a great moment of relief. I remember exhaling deeply at that point. Because I felt that we could get through every other parliamentary contingency and eventuality if we could just make sure that the vice president didn't just knock over the nightstand. History plays tricks on everybody, and I had been so worried about Vice President Pence. And in fact, I should have been worried about the people who wanted to hang Mike Pence.

Paul Irving, House sergeant at arms: I started the day believing that my official duties on the House floor for the joint session would predominate my day. At around 1 p.m., I announced to the speaker in the House chamber the arrival of the vice president and the Senate.

The Senate's arrival at any joint session, including the annual State of the Union, is usually an exuberant affair. House members clap and cheer and line the center aisle to shake the hands of senators, who bask in the attention and walk to the front like visiting royalty. But the mood was more sober than usual. All eyes were on Pence, who walked down the center aisle alone and then stepped up to the rostrum next to Pelosi. There had been occasional tension in the past when the two had sat there together, including a year earlier, when Pelosi had angrily ripped up her copy of Trump's State of the Union speech. But this time she gave Pence a friendly nod as he took his seat.

Rep. Ronny Jackson, R-TX: It was pretty neat. The Senate came in and everything, they just filed in, and I was sitting down there and they all filed in. We met together, a joint session of Congress with the House and Senate together. Everything was going fine.

Just before the Senate entered, Pelosi had started with an admonishment for Republicans, who packed their side of the chamber despite pandemic rules for spacing set by the Capitol physician. She had asked that members leave the floor so it would be less crowded—meaning they would watch from their offices—but few did. She was clearly annoyed that members weren't following the protocol.

Joe Novotny, House reading clerk: Speaker Pelosi when she presides has a certain style, and I did notice how agitated she was. Not with staff or anybody; it was just more—it was a nervousness. Asking questions. Remaining cool as a cucumber as she's acknowledging members, but behind the scenes I could sense this, almost like a jittery feeling. All of us were starting to pick up on the vibe.

As the session began, Pence took the microphone to present the certificates of the electoral votes in alphabetical order. Senate Rules Committee Chairman Roy Blunt, R-MO, was the first of the four bipartisan "tellers" to speak, presenting Alabama's electoral votes. House Administration Committee Chairwoman Zoe Lofgren, D-CA, read Alaska. As each state's certificate was presented, Pence announced that the parliamentarians had advised him it was the "only certificate of vote from that state"—new language that Pence had added himself to head off any attempts to present alternative slates of electors.[1] *Next was Minnesota Sen. Amy Klobuchar, the top Democrat on the Senate Rules panel, who presented Arizona.*

Rep. Rodney Davis, R-IL, the top Republican on the House Administration Committee: We had opened up the ceremony, and we had certified two states. Before we could get to Arkansas, which I was supposed to read and nobody was objecting to, the first objection came up. Senator Cruz stood along with the objectors in the House, and we then went into the debate.

Fewer than fifteen minutes after the joint session had started—as Trump was finishing his speech and as the violence was escalating outside—the Senate left the House and walked back across the Capitol for up to two hours of debate on the Arizona electors.

House lawmakers—mostly Democrats—had spread into the second floor of the chamber, where they rarely sit, to create the social distance suggested by the Capitol physician. Pelosi had invited some members of her caucus to speak on the floor, and several of those Democrats were sitting together in the upper galleries to wait their turn.

Rep. Bennie Thompson, D-MS: I got what I called a bird's-eye view of the process. And I thought it would be something that I could tell my grandchildren, that I was there when the certification of the election took place.

Rep. Pramila Jayapal, D-WA: I had had a knee replacement surgery just five weeks before, and so I was walking with a cane. And I was given a place in the gallery.

Rep. Annie Kuster, D-NH: I have a photo of me sitting. I had a little pocket Constitution. And I'm looking out at the scene, and I sent it to my family. We have a family text chain with all my nieces and my kids. And I sent it to my family to say I have this tremendous honor to witness history today. And little did I realize that they all were at a total tailspin later because they knew I was there and they kept texting, "Are you okay, where are you?"

At first, the House debate proceeded as expected. The Democrats, who had been meeting for weeks, laid out their arguments in defense of the Constitution. Raskin was one of the first to speak, and he started out by thanking colleagues for their kindness after the death of his son—a momentary interlude from the tension. The entire chamber, members of both parties, suddenly erupted in applause. Surprised by the response, Raskin looked down and put his hand on his heart.

Rep. Jamie Raskin, D-MD: Everybody clapped, and it was a standing ovation. I was so shocked and taken aback by the emotion in the chamber that I just had this almost hallucinatory thought that maybe all of the division and conflict that was about to happen might be dispelled. It was just magical thinking. But I just kept thinking, maybe because of Tommy they'll just let all of this rancor go. But obviously not.

As the Democrats laid out their arguments, it was clear that the objectors were prepared as well. Jen Daulby, the Republican staff director of the House Administration Committee, was watching ringleader Jim Jordan, an Ohio Republican who had been strategizing with Trump.

Jen Daulby, Republican staff director, House Administration Committee: Jim Jordan and a bunch of those members walked in, and they were super-organized and together.

As the debate got underway, members started nervously looking at their phones. Some of their offices had been evacuated because of the pipe bombs discovered at the RNC and DNC—though they didn't yet know that was the reason—and there were reports of a growing number of protesters outside. Few people realized that the outer perimeter had been breached.

Joe Novotny, House reading clerk: All of a sudden, you start hearing chatter within the chamber. And you started to pick up on the fact that members were not talking about what was happening within the chamber.

Rep. Lisa Blunt Rochester, D-DE: I was wanting to say, why do people have their phones out during this really important time?

Emily Cochrane, congressional reporter, *The New York Times*: As they often do on the floor, they had this very choreographed schedule of who was going to deliver the challenge, who was going to condemn it from the Democratic side, who was going to weigh in one way or another from the Republican side. And that choreography was going on like nothing was happening outside, because they were so focused on what they were doing.

Terri McCullough, chief of staff, House Speaker Nancy Pelosi: Our staff had a daily text chain where we shared information, made sure everybody was up to speed. Somebody texted that they pulled down the bike racks, or that the bike racks had been turned over. I didn't immediately make a connection in my head that that was a barrier to entry.

Across the Capitol, senators were also largely unaware of the clashes outside. Senate Republican Leader Mitch McConnell was making a final plea to any of his Republican colleagues who were considering a vote for the Arizona objection:

> My colleagues, nothing before us proves illegality anywhere near the massive scale—the massive scale that would have tipped the entire election, nor can public doubt alone justify a radical break when the doubt itself was incited without any evidence.
>
> The Constitution gives us here in Congress a limited role. We cannot simply declare ourselves a national board of elections on steroids. The voters, the courts, and the states have all spoken. They have all spoken. If we overrule them, it would damage our republic forever. This election actually was not unusually close. Just in recent history, 1976, 2000, and 2004 were all closer than this one. The electoral college margin is almost identical to what it was in 2016. If this election were overturned by mere allegations from the losing side, our democracy would enter a death spiral.

Arguing for the objection, Texas Sen. Ted Cruz made the case that public doubt was indeed enough justification:

> We gather together at a moment of great division, at a moment of great passion. We have seen and, no doubt, will continue to see a great deal of moralizing from both sides of the aisle, but I would urge to both sides perhaps a bit less certitude and a bit more recognition that we are gathered at a time when democracy is in crisis. Recent polling shows that 39 percent of Americans believe the election that just occurred "was rigged." You may not agree

with that assessment, but it is, nonetheless, a reality for nearly half the country.

Outside the chamber and around the Capitol, senators and staff started to notice the ruckus outside the building. Senate Chaplain Barry Black was watching the crowd from his large, round third-floor window, where he has one of the most spectacular views from the Capitol—all the way down the National Mall to the Lincoln Memorial.

Senate Chaplain Barry Black: When I looked out the window, I saw a gathering of people coming toward the Capitol, and it was a very impressive size for a crowd. And they seemed ready for—let's just say they did not seem interested in nonviolent direct action of the kind I participated in in the 1960s, when I was a university student in Huntsville, Alabama. This was obviously going to be a physical confrontation.

Three floors down, in the basement near her Capitol "hideaway" office—one of the small rooms near the Senate chamber assigned to each senator—Democratic Sen. Catherine Cortez Masto of Nevada found Sens. Tina Smith, D-MN, and Lisa Murkowski, R-AK, standing outside a restroom, looking concerned.

Sen. Catherine Cortez Masto, D-NV: They said, "There's a Capitol Police officer in there, he's got something in his eyes and he is flushing his eyes out with water." And I leaned in and I saw the officer at the bathroom sink and I thought to myself, and I said aloud to my colleagues, "I think he's been pepper sprayed." And I asked him, "Have you been pepper sprayed?" And he said, "Yes, but don't worry. Everything's fine. I am going to keep you all safe." And with that, he dashed back out the door and up the stairs.

The Trump supporters who had just broken through the barricades at Peace Circle were spreading out, and they quickly breached another police line as they moved toward the building. Joseph Biggs and some of the other Proud Boys, including Dominic Pezzola, a man in his mid-forties from New York, frequently stopped to take selfies or shoot videos. "Dude, we're right in front of the Capitol right now," Biggs said in one video. "American citizens are storming the Capitol—taking it back right now. There's millions of people out here. This is fucking crazy. Oh my God! This is such history!"[2]

Captain Jessica Baboulis, US Capitol Police: The initial call for help came out in the area of Peace Circle, which is in the northwest grounds of the US Capitol complex. And then it was repeated. I mean, just through radio, you could hear where the crowd was moving and approaching the Capitol, and officers were retreating to try and gain more coverage of the building itself as opposed to the very broad grounds. So you can hear these multiple breaches occurring.

Officer Harry Dunn, US Capitol Police: I heard urgent radio calls for additional officers to respond to the west side, and an exclamation, in a desperate voice, that demonstrators on the west side had "breached the fence!"

Officer Shae Cooney, US Capitol Police: The panic I heard on the radio justified me getting there as fast as possible.

Inspector Thomas Loyd, US Capitol Police: I went into Senator McConnell's office, the majority leader at the time, because his office had a bird's-eye view of the breach. I went in there, looked out of the window, saw that it was very bad, and then I made my way onto the West Front, onto the stage.

Officer Winston Pingeon, US Capitol Police: At that point it was like, okay, this is "game on." And you get that adrenaline pumping. This is what we're trained to do.

Perched on the terrace, Capitol Police Officer Shae Cooney saw the large group of protesters coming down Pennsylvania Avenue. She felt paralyzed for a moment, overwhelmed by the size of the crowd.

Officer Shae Cooney, US Capitol Police: A little panic came through, knowing how many people there were and how many officers we had. We knew that we weren't going to have enough.

Officer Winston Pingeon, US Capitol Police: We formed up and marched right up to the West Front. And at that point things were kind of going crazy.

Officer Shae Cooney, US Capitol Police: Once they broke through the fence, we saw that they were growing more agitated, more angry at us.

Members of the Capitol Police Civil Disturbance Unit had formed a line on the Upper West Terrace, above the crowd as people were pushing toward the Senate side of the building. Some of the officers were holding grenade launchers and prepared to deploy chemical munitions—"PepperBall" irritants made from the resin of chili peppers—if told to do so. At 1:06, as the joint session was just starting inside, they got the order to deploy.[3]

Officer Shauni Kerkhoff, US Capitol Police, Civil Disturbance Unit: The PepperBall system is powered by compressed air, and it launches a projectile at an individual, and it causes both a pain compliance but also releases that irritant, that PAVA powder, in the air. It's basically a paintball gun.

It was the first time that those chemical projectiles—known as "less lethal" because they are designed to disperse rather than kill—had been used at the Capitol.[4] *Police would also use OC spray (made of oleoresin capsicum, a product derived from peppers) and other deterrents. They slowed the rioters' advance, but they weren't enough. Many of the first people to charge the building were wearing tactical gear or gas masks and pushed forward despite the projectiles and the spray. Some were firing their own chemical irritants back at the police.*

Sergeant Adam DesCamp, US Capitol Police, Civil Disturbance Unit: My mask was pushed aside, and I was sprayed with a couple different chemicals, one of which I don't even know what it was.

Inspector Thomas Loyd, US Capitol Police: We were greatly outnumbered. You're seeing thousands of people in the crowd to a couple dozen officers on the line.

Officer Shae Cooney, US Capitol Police: They were screaming at us, calling us names, shouting out, "USA, Trump, MAGA" over and over again. We were getting called pigs, traitors throughout the day.

Inspector Thomas Loyd, US Capitol Police: I was getting ready to evacuate—give up the entire stage and evacuate into the building because we were getting beaten up so bad. And then Metropolitan Police showed up and took over the line.

Inspector Robert Glover, Metropolitan Police Department: Upon my arrival, I noted that there were very few uniforms of the United States Capitol Police visible on the grass area, the West Front, or around the two circles, Peace and Grant Circle. I noticed the officers that I encountered on my walk up toward the West Front seemed to be very hectic and scattered, with no clear direction.

Chief Robert Contee, Metropolitan Police Department: Our members arrived at a chaotic scene. The violent mob overran protective measures at the Capitol in an attempted insurrection.

Inspector Robert Glover, Metropolitan Police Department: They [Capitol Police] weren't running toward the problem, and it almost seemed like they didn't really have an assignment at that point. And when I did get onto the West Front plaza, the officers that were there were fighting for every inch on the line.

Officer Winston Pingeon, US Capitol Police: We lined up, trying to defend the base of the building. But I remember thinking we weren't in a super-effective position, and I remember a whole squad of DC officers marching right by us. It was kind of like, wait, why aren't we going with them? But I was just the officer. I'm going to just do what I'm told.

Inspector Robert Glover, Metropolitan Police Department: I would estimate the crowd size at that moment in time [at] a couple thousand. They were hostile toward law enforcement. They were pushing and shoving. They were going hand to hand with the officers, the Capitol

Police officers that were already deployed. I did see Capitol Police officers were already hurt.

Chief Robert Contee, Metropolitan Police Department: Shortly after MPD officers arrived on the scene, I was able to stand on the West Front of the Capitol to get a broad view of the riot as many of MPD's brave officers made their way to the front line. Our police officers were under attack, the Capitol—hallowed ground for our country—was under attack, and the constitutional electoral process—the very foundation of our democracy—was under attack.

Officer Adam Eveland, Metropolitan Police Department: During Trump's speech, most of the questions were like, "Hey, where are the bathrooms?" "Which way is Trump speaking?" But after Trump's speech ended, people started coming up and asking, "Hey, which way is the US Capitol?" Well, that's an easy one. "It's just down Constitution Avenue. But it's closed to tourists today."

When Trump's speech ended at 1:10 p.m., an hour and thirteen minutes after he had started, another large wave of protesters headed to the Capitol. Trump had said he would go with them, but he had gone back to the White House instead.

Janet Buhler, music teacher and college fashion instructor, Utah: I think he suggested that he was going to do that, but in my mind I'm thinking, how could he do that? That would be—seems like that would be dangerous. Like, how could you have enough security around him?

Doug Jensen, Iowa: I was just hoping it was showtime basically, and then he gets done with this rally and I'm just kind of like—he's like, oh, let's all go march down peacefully, you know. He didn't tell us to go storm the building.

Robert Schornack, business development manager, Michigan: As far as making the decision to go down to the Capitol, yeah, it was probably when Trump said, hey, you know, "peacefully and patriotically" go down and protest at the Capitol.

Annie Howell, Pennsylvania: I think it was like a car accident. I wanted to see it, truthfully.

Jessica Watkins, US Army veteran and bar owner, Oath Keepers, Ohio: So before we left the Ellipse, like, the crowd was real, real thick. And then, like, everybody—like, literally everybody—just started pulling out their phones. They were like, "Pence betrayed us. Pence betrayed us." Like, we have to go.

Annie Howell, Pennsylvania: It was at that moment I think people turned on Vice President Pence, because I remember as we were walking to the Capitol building, people in the street were screaming, "Pence is a traitor!"

Jason Dolan, former marine, Oath Keepers, Florida: I think you kind of felt a palpable feeling where the crowd went from being pretty—a pretty happy, joyful crowd to a pretty kind of pissed-off crowd.

Robert Schornack, business development manager, Michigan: I did hear people say, "Hang Mike Pence." I wasn't going to get involved in that one. You know, they were saying other stuff like "Drag him out," and it was kind of humorous, to be honest.

Stephen Ayres, Ohio: There was a bunch of people that had bullhorns kind of like directing traffic, and just—we were just kind of going with the flow. You kind of got packed in like sardines.

Jessica Watkins, US Army veteran and bar owner, Oath Keepers, Ohio: It was like Fourth of July. It was awesome.

Doug Jensen, Iowa: [My friend Anthony] was walking with me and he's like, I don't want to go, I'm kind of scared. He's like, can I just go back to the room? And I'm like, sure. So he ditched me. He was like, I came here for—to be your friend, but I'm not going to that Capitol.

As Doug Jensen neared the building, another friend texted him with the incorrect information that it was already over. Jensen responded, "Lmao I'm here. Who the fuck told you that. We are headed to the White House."[5]

It was the first of many times that day that Jensen would confuse the Capitol and the White House, but it didn't really matter. Jensen knew he was there to protest Trump's defeat, and he was ready.

He also wanted to be a "poster boy" for QAnon, the group he followed that espoused the theory that Trump is saving the nation from a satanic cult of child sex traffickers. Jensen had closely monitored the mysterious online figure called "Q," and the letter was emblazoned on his dark shirt in the colors of an American flag, with an eagle in the center and two QAnon phrases: "Trust the Plan" and "Where we go one, we go all."

Around 1:30 p.m., the friend texted back with another incorrect update: "CNN pence banged the gavel[.] Joint sessions [sic] *certified all electoral votes as is." Jensen texted back, "That's all about to change."*[6]

Ashli Babbitt was a veteran of the US Air Force who had been deployed to Iraq and Afghanistan, but the thirty-five-year-old's last post had been in Washington, serving in the 113th Wing of the District of Columbia Air National Guard[7]*—nicknamed the "Capital Guardians."*[8]

Now, walking toward the Capitol after Trump's speech, the military veteran posted a video of herself to her Facebook page. "We are walking to the Capitol in a mob," she said. Decked out in jeans and a black jacket, she had a Trump flag tied around her neck, cascading down her back and draped over an American flag backpack.[9]

Like Jensen, Babbitt was an avid follower of QAnon, and she had been tweeting about the "storm"—a central QAnon belief that Trump would have a final victory over his political enemies. "The storm is here and it is descending upon DC in less than 24 hours," she had posted the day before.[10]

"There's an estimated over 3 million people here today," Babbitt said in the Facebook video, energized and almost giddy. "So despite what the media tells you, boots on ground definitely say something different."

Babbitt's numbers were off—she was in a group of tens of thousands of people rather than three million[11]*—but no one could have convinced her otherwise.*

"There is a sea of nothing but red white and blue patriots," she said. "God bless America."

Stewart Rhodes, the founder of the Oath Keepers, had called on Trump weeks earlier to invoke the Insurrection Act and form his own militia. And the group was storing weapons in Virginia, just outside Washington, just in case. Only two days after the election, before it was called for Biden, Rhodes had written to others in the group, "We aren't getting through this without a civil war. Too late for that. Prepare your mind, body, spirit."[12]

Now several groups of Oath Keepers were headed toward the Capitol. One group had equipped themselves with communication devices and reinforced vests, helmets, goggles, and other tactical gear. A second group, speeding toward the Capitol on golf carts, was not only wearing battle gear but also had hard-knuckle tactical gloves, ballistic goggles, radios, chemical sprays, cord, scissors, a large stick, and a huge German shepherd named Warrior.[13]

Jessica Watkins, an Ohio bar owner, was part of the first group. Using an application that mimicked walkie-talkies over cellular telephone networks, Watkins made an announcement on a "Stop the Steal J6" channel: "It has spread like wildfire that Pence has betrayed us, and everybody's marching on the Capitol. . . . We have about 30–40 of us. We are sticking together and sticking to the plan." Later, Watkins said, "Y'all, we're one block away from the Capitol right now. I'm probably gonna go silent when we get there, because I'm gonna be a little busy."[14]

Captain Carneysha C. Mendoza, US Capitol Police: It was approximately 1:30 in the afternoon. I was at home eating with my ten-year-old, spending time with him before what I knew would likely be a long day, when a fellow captain contacted me and told me things were bad and that I needed to respond in.

Julio Cortez, photographer, The Associated Press: It erupted really fast—all of a sudden it was like there were a thousand people pushing and shoving against the cops.

Officer Harry Dunn, US Capitol Police: I quickly put on a steel chest plate, which weighs about twenty pounds, and, carrying my M4 rifle, sprinted around the north side of the Capitol to the West Terrace and the railing of the inaugural stage, where I had a broad view of what was going on. I was stunned by what I saw. In what seemed like a sea of people, Capitol Police officers and Metropolitan DC Police officers were engaged in desperate hand-to-hand fighting with rioters across the west lawn.

Julio Cortez, photographer, The Associated Press: Everywhere you looked, there was hand-to-hand combat.

Officer Eugene Goodman, US Capitol Police: I've never seen something like that ever. One side was police officers. The other side was protesters.

Officer Caroline Edwards, US Capitol Police: I can just remember my breath catching in my throat, because what I saw was just a war scene. It was something like I'd seen out of the movies. I couldn't believe my eyes. There were officers on the ground. You know, they were bleeding. They were throwing up. I saw friends with blood all over their faces. I was slipping in people's blood. I was catching people as they fell. It was carnage. It was chaos. I can't even describe what I saw.

Officer Eugene Goodman, US Capitol Police: It looked like medieval times. It was just fighting and punching and force clashing against force.

Officer Caroline Edwards, US Capitol Police: Never in my wildest dreams did I think that, as a police officer, as a law enforcement officer, I would find myself in the middle of a battle.

Officer Eugene Goodman, US Capitol Police: Metropolitan Police began to deploy their tear gas at that point, and a lot of the blowback from the tear gas came back on a lot of us, and it kind of had a pretty bad effect on me. So I came back into the Lower West Terrace door. I went back upstairs to the first floor, where a few of our officers along with the Office of the Attending Physician had set up a sort of triage point for us to rinse our faces off or do what we needed to do to get back into the fray of things. I sat down. I rinsed my face. I threw up a couple of times from the reaction from the tear gas. And then I went back outside.

Protesters climbed up the tall media tower standing in front of the inaugural stage and started to dismantle parts of the stage to make a pathway and evade the officers—and to create makeshift weapons. As the crowd grew larger and angrier, the MPD quickly reinforced the long line of officers preventing access to the upper terrace closest to the building.

Inspector Thomas Loyd, US Capitol Police: Baseball bats, flagpoles were thrown at us. The temporary fence, that was thrown at us. It was a construction site. There was a full construction team on the stage when the first breach was called out. The construction team fled, but they left their tools, so all their tools, fire extinguishers, anything and everything was thrown at us. It can be deadly, depending on what's thrown and the lack of equipment that you have.

Officer Eugene Goodman, US Capitol Police: I ran up and down scaffolding, chasing rioters off the scaffolding. And it was at that point where a few of us were on top of the scaffolding and they started shaking the scaffolding, trying to rock us down off the scaffolding. And by that point is when we sort of started to become overrun.

Detective Phuson Nguyen, Metropolitan Police Department: I saw this guy that had a knife. And they were cutting—so when they build the inaugural stand, they have these big sheets of fabric that cover the bottom so that nobody can get under. But there's a guy with a knife, and he was cutting the sheet of fabric up to open up the hole.

Officer Harry Dunn, US Capitol Police: I witnessed the rioters using all kinds of weapons against the officers, including flagpoles, metal bike racks they had torn apart, and various kinds of projectiles. Officers were being bloodied in the fighting, many were screaming, and many were blinded and coughing from chemical irritants being sprayed in their faces.

I gave decontamination aid to as many officers as I could, flushing their eyes with water to dilute the chemical irritants.

Officer Caroline Edwards, US Capitol Police: They were using the flagpoles. I remember at one time just seeing people getting hit with blue line flags, and just thinking like, is this real life? Like are these people serious? American flags, blue line flags—they were using these flagpoles as weapons.

Officer Mark Ode, US Capitol Police, Civil Disturbance Unit: At the other side of the line, there was wrestling for possession of the bike racks. There were things thrown, projectiles thrown at us. There were individuals walking around spraying unknown chemical substances in police officers' eyes.

Officer Shauni Kerkhoff, US Capitol Police: I've never seen a crowd that size before. It was extremely loud. I remember hearing flash-bangs, people yelling, people throwing stuff, things hit—like objects hitting officers' shields and gear. It wasn't just the roar of a peaceful crowd. There was violence happening.

Officer Winston Pingeon, US Capitol Police: Members of the crowd were yelling at us and starting to assault us. There were a couple of people trying to agitate me. I had my hand resting on my baton, and they're like, "Oh, you're scared." There was one guy I remember specifically telling me that he was a veteran, I think of the Navy. And he's like, "I took an oath to the Constitution. I served my country. You took an oath, and you're a traitor. You're on the wrong side of history. You need to take your badge off and come and join us."

Inspector Thomas Loyd, US Capitol Police: The crowd was very angry. They hated the cops. They accused us of being traitors, protecting the criminals, referring to the politicians in the building.

Officer Winston Pingeon, US Capitol Police: That same veteran was saying something like, "Trump is your boss, so why are you doing this?" And I'm thinking, you have no idea how basic government works, I guess, because we don't answer to him.

Captain Jessica Baboulis, US Capitol Police: When the outermost perimeter has been broken with that many people, with the numbers of officers that were present that day, it was going to present a significant challenge for us to regain that back.

Officer Winston Pingeon, US Capitol Police: They were saying things like "We don't want to hurt you all, but we will. We're getting inside that building." And even in that moment, I'm thinking, there's no way that they will be so violent or aggressive or brazen to actually make their way in. But of course I was wrong, because really it was just us between them and the building.

Capitol Police Officer Mark Ode was part of the long police line along the West Front. When an officer next to him was assaulted and fell to the ground, he reached down to help him up.

Officer Mark Ode, US Capitol Police: When I came out to assist him and create space from rioters, there's individuals that grabbed—violently and forcefully grabbed my shield and pulled me down to the ground. Instantaneously, as I was being pulled down, another individual sprayed me with an unknown chemical substance, and as I was going down, I fell down on my stomach and there were multiple people that were on top of me. And at that specific moment, I was incapable of moving most of my limbs, including my legs.

Ode was wearing a medical face mask to protect himself from COVID-19, but he was now struggling to breathe after being sprayed. As he was trying to remove the mask, he felt pressure on his neck and realized someone was pulling on his helmet to try to choke him with the strap.

Officer Mark Ode, US Capitol Police: I thought that I'll not make it out alive out of that pile. It was very difficult for me to breathe.

Another officer eventually pulled Ode out and helped him to safety.

Officer Mark Ode, US Capitol Police: I couldn't really see very well because my eyes were shut, it was burning. I was able to find my way up to the stairs and try to decontaminate my eyes using water, and as I was doing that, I realized that I no longer held my shield and I no longer had in my possession my gas mask and my PR-24 baton.

Proud Boy Dominic Pezzola, one of the first rioters to breach the Capitol perimeter, had been part of the scuffle and was now carrying Ode's shield. Another Proud Boy took a photo of him holding it and flashing a Proud Boys sign with his hand.[15]

Many other Capitol Police officers were without equipment, either because rioters had wrested it away or because of poor planning by superiors. In some cases, they did have equipment, but it failed—old riot shields shattered upon impact, or chemical sprays had expired and the officers didn't feel comfortable using them.[16] *Many in the Civil Disturbance Unit weren't sure what to do or where to go. On the radio, officers were screaming for help, but there was little direction from Sund or other leaders who were managing the crisis at headquarters a few blocks away. A voice on the radio cried, "Does anybody have a plan?"*[17]

Officer Kyle Yetter, US Capitol Police: Throughout that day, the radio calls were—you couldn't understand the radio. So there were no formal assignments given. It was constant, just respond where you think you could help.

Officer Eugene Goodman, US Capitol Police: The radio was haywire. I could just hear officers trying to come across and I guess give their positions or individual battles that they happened to be dealing with around the Capitol. Not too many people could get across the radio.

Officer Kyle Yetter, US Capitol Police: There were hundreds of "officer down" calls, as well as people requesting assistance, but it was all too much to comprehend.

Captain Jessica Baboulis, US Capitol Police: It was extremely difficult, particularly that day at the initial breach. I was the incident commander, meaning in charge of two pipe bombs that had been placed, and so listening to explosions going off on the west side of the Capitol and not knowing whether those were weapons or explosive devices and hearing the screams from my officers for help—"We need help, we need backup"—but being in a fixed location that I couldn't leave because I was working with two bombs, it was difficult.

Inspector Thomas Loyd, US Capitol Police: We were on different radio channels, and it was just complete chaos. I was assuming that headquarters would take control of the radio system, but they never did.

Inspector Loyd had worked at the Capitol Police for more than thirty years and was a well-known, commanding presence at the Capitol. As a higher-ranking official, he wore a white shirt—a "Class A uniform"—distinguishing him from the rank-and-file officers on the force who wore blue. But unlike some of the top officials who were still at headquarters, he was in the fray with the men and women who worked for him. Once the MPD arrived, he evacuated some of his officers who had been beaten up and made sure they were treated for their injuries. He then went back outside and joined the DC police himself, physically engaging the rioters and taking hits of chemical spray despite his white-shirt status.

Inspector Thomas Loyd, US Capitol Police: Most of my team was going into the building to get rehabilitated. I stayed out there with Metropolitan and assisted them. And whenever there was a gap in the line, I would step up and fill in that gap.

The line across the West Front was barely holding. Metropolitan Police Inspector Robert Glover was frantically calling on the radio for more help: "Multiple Capitol injuries! Multiple Capitol injuries!"[18]

"Be advised, the speech has ended," the dispatcher replied. Another voice said, "Be advised you've got a group of about fifty up the hill on the West Front just north of the stairs. They are approaching the wall now."

The crowd on the other side of the line was becoming larger and angrier, and Glover needed reinforcements. One officer told the dispatcher that the protesters were starting to dismantle the reviewing stand set up for the inauguration. Glover begged for more help.

"We're thirty seconds out," replied another officer.

"We need some reinforcements up here now!" someone screamed into the radio. "They're starting to pull the gates down! They're throwing metal poles at us!"[19]

Down the National Mall, Hodges and other members of his MPD unit were still near the site of the rally, listening to the chaos unfold on the radio.

Officer Daniel Hodges, Metropolitan Police Department: I could hear Inspector Glover leading the defense efforts at the Capitol as the protesters began their transition from peaceful assembly into terrorism. I became agitated and wished we could move in to support, as I could hear the increasing desperation in his voice, yet we still had to wait for our orders to change. Eventually they did.

Officer Jesse Leasure, Metropolitan Police Department: We're just listening to the radio and hearing the panic in the voices. When you do this stuff as much as we do, and how often we have done it, you kind of know something's happening. We were just anxious to get in the fight. It's almost like a racehorse in the pen before the race starts. It's not like you want to fight anybody, it's just like the adrenaline's building up, and it's that natural fight-or-flight kicking in.

Officer Daniel Hodges, Metropolitan Police Department: Navigating alternate routes to avoid the foot traffic, we drove as close as we could to the Capitol, disembarking at the northwest side of the Capitol grounds. We gave our gear a final check and marched toward the West Terrace.

Officer Jesse Leasure, Metropolitan Police Department: As we're marching, we start to see the vastness of this crowd, and it's just wild.

Officer Daniel Hodges, Metropolitan Police Department: The crowd was thinner the further out from the Capitol you were, so as we marched, the resistance we initially met was verbal.

Officer Jesse Leasure, Metropolitan Police Department: These idiots were yelling, "Traitor! Traitor!" And I'm just like, what the hell is wrong with you people?

Officer Daniel Hodges, Metropolitan Police Department: A man sarcastically yelled, "Here come the boys in blue! So brave!" Another called on us to "remember your oath." There was plenty of booing. A woman called us "storm troopers."

Officer Jesse Leasure, Metropolitan Police Department: We're kind of like scrapping, and I'm just trying to be as polite as possible, because I don't want to set these people off. We know these people have weapons, and we're outnumbered.

Officer Daniel Hodges, Metropolitan Police Department: And then as we got closer to the West Terrace, we were attacked.

Officer Michael Fanone, Metropolitan Police Department: You could hear the tone of the individual officers' voices [on the radio]. They were scared. They were clearly outnumbered and being violently assaulted.

Jason Riddle, former correctional officer and mail carrier, New Hampshire: The walk to the Capitol building was pretty quiet. But it wasn't quiet by the time I got to where the police were. There were tear-gas grenades going off, people screaming and yelling.

Daniel Rodriguez, California: There's no leaders. There's no playbook. There's no guidance. You don't know what's going on. You just look around, and you got people over here singing a song or doing an interview, waving their flags. And then you go up to the Capitol building and they're getting sprayed in their eyes and just—it's totally, like, chaos and havoc and all this stuff. And it's, like, a whole mixture of everybody.

Lewis "Easton" Cantwell, North Carolina: I was just walking up, there was, like, people on loudspeakers. It was so loud. Like, it was so loud.

Janet Buhler, music teacher and college fashion instructor, Utah: It was getting really noisy. People were playing music. People were chanting things like "Trump! Trump! Trump!"

Christopher Grider, winery owner, Texas: Up until I think the tear gas came, it felt like—it did feel like a rally.

Janet Buhler, music teacher and college fashion instructor, Utah: So this woman came up to the side of us, and she says, "Pence folded." So it was kind of, like, okay. In my mind I was thinking, Well, that's it, you know. Well, my son-in-law looks at me, and he says, "I want to go in."

Jason Riddle, former correctional officer and mail carrier, New Hampshire: We came up to where I had to step up, like, onto a wall a little bit. And that's when my two friends stopped following me. And then I approached up towards the scaffolding. That's where all the police and the protesters were squaring off. And when I walked up, there were tear-gas grenades kind of blowing up. I saw the police shooting the tear gas into the scaffolding, and it turned the scaffolding into like this giant gas chamber.

Dominic Pezzola, flooring contractor, Proud Boys, New York: My first reaction was disbelief that this type of force was actually being used on an unarmed crowd of people who were just pushing against riot shields.

The protesters were becoming increasingly angry as the police fought them and tried to push them back. Instead of deescalating, many of the protesters became more violent and more determined to push ahead—especially after a rioter named Joshua Matthew Black was shot in the face with a crowd control munition.[20]

Julio Cortez, photographer, The Associated Press: A man wearing a "Make America Great Again" blue beanie cap was shot with a rubber bullet that pierced his left cheek. With the pellet still in the hole, he chewed on a gauze wrap while a bystander told him to stay calm because he was going into shock.

Black, who carried a concealed knife on his hip, was an evangelical Christian from Alabama who believed God had directed him to go to Washington. He had been the first rioter to breach the barricade at the Lower West Terrace, shortly after the initial breach at Peace Circle, and other rioters had soon followed his lead. He was shot shortly after that with the munition that lodged in his cheek. The wound was bleeding profusely.

Dominic Pezzola, flooring contractor, Proud Boys, New York: After people started getting shot in the head and, you know, Mr. Black was ultimately shot in the face, it turned more into a dire situation where it became quite deadly, you know? There was more concern, and there was a palpable feel of panic in the air.

Jason Riddle, former correctional officer and mail carrier, New Hampshire: In my mind, the police are shooting tear gas at peaceful protesters, even though I'm no longer a peaceful protester because I walked past the barricade at that point. But I didn't understand. In my head, they're escalating and they shouldn't be doing that.

Dominic Pezzola, flooring contractor, Proud Boys, New York: Military training, and especially in the Marine Corps, you don't ever turn around and run.

Jason Riddle, former correctional officer and mail carrier, New Hampshire: I've always just been someone who's kind of drawn to fire. I want to see it.

Julio Cortez, photographer, The Associated Press: I stopped to take a photograph of protesters playing tug-of-war with a barricade against authorities. I framed my image of the moment with the Capitol building in the background. As I pressed the shutter, I thought about how surreal that scene was and how I really couldn't believe this was happening. Framing the building as a backdrop allowed me to show the world exactly how this moment was unfolding.

Associated Press photographers Julio Cortez and John Minchillo were now in the thick of the fighting crowd. Because they were sticking close together, Cortez knew immediately when Minchillo was in danger.

Julio Cortez, photographer, The Associated Press: They aggressively dragged him down a few steps, punched him, shoved him, threatened his life.

John Minchillo, photographer, The Associated Press: I knew implicitly, don't hit the ground and don't fight back. You need to deescalate.

Julio Cortez, photographer, The Associated Press: For me, it was a really scary moment. John and I have known each other for about twelve or thirteen years, and we have become really good friends. He was invited to my wedding; he's a family friend.

Cortez quickly looked around for a friendly face who could help. But he was unable to find anyone, so he got between Minchillo and his attackers.

Julio Cortez, photographer, The Associated Press: It worked for a minute, but then somebody in the crowd yelled that he was antifa, and it just gaslit the situation.

John Minchillo, photographer, The Associated Press: I was holding my press pass and showing them my press pass. It was only after I calmed them down and I was able to get a pause in the violence that somebody said I was antifa, which is what gave them the impetus that they needed—the motivation they needed to continue attacking.

Julio Cortez, photographer, The Associated Press: And that's when they threw him over the retaining wall.

John Minchillo, photographer, The Associated Press: I'm thinking to myself, if I do anything to get these guys to start swinging at me, they're going to turn on everybody else. I knew that if I started swinging, they're going to kill me, right? They'll stomp on your neck, and you're done. And they were going to grab everybody that had a press credential.

Julio Cortez, photographer, The Associated Press: Some people came to help him up. We have no idea who they were.

John Minchillo, photographer, The Associated Press: I was relieved that we got out. And then I was angry that we were pulled from the front.

Julio Cortez, photographer, The Associated Press: The minute John got beat up, I thought to myself, this is it, like, I'm no longer going to do this. Screw journalism. I'm going to go find a construction job, do something else. Like, I'm done. This is scary.

John Minchillo, photographer, The Associated Press: I went into it with the understanding that there was going to be potential violence. That's why I was there in the first place.

At 1:48 p.m., an hour after the first breach of the perimeter, protesters broke past police at a critical access point—a stairway covered by scaffolding that led directly up to the Senate side of the building. Police were still holding the long line along the West Front, but just barely.

Captain Ronald Ortega, assistant commander of the Senate division, US Capitol Police: The rioters at that point were starting to go under the scaffolding. The scaffolding is these metal poles, and it was covered by a tarp. The crowd was able to figure out how to get under the tarp and started to enter inside the tarp. And at that point, slowly the crowd was starting to come in. At one point, they threw some sort of orange liquid at my face, and then they eventually started to surround us and we had to engage in combat with them.

Inspector Thomas Loyd, US Capitol Police: My original concern when they entered the scaffolding was that they were going to topple the scaffolding, topple the main part of the stage.

Captain Ronald Ortega, US Capitol Police: If they were able to get through the scaffolding, they were going to have immediate access to the Lower West Terrace door. If they were to get up to the stairs on the other side, they'd have access to the Capitol building, to the first floor through the doors.

On Metropolitan Police radios, officers heard Inspector Glover tell dispatch that the scene was "now effectively a riot."

The dispatcher replied, "1349 hours. Declaring it a riot."[21]

Inspector Robert Glover, Metropolitan Police Department: It was a riot much earlier before I declared it. I kind of lost track, but that was a matter of formality.

As members of the mob ran through the scaffolding and up the stairs, they were now only steps away from an entrance to the Senate side of the building, separated from it only by a few officers. Capitol Police Officer Shauni Kerkhoff was desperately firing chemical munitions at the crowd. But the officers were outnumbered. "They're breaching the West Terrace," she yelled over the deafening roar of the crowd. "We need backup!"

Officer Shauni Kerkhoff, US Capitol Police: They're now within arm's reach of us, and they're getting closer and closer to members of Congress.

House Speaker Nancy Pelosi was presiding as the House debated the Republican objection to Arizona's electors. As it became clear that the situation was escalating outside, members of her staff congregated several times just outside the chamber, in the Speaker's Lobby, to get security updates from Sergeant at Arms Paul Irving and other officials. Irving was also having separate conversations with members, assuring them the situation was under control.

Keith Stern, House director of floor operations: We got pulled out four or five times. And at some point, they would tell us that "it's okay, we've got the barricades up. It's okay, they can't get in the building."

Drew Hammill, deputy chief of staff, House Speaker Nancy Pelosi: We were told over and over again by the sergeant at arms that there was no way the Capitol could be breached. He was reiterating what he had been saying for probably a week, because members had been raising concerns. And these are security professionals, so you tend to take their word.

Keith Stern, House director of floor operations: We're starting to hear about the things that are happening on the outside. "There's a group of people coming down the mall, coming to the Capitol, and everything's fine. We have things under control. But just so you know, this is happening." Then it becomes the next step of "Okay, they're here."

Rep. Zoe Lofgren, D-CA, chairwoman of the House Administration Committee, which oversees Capitol security: The sergeant at arms assured me that the mob would not be able to get in.

Jamie Fleet, Democratic staff director, House Administration Committee: The chamber was like its own little island. We were sort of clueless as to what was going on. We were focused on what was happening there. And then it got more serious when the sergeant at arms was like, "We have a situation here."

Keith Stern, House director of floor operations: It is becoming more and more chaotic. At some point, the speaker's detail says we may have to pull the speaker off and get her out. I said, "Whatever you guys need, I'm not going to stop you. But if you give me the most amount of time, I can make it look a little bit more coordinated, rather than you just whisking her off." Fifteen, twenty, thirty seconds matters at this point.

Chief Steven Sund, US Capitol Police: I called [Sergeant at Arms Paul] Irving and it was a very short call. He picked up. I said, we are getting overrun on the West Front by thousands. We need the National Guard now. It was clear. We need the National Guard now. He said, I'll run it up the chain. Click.

Terri McCullough, chief of staff, House Speaker Nancy Pelosi: The sergeant at arms said something to the effect of, we need to get the speaker and [Senate Majority Leader] McConnell to sign off on getting the National Guard in. So I thought, that's my job to do and I'm going to do it. So I scribbled down a note to the speaker explaining to her what the situation was and I asked another aide to go and hand it to her on the rostrum. She said immediately, "Yes. Make sure McConnell says yes as well."

Across the Capitol, House Sergeant at Arms Paul Irving and Senate Sergeant at Arms Michael Stenger were holding an emergency meeting in Stenger's office to figure out the next steps. McCullough and Fleet hurried over, leaving the House floor despite the growing uncertainty. As McCullough left, a staff member warned her that Pelosi might have to be evacuated soon.

When McCullough and Fleet rushed into Stenger's first-floor office, McConnell's staff were also there, including his chief of staff, Sharon Soderstrom. Stenger was standing at his West Front window, staring outside.

Jamie Fleet, Democratic staff director, House Administration Committee: He's like, "Jamie, get over here." And I walk over to the window, and I was like, "Jesus Christ. Like, what is happening out there?" And it was just, like, a thin line of law enforcement and a mass of people. And the line was just, like, swaying.

Fleet saw the rioters attacking the officers and people pouring water on their eyes to wash out the chemicals.

Jamie Fleet, Democratic staff director, House Administration Committee: That was the first time that day I had laid eyes on the extent of the violence. And I was shaken by it. It was dramatic.

Terri McCullough, chief of staff, House Speaker Nancy Pelosi: You could see from the windows in his office, people starting to run toward the Capitol. It felt so surreal, like, how could this be happening?

McConnell's staff and Pelosi's staff all agreed that they needed to call the National Guard immediately.[22]

Jamie Fleet, Democratic staff director, House Administration Committee: Ms. McCullough made very plain at that moment that the speaker was aware and whatever we needed to do to get the Guard here, that Mr. Irving had alerted her to that effect.

Terri McCullough, chief of staff, House Speaker Nancy Pelosi: I reiterated strongly again, "Yes, we want the National Guard to come."

Jamie Fleet, Democratic staff director, House Administration Committee: It was like, we've got to get as much help here as we can, as quickly as we can, from all the people that we can.

Terri McCullough, chief of staff, House Speaker Nancy Pelosi: I then got a text from one of our staff saying, "You need to come back up here now." So I left Jamie in the room and said, "Just please keep me updated." And ran back up to the floor. When I got there, our detail said, "We are leaving now."

While Pelosi presided on the floor, only a handful of her staff remained in her office.

Alisa La, special assistant to House Speaker Nancy Pelosi: I was Pelosi's "body" person. She had a two-person executive office with a couple of staff assistants, and we would just basically run her day, make sure it went smoothly, keep her on schedule, keep a running to-do list for her. So typically I would be bodying the speaker, but my colleague Emily did that instead. We planned to be two hours on, two hours off and switch throughout that day, which is very typical. On big event days, there was a small army of people that kept up with this one woman.

The speaker's suite is dead center on the West Front of the Capitol. The Speaker's Balcony, as it is known, looks directly out on the terrace, where rioters were starting to fill in, having breached the stairway from below. Alone in her office, La was watching things get worse outside and trying to figure out what to do.

Alisa La, special assistant to House Speaker Nancy Pelosi: At this point, the West Front was overrun with rioters. I could almost see eye to eye with rioters on the media tower of the inaugural platform.

One floor down, Pelosi's communications director, Henry Connelly, was also alone in his office. He didn't have much of a view, though, as his first-floor window was covered with inaugural scaffolding. At 1:55 p.m., as Pelosi's other aides were getting increasingly urgent security updates, they called Connelly and La and told them to lock themselves in their offices.

Terri McCullough, chief of staff, House Speaker Nancy Pelosi: I picked up my phone and I called one of our staff in our office, and I said something to the effect of "Shut it down now."

Alisa La, special assistant to House Speaker Nancy Pelosi: I had to go lock [the Speaker's Balcony]. And I was really scared.

Henry Connelly, communications director, House Speaker Nancy Pelosi: The doors into the press office are, like, I guess they're lockable, but they're not particularly sturdy. So I started thinking about, like, okay, if I was going to barricade myself in the office here, what would I have to do?

Alisa La, special assistant to House Speaker Nancy Pelosi: We started hearing flash-bangs. I realized they were at the west door under us, and they were really close to breaching.

Andrew Harnik, photographer, The Associated Press: I was sending pictures from my laptop in the media filing area off of the House chamber, and I got a phone call from one of my editors. He said, "I'm hearing that the protests on the east side of the Capitol are getting pretty intense. Would you mind seeing if you can get to a window and see what you can?" So I left most of my gear, grabbed two cameras, and went out into the hallways.

Harnik eventually found a giant circular window hidden in a men's restroom on the third floor that had a direct view of the East Front plaza.

Andrew Harnik, photographer, The Associated Press: As soon as I got to the window and looked out, the crowd surged and broke the police line and ran up the center steps of the Capitol, which—obviously I had never seen anything like that since I've covered Congress. The center steps are a place always reserved for Capitol Hill police. It's not open to the public.

The huge crowd that had amassed at the West Front had spilled around the Capitol's north side and to the East Front, agitating the more peaceful crowd that was already there. The protesters were now rushing toward the building and gathering on the central stairway that leads to the Capitol Rotunda.

Andrew Harnik, photographer, The Associated Press: Pretty shortly thereafter I heard a huge explosion, which I took to be some sort of police flash grenade at the steps. It was out of my field of view from where I was. Then I could hear breaking glass and yelling.

2:00 p.m.

Assistant Chief Yogananda Pittman, US Capitol Police: When the East Front plaza was breached, I directed an immediate lockdown of the US Capitol building, which means all entrances and exits are sealed, preventing anyone from entering or exiting the building, including police officers.

Officer Winston Pingeon, US Capitol Police: I do remember hearing Pittman say "Lock down the building." But it was almost funny, because the building was being overrun.

At 2:04 p.m., an announcement blared on security speakers throughout the Capitol: "Due to an external security threat, no entry or exit is permitted at this time in the US Capitol building. You may move throughout the buildings, but stay away from exterior windows and doors." For many inside, it was the first indication that something was seriously wrong.

Manu Raju, anchor and chief congressional correspondent, CNN: We have a booth in the Radio-TV Gallery on the third floor of the Senate. We can watch on our TVs what's happening in the Senate and in the House. I have a television camera there in case I need to go live. We were rolling coverage of the debate in the House and the Senate, so I wasn't really anticipating to go live until later. The Capitol being locked down, that's when we decided to break into our live coverage, and that was our first report.

Henry Connelly, communications director, House Speaker Nancy Pelosi: At 2:02 p.m., I wrote down in my notes, "What a dark day this will be in the history of our democracy."

Manu Raju, anchor and chief congressional correspondent, CNN: I remember Wolf Blitzer asked me something along the lines of "What are the chances they're going to get inside the building?" And I was like, "Well, that does not seem likely, Wolf. This is one of the most fortified buildings, there's so many police everywhere." And obviously the events later contradicted my false sense of security.

Henry Connelly, communications director, House Speaker Nancy Pelosi: I looked outside the window, and I could see a Capitol police officer running with an assault rifle. Not pointed at anybody, but that felt like a sign of escalation. At 2:08 p.m., I wrote, "MAGA people storm the East Senate steps. MSNBC shows protesters on the face of the Capitol." And then that's the last record that I have until 9:34 p.m.

Alisa La, special assistant to House Speaker Nancy Pelosi: My mind started going into survivor mode for all of us. No resources were going to be sent over to us. I'm looking outside, and I'm like, this is insane. So then Emily texts, "We're evacuating. Lock everything down."

The Senate was debating the Arizona objection, but it was clear by now that there was violence outside. Senators broke the strict rules against using their phones on the floor and peeked at their devices. They were also discussing privately what would happen if Trump tried to come to the Capitol, as he had just told the crowd on the Ellipse that he would.

Senate Rules Committee Chairman Roy Blunt, R-MO: Under Senate rules, the president can come to the Senate any time he wants to. If he came to the Senate door, he'd have to be admitted. We made some quick arrangements that if that does happen, we don't have a rule about this that could keep the president from coming on the floor. We made sure that the vice president was aware.

Andrew Taylor, reporter, The Associated Press: If you've seen *Mr. Smith Goes to Washington*, you've seen my work area, since a press gallery scene from the movie was filmed there more than seventy years ago. It overlooks the north lawn of the Capitol, where a steady march of insurgents began ominously arriving. The Senate pros who have offices near the chamber started getting nervous.

Greg Jacob, counsel to Vice President Pence: As the debate proceeded, we started noticing that there were people starting to stream around the back side of the building.

Sen. Patty Murray, D-WA: I was preparing myself in an office very close to the Senate floor when, all of a sudden, I could see out the window the people who were protesting were no longer protesting. They were breaking through.

Doug Jensen had arrived at the Capitol after the outer barriers had already been breached. He easily made his way past the broken fences and scrambled up the side of a twenty-foot retaining wall. Once he got to the top, close to the doors of the Senate, he climbed over the steep marble railing and raised his arms overhead like a boxing champ who'd just leveled a knockout punch, riling up the rioters who were surging past the officers nearby. His black shirt with the "Q" on it faced outward toward the National Mall for all the world to see, just as he had wanted.

Jensen joined a group of rioters who had broken past police on the lower terrace and climbed a staircase inside the scaffolding.[1] *The group was now close to a Senate doorway, and Capitol Police officers were trying to push them back with rounds of pepper spray.*

Officer Shauni Kerkhoff, US Capitol Police: I've never seen anything like this. My heart rate was like—you know, I'd never been this anxious or this stressed out. I was just worried that we wouldn't be able to hold them back.

Christopher Alberts, handyman and former National Guardsman, Maryland: I wonder why everybody is being gassed. You know, there's no warning of the crowd control devices. I'm wondering why we can't be there to speak. We were being silenced right here. This was an immediate attack on a crowd to be silenced.

As the protesters were sprayed with chemicals, they started to fight back, spraying their own bear spray and other chemicals at the officers. Alberts, the Maryland man with a concealed gun on his hip, used a wooden pallet he had picked up from the inauguration construction to ram into Capitol Police Officer Stephen Sherman, trapping him as other rioters pushed forward.

Christopher Alberts, handyman and former National Guardsman, Maryland: I felt that there was lives at risk behind me, that the police in front of me were not going to stop at any point in time, and that somebody had to build a wall—I mean, I don't know how else to say it—to protect them.

As Alberts pushed toward Officer Sherman with the board, another rioter had grabbed Sherman's shield and was pulling him down the staircase. As Sherman was losing his balance and caught between the two, he was forced to let go of his shield. Shortly afterward, he was sprayed in the face with a chemical agent. He thought he was going to die.

Officer Stephen Sherman, US Capitol Police: I felt as though someone in the crowd was going to take out a firearm and start assassinating myself and other fellow officers.

Christopher Alberts, handyman and former National Guardsman, Maryland: I've always been known to stand and, you know, defend myself.

Also on the terrace was Proud Boy Dominic Pezzola, who was taunting the officers, yelling, "You better be fucking scared!" and "We ain't fucking stopping! Fuck you!"[2] *At 2:13 p.m., the crowd had pushed through a final, weak line of police and reached a doorway on the first floor of the Capitol, one floor below the Senate chamber. Pezzola used the shield he had taken from Officer Mark Ode to break a window next to the door. Another rioter climbed through, then another, and the people inside opened a door to let the rest in.*[3]

The first members of the mob entered the building. The Capitol was breached. The Senate was still in session one floor above.

Doug Jensen, Iowa: We are on the verge, this is it. We're at the end of the story, you know what I mean? Biden's about to be our president, and Pence was supposed to be the hero to save the day.

Jensen and several other rioters turned left, then right down another hallway.

Doug Jensen, Iowa: I wanted to be the first one in that door, you know, with my "Q" shirt. The only thing I had on me was a knife, and that was protection from if there was going to be some kind of showdown. What I thought, when I went there, was that there's gonna be a hundred thousand of us.

Oklahoma Sen. Jim Lankford surprised many of his colleagues when he decided to join Cruz and the other GOP senators supporting objections to Biden's legitimate win. The former youth pastor had been supportive of Trump, but he has a reputation as a sincerely religious man who had questioned the president's false allegations in 2016 that "millions of people" had voted illegally for Democrat Hillary Clinton.[4] *Lankford, remarkably, was now calling for a "pause" in Biden's certification on the Senate floor as the Senate debated the Arizona objection.*

Roy Blunt, the Senate Rules Committee chairman, was sitting at his desk on the Senate floor listening to Lankford's speech when his phone vibrated.

Sen. Roy Blunt, R-MO: The hardest rule to enforce was phones on the floor. But it was still the rule, so I was usually pretty careful about that. But it's just odd. I think what I thought was maybe the president's headed this way. So I look at my phone, and it's from Fitz Elder, who was running the Rules Committee for me at the time. And the message was "Protesters have seized the south media tower." I'll probably never get any message quite like that again. And within a minute, it was "Protesters are fighting the Capitol Police on the inaugural platform."

Officer Mark Gazelle, US Capitol Police, Senate Chamber Section: It was one big fluid motion. I came onto the Senate floor because I knew we were facing a problem, and I saw [Pence] still sitting in the chair, which I was a little shocked. At this point I saw him get up. His Secret Service team meets him at the door to his left.

Greg Jacob, counsel to Vice President Pence: The vice president had been pulled off of the floor and into his personal office behind the Senate floor.

Sen. Susan Collins, R-ME: Chuck Grassley then went up to replace the vice president, and you could see he was sort of puzzled by what was going on.

Iowa Sen. Chuck Grassley, the most senior Republican and Senate president pro tempore, replaced Pence in the chair and began to preside. But he quickly interrupted Lankford midsentence and frantically banged the gavel. "The Senate will stand in recess until the call of the chair!" Grassley said.

A young aide ran up to Lankford. "Protestors are in the building," he whispered. Grassley, third in the line of presidential succession, was quickly whisked away by police. The C-SPAN cameras went dark, but senators didn't immediately leave. Police yelled to lock doors and asked senators to move away from them.

Sen. James Lankford, R-OK: All of that chaos was happening, and I was watching as I was speaking, and thought, okay, we've got something really serious going on, to say the least, around us because this is obviously not normal.

Mark Gazelle, a Capitol Police officer who had been assigned to the Senate chamber for more than twenty-five years, took Grassley's spot on the dais and banged the gavel, trying to restore order. For a police officer to take the gavel was extraordinary—but Gazelle knew that these were extreme circumstances and that they would soon have to lock down the chamber.

Officer Mark Gazelle, US Capitol Police: The parliamentarian gave me the gavel because that's the thing you slam on to get everybody's attention. And at this point I am trying to get the Senate under control. There's a lot of commotion.

Sen. Richard Burr, R-NC: I've been through 9/11 and a lot of events. I won't tell you that I immediately thought about a threat because I've never perceived, up to that time, people in the Capitol being a threat. Incoming airplanes? Yeah, that's a different situation.

Minnesota Sen. Amy Klobuchar, top Democrat on the Senate Rules Committee: Suddenly my staff let me know that something was going wrong. A cop told me that people had to get away from the windows.

Sen. Richard Burr, R-NC: My wife called me and said, "You realize they're entering the Capitol?" Up until that point, there was no visible sign of any type of confrontation or threat. But I don't think there's anybody that was in the Senate that had a full sense of how many people were in the Capitol or whether there should be any concern with anybody's safety.

Sen. Bob Casey, D-PA: I do remember hearing noise or a disturbance of some kind, but it was really muted. It didn't sound like much. And then it got a little bit louder.

Sen. Mike Rounds, R-SD: We started hearing noises. We started hearing stuff that wasn't normal. There were [security] people that came in who had guns into the chamber.

Greg Jacob, counsel to Vice President Pence: There's a self-serve coffee kiosk down on the first floor of the Senate on that side. And as we were getting coffee, suddenly there was a loud banging sound that started. We sort of wandered out of the coffee kiosk. "What in the world is that?"

Marc Short, chief of staff, Vice President Pence: I started the morning early, and, unfortunately, had not had lunch. And I eat a lot. And so, at that point, when the vice president had resumed his position in the Senate, I felt like I had two hours. I escaped down to the basement of the Capitol to the Senate carryout to order a cheeseburger. That's where I was when it all happened.

Greg Jacob, counsel to Vice President Pence: I think I now know, based on videos that I've seen, that that was the police riot shield that folks had stolen and were banging on the window right there. Glass then shattered. And I said, "All right, everybody upstairs," because there was no security that I could see down there, and the glass had shattered just down the hallway from where we are, probably sixty feet away.

Marc Short, chief of staff, Vice President Pence: At that point, police were running by, and they asked us to evacuate. Rather than evacuating, I went back upstairs and met the vice president in the ceremonial office off the Senate floor. I never got my cheeseburger.

Greg Jacob, counsel to Vice President Pence: I quickly hightailed it upstairs to the vice president's staff office. The younger guys who didn't have young kids at home evidently decided, "Oh, glass shatter, we should go check that out." So they had evidently gone towards the window, seen a two-by-four come flying through the window, and then saw people start clambering through. I think a security person had showed up by that point. They then followed me up to the staff office. Two or three minutes after I got into the staff office, I think it was Capitol security came in and said, "We can't secure this area. We need you all to get onto the Senate floor."

Emily Berret, director of operations, House Speaker Nancy Pelosi: My chief of staff slipped the speaker a note, and we pulled her down. We did a quick transfer.

2:00 p.m.

Nancy Pelosi did not go easily when security people swooped onto the rostrum to pull her out of the chair. She told the officers she could handle the situation on her own.

House Speaker Nancy Pelosi, D-CA: And they said, "No, this is different." And they just pulled me off. I even left my phone, my purse; I didn't have anything. I was just like that, pulled off.

Joe Novotny, House reading clerk: I turn around and she's gone.

Rep. Jim McGovern, D-MA: She seemed a little bit frustrated that she had to leave.

House Speaker Nancy Pelosi, D-CA: I thought maybe it was something specific with me, and it probably was because they were going to put a bullet in my head. But I didn't know that at that time.

Thomas Wickham, former House parliamentarian and senior adviser to the parliamentarian: I'd not seen that happen before—to see the speaker taken from the speaker's chair during the proceedings. I've seen the speaker and other detailees removed from the floor, but never the speaker from the speaker's chair.

Rep. Zoe Lofgren, D-CA: I look and realize that the speaker, who had been presiding, was being whisked away by her security team. She's second in line to the presidency. You know, the vice president and then the speaker in terms of line of succession. And I thought, we're in trouble here. Jim McGovern, the chairman of the Rules Committee, went to preside to try and keep matters going.

Emily Berret, director of operations, House Speaker Nancy Pelosi: We did not want to stop the proceedings. And the speaker can designate another member to take over, as you would call it, speaker pro tem, so they could step into her place if she needed to leave. So we got another member up to the rostrum.

Rep. Jim McGovern, D-MA: Although she was being called away, I still had no idea what was happening. I went up to the speaker's chair, and Nancy Pelosi said, "Thank you very much." I think she said, "I'll be right back." She left her phone there. So I began to take over the procedure overseeing the House.

Keith Stern, House director of floor operations: She left her phone there, and so Jim thought she was going to the bathroom.

Emily Berret, director of operations, House Speaker Nancy Pelosi: We pulled the speaker out into the hallway, and we started running.

Jen Daulby, Republican staff director, House Administration Committee: There's a hierarchy of when things get bad. And I know that the moment before it really gets bad, you pull out the leaders.

Rep. Elise Stefanik, R-NY: The way she was removed was not normal. And then Steve Scalise, who is minority whip, was seated behind me, and he was removed from the chamber, so it was very clear that something was not right.

House Majority Leader Steny Hoyer, D-MD: David Bohn, who was on my detail, came to where I was sitting. He said, "We have to leave now." Pelosi had just been taken out a minute or two before, so I knew something was radically wrong. We walked out into the Speaker's Lobby, and I said, "What's up?" He said, "The Capitol has been breached. They're coming this way, and we need to get out."

Emily Berret, director of operations, House Speaker Nancy Pelosi: We moved through the Capitol into a tunnel into her vehicle. I started to know how serious this was because other members of leadership were going past us. So other members of Congress with security details had also been pulled from the floor at that time. So all of the details were going to their location to get into their vehicles. We all jumped into the speaker's vehicles and left the building, and we headed to our secure location.

Rep. Rodney Davis, R-IL: I left the floor when the debate started happening because I thought it was absurd. I started to see Capitol Police officers running inside the Capitol building. And I walked into the sergeant at arms office; that's when I saw the screen—I saw on the screens the breaches of the bike racks and the Capitol police officers being attacked and the fighting that they had zoomed in on certain screens.

Rep. Zoe Lofgren, D-CA: There are TVs in the cloakroom, and one was turned on to the floor proceedings. And I thought, well, I'll turn the other one on to the news and see what's going on. And when I did, I saw that there was this tremendous mob outside the Congress, and that they appeared to be breaking into the Congress. And in fact, it looked like they had broken into the Congress.

Rep. Markwayne Mullin, R-OK: I started noticing a lot of activity with the Capitol Police and with the sergeant of arms. You can hear their earpieces, which is unusual. Usually there's no traffic in the earpieces.

Rep. Zoe Lofgren, D-CA: I went out back on the floor. By then it seemed pretty apparent that there was a big problem. I remember talking to [Rep.] Tom O'Halleran, who is a former sheriff and really an expert in security. And I said, "Tom, I think there's a problem. I think there's a mob that's broken in." And he said, "Well, don't worry about that. There'll be a SWAT team on them very soon." And I thought, I'm not adequately explaining what's going on here.

Rep. Rodney Davis, R-IL: I walked back to Rayburn [House Office Building], and that's when I decided that I was going to grab something for lunch and I'm going to get another sandwich and put it in the fridge for dinner. And I remember I got back [to my office], and I was eating a warm steak-and-cheese sandwich and I stored a cold tuna-salad sandwich. And while I was eating that sandwich, I got a call from my staff director, and she said, you need to get back to the floor because they're about ready to seal the floor.

Rep. Jim McGovern, D-MA: I just remember my phone vibrating and my daughter sending me texts like "What are you doing there?" I had no clue what she was talking about. I'm saying, "I'm in the speaker's chair." She says, "You should leave." I put in a question mark, as in stop texting because I'm not supposed to be texting from here. And shortly after that, it became clear that she was seeing things that I wasn't seeing.

Rep. Rodney Davis, R-IL: And so I run back towards the Capitol, and I'm running down through the hallways toward the House floor. And right when I get to the doors to enter the House floor, I run into my good friend Steve Scalise, who was part of the leadership evacuation. And Scalise was being evacuated out by his detail, and I was going in. And I remember looking at Steve saying, "What the fuck, man?" And he looked at me and he shook his head too. And he went out and I went in. Bam, the doors are shut.

After more than an hour of fighting on the West Front, US Capitol Police Officer Eugene Goodman was called inside by a supervisor. He ran to the Rotunda, where he saw that rioters were trying to break in on the east side of the building and were pushed up against the doors.

Officer Eugene Goodman, US Capitol Police: I looked out the Rotunda door and I could see officers in riot gear outside of the door with their backs pressed up against the door and just a mob of people pressing up against them.

An alert on his radio diverted his attention: "Breach of the Senate!"

Officer Eugene Goodman, US Capitol Police: I ran down from the Rotunda to the Senate wing of the building, which is where I passed by a leadership office and also passed by Senator Romney on the way. And I round the corner.

Sen. Mitt Romney, R-UT, was running with a member of his staff away from the Senate and in the direction of the Rotunda. Without breaking stride, Goodman yelled and gestured at Romney to get back in the chamber, where it was more secure, away from the mob that he had just seen trying to break in.[5] *As Romney ran back into the chamber, Goodman ran through another hallway and down a winding staircase to the first floor.*

At the bottom of the stairs, Goodman found one person—Kevin Seefried, a Delaware man who was carrying a Confederate flag.

Officer Eugene Goodman, US Capitol Police: I approach him and I tell him, "You need to get out. You need to leave." And that's when he uses the base of his flagpole in a jabbing motion sort of to create space between he and I. I'm advancing to him. I'm telling him to back up, to leave.

Soon Seefried was joined by a group of angry rioters that quickly filled the doorway. They were all yelling. One screamed at Goodman, "Where are they counting the fucking votes?"[6]

In the Senate press gallery on the third floor, longtime Washington Post *reporter Paul Kane was watching the proceedings when he saw Pence pulled from the chair.*

Paul Kane, reporter, *The Washington Post*: I jumped up and ran out of the chamber into our office portion of the gallery, and I just kind of ran through—I don't know if it was like full sprint, fast walking, whatever—and I was yelling, "They just pulled Pence out of the chair! They just pulled Pence out of the chair!"

Igor Bobic, reporter, HuffPost: Up until that point, I didn't really notice anything was wrong until Paul, out of nowhere, came barreling through the press gallery from my right to the left, screaming, "Pence just left the chair!"

Paul Kane, reporter, *The Washington Post*: I then went down the steps to the second floor because I wanted to figure out whether or not Mike Pence was being pulled out of the chair because there was danger. Or maybe he just had a pee break.

Igor Bobic, reporter, HuffPost: As soon as I saw Paul, who's this veteran who's been there for decades, screaming that, I got up and followed him downstairs.

Paul Kane, reporter, *The Washington Post*: Igor was the only other reporter who came down, and we stood there for a split second, like, where is he? What's going on? And we heard this loud crash one floor below us.

Igor Bobic, reporter, HuffPost: I didn't know where it was coming from. I just knew it was downstairs. People shouting and yelling, which is not something you normally hear in the Senate halls. I kept going downstairs to the first floor.

Paul Kane, reporter, *The Washington Post*: I kind of froze. I did not want to see cops beating up protesters. That was what I thought in my brain—I thought everything was so secure in our building. And I had no notebook, I didn't have my phone, I was just useless. Igor had his phone, and he looked at me and bolted down the steps.

Igor Bobic, reporter, HuffPost: I remember opening my iPhone camera and debating for the briefest second, as I'm sprinting down these marble stairs, whether I should put it in video or photo. Because I knew that we're not allowed to take videos in the halls. In that split second, I kept it on the video camera.

Paul Kane, reporter, *The Washington Post*: I didn't know until later that night, or even the next day, in the fog of everything. I realized that Igor did one of the most important historical things of that day that anyone in the media did—he hit record on his video and went down those steps. And it was not cops roughing up protesters.

The crowd confronting Officer Goodman was loud, and they advanced quickly. Doug Jensen pushed to the front of the crowd, his "Q" shirt leading the way.

Officer Eugene Goodman, US Capitol Police: It's a small sort of hallway. It's tight. The archway that exits that little hallway is even tighter, about the size of a doorway. And so it's really a confined space.

Doug Jensen, Iowa: The reason I made sure I was at the front was because I wanted that "Q" to be on TV. I wanted Q to get the attention.

Officer Eugene Goodman, US Capitol Police: They were there to interrupt the process.

Jensen yelled and gestured at Goodman, shaking his head as he walked toward him. The crowd followed behind, shouting. Igor Bobic, the reporter for HuffPost, was on the stairwell, recording the interaction on his iPhone.

Officer Eugene Goodman, US Capitol Police: I put my hand on the weapon. It means compliance. Back up. They kept advancing.

Igor Bobic, reporter, HuffPost: They were sort of threatening him, and he was wanting them not to go forward.

Officer Eugene Goodman, US Capitol Police: I had a large group of people yelling. They are angry. I'm outnumbered. One guy has the sharpened point on the flag, and I'm boxed in. I have no out other than the stairs from this point.

Igor Bobic, reporter, HuffPost: They were yelling, "Where the hell are they? Where the f are they? We're doing this for democracy! You're on our side!"

Senators and staff were still in the chamber, and Vice President Pence was huddled in an office nearby. Goodman bolted up the stairs, with Jensen immediately behind him. One of the rioters yelled, "Keep running, motherfucker!" Goodman stopped at a landing, turned around, and raised his baton.

Doug Jensen, Iowa: He pulled his baton out at the top of those stairs, and I was like, hit me, I'll take it. I'll take it for this country, you know.

Igor Bobic, reporter, HuffPost: There was this mad scramble up the stairs, and I'm trying not to fall over backwards and eat it while this mob of a dozen, maybe twenty guys is advancing up the steps menacingly. And at that point, I still had no idea what was going on outside. I just thought it was this group of people who got in.

Running up the second half of the stairway, Goodman called for assistance—"Second floor!" Jensen and the rioters kept up the chase.

Goodman stopped at the top of the stairwell and turned around. The officer briefly glanced toward the closed door to the Senate chamber, which was now just feet away from the crowd. There was no security posted outside. Goodman led the crowd to his right, away from the door.

Doug Jensen, Iowa: I had no idea where I was going. I was being directed.

Inspector Thomas Loyd, US Capitol Police: If the demonstrators had gone to where Officer Goodman looked over his left shoulder, that leads you to the rear of the Senate lobby, where the vice president and the senators were located.

Igor Bobic, reporter, HuffPost: I think he did very well in the sense that he didn't announce in their presence that there was a breach by the Senate doors or anything like that. He didn't use any identifying language.

Inspector Thomas Loyd, US Capitol Police: The doors that lead into the Senate—back of the Senate chamber, the Senate lobby—are made of nothing but glass, mostly glass. So they're easily breachable. And if those doors had been breached, more than likely there would have been gunfire at that point.

Goodman led the crowd around the corner to what is known as the Ohio Clock Corridor, the same spot where he had just run by Sen. Romney. The group was now close to another set of doors that led into the chamber, but there were several officers there to back Goodman up. One of them was Inspector Loyd, who had left the fight outside when he heard Goodman's urgent calls on the radio.

Igor Bobic, reporter, HuffPost: Goodman and the other police officers formed a line, preventing them from advancing further into the corridor.

Now in a standoff with multiple officers, Jensen and the rest of the crowd tried to push forward. They screamed at the officers to back up, their voices reverberating on the other side of the walls, where almost the entire Senate was sheltering in place. "Go arrest the vice president," Jensen ordered Loyd, who was blocking him from moving further down the hallway. Another rioter yelled, "We want justice!"[7]

Capitol Police officer Mark Gazelle stood at the Senate dais as the sounds outside became louder. He and other security officials were talking to headquarters, trying to figure out what they were going to do as the rioters approached the doors. Around ninety senators were in the room—an unusually large number on any other day.

Officer Mark Gazelle, US Capitol Police: At this point, we are telling them we are locking ourselves inside the Senate chamber and that we were going to stay in there. And we are trying to find out if we can find another place—if we are going to stay there or go to another place.

Staffers who had been in the halls outside spilled into the room, shaken. Reporters who had been in the press gallery offices gathered in the press balcony, watching the scene from above.

Chris Hodgson, director of legislative affairs, Vice President Pence: Chaotic was a pretty good way to describe it just because you go from the Senate floor, which is very orderly and organized, and all the sudden there's staff being brought in.

Andrew Taylor, congressional reporter, The Associated Press: Maybe a dozen reporters and aides in the gallery and virtually the entire Senate huddled inside. Tight COVID-19 quarters despite the masks. The police were in charge. "Move away from the doors," they ordered. Staff was squeezed into a corner.

Sen. Bob Casey, D-PA: And then it was loud enough where you knew there was some kind of a problem. And then as it went on from there, it was more like a threat. And then eventually they just closed the doors.

Sen. Mark Warner, D-VA: I distinctly remember the slamming of the doors in the gallery. And those doors are those little thin wooden doors. And there was kind of a "holy heck" moment.

Paul Kane, reporter, *The Washington Post*: I looked around, and I could see cops running around with guns and sergeant at arms staff locking the doors.

Andrew Taylor, reporter, The Associated Press: In the center aisle, right between McConnell and Senate Democratic Leader Chuck Schumer of New York, stood an officer with an identifying sash. His back was to us as he faced the center Senate door. He had a large rifle, it seemed, but he was trying to hide it. Behind him were three boxes holding electoral college vote certificates.

Sen. Bob Casey, D-PA: It seemed like a huge weapon at the time. Maybe that's just my recollection. I thought, this is something I've never seen before. Like, why does he need to be here? Why does he need that kind of a weapon?

Sen. Chris Murphy, D-CT: It was a really frightening scene inside the Senate chamber because they had evacuated a lot of staff into the Senate who had confronted the rioters. And so you had a lot of very shaken staff who were in the chamber with us. There's a lot of people sort of crying. The doors were locked, and we obviously knew something terrible could be happening.

Sen. Bob Casey, D-PA: I just assumed that the doors would be closed for a period of time and whatever disturbance there was in the building would be quelled. And we would just go on with our work. But wow, did I underestimate what was happening. And I had no concern that our lives were at risk or even that the proceeding wouldn't go forward. I just assumed that they would deal with it and we'd get back in fifteen or twenty minutes. But then it kept getting worse. The chamber was getting rather crowded.

Sen. Amy Klobuchar, D-MN: I told people to get away from the windows or doors because the cops told me there was someone with guns.

Officer Mark Gazelle, US Capitol Police: There's a lot of nervousness. You can start to see certain members looking with fear wondering what's going on.

Sen. Tim Kaine, D-VA: A lot of us are looking up and seeing that the doors up in the gallery are not closed, where the press and everybody is. And so people were shouting up, "Hey, shut the doors up there too."

Sen. Susan Collins, R-ME: The press gallery above us is completely open. Which showed to me how completely unprepared the Capitol Police and the sergeant at arms were.

Officer Mark Gazelle, US Capitol Police: At this point, we were trying to communicate with our headquarters to find out if there was an option for us to stay or go. And if we go, how we are going to do this?

Sen. Tim Kaine, D-VA: There was sort of a gallows humor component to it. Mark Warner sits about fifteen people away from me, and I said, "Hey, Mark!" And he looks at me, and I said, "I love you, man." And that made a lot of people laugh. And I was trying to make people laugh. I felt a need to lighten the mood.

Sen. Susan Collins, R-ME: Lisa [Murkowski] and I were seated next to each other, and [Indiana Sen.] Todd Young came over and talked to us about what was going on. Later, I learned from him that he was positioning himself to defend us because he was sure that the rioters were going to breach the Senate doors. We could hear them.

Outside the Senate chamber, more rioters were streaming into the Ohio Clock Corridor. Officer Goodman, Inspector Loyd, and the other officers were trying to hold them off and not let on that senators were just on the other side of the doors.

Inspector Thomas Loyd, US Capitol Police: [The crowd was] very angry and very upset. The first thing is I'm fully aware they will have not been screened. They're there for nefarious purposes. I'm worried about weapons.

Doug Jensen, the rioter with the "Q" shirt who chased Goodman up the stairs, was face-to-face with Loyd.

Inspector Thomas Loyd, US Capitol Police: He had the big "Q" on the front of his shirt—he was trying to tell me to surrender the building so the mob could get to Pence. I said that wasn't happening. When I told him no, he wanted me to go find the vice president and arrest him myself.

Doug Jensen, Iowa: This guy had blue eyes and gray hair, and that's about all I can remember. I was so locked on to those eyes.

Inspector Thomas Loyd, US Capitol Police: We were there together for several minutes.

As Jensen shouted orders, the rest of the group filled the hallway. They were angry and loud.

Inspector Thomas Loyd, US Capitol Police: There was a lot of danger to observe in that small amount of time.

Officer Brian Morgan, who had worked the same shift with Goodman for more than a decade, had run down from his post on the third floor.

Officer Brian Morgan, US Capitol Police: We had no idea if the doors behind us were locked. And if they were not locked, that would be easy access to the Senate chamber.

Bobic, the HuffPost reporter, had run to safety behind the line of officers after following Goodman and the crowd into the Ohio Clock Corridor. He looked out a second-floor window that had views down the National Mall and saw the enormous crowd up against the building. Two rioters had commandeered a window-washing lift and were banging on second-floor windows from the outside.

Igor Bobic, reporter, HuffPost: I realize, holy shit, this is really happening. I'm there, I'm trying my best to record and take videos and photos. Suddenly somebody sets off like a smoke grenade or something like that. And it looked like a scene out of a war movie. You had cops who were dazed and shell-shocked.

Manu Raju, anchor and chief congressional correspondent, CNN: A producer of ours on the Hill, Ali Zaslav, walked into the booth and said, "Oh my God, look at this." And she showed me a tweet from Igor Bobic with pictures of the rioters on the second floor of the Senate, which was one floor below us. I was stunned. I was like, this cannot be real.

Chad Pergram, senior congressional correspondent, Fox News: I'm struggling at that moment, from a reporting standpoint, to put this into context. So I run through all these different security scenarios, and the only one that I come up with that was on par is ancient, more than two hundred years ago. I went on the air and I said, "This is the worst incursion of an American government institution since the British invaded the White House and the Capitol during the War of 1812."

As police tried to hold off the rioters, phones lit up inside the Senate chamber with Trump's latest tweet:

> Mike Pence didn't have the courage to do what should have been done to protect our Country and our Constitution, giving States a chance to certify a corrected set of facts, not the fraudulent or inaccurate ones which they were asked to previously certify. USA demands the truth!

The tweet came at 2:24, thirteen minutes after Pence had been evacuated from the Senate floor and eleven minutes after the first rioters had broken into the building.

Sen. Chris Murphy, D-CT: When Trump sent out that tweet about Pence, I remember that being the sort of panic moment. We could hear the protesters outside. I remember that being the moment where it's like, oh, crap, he's behind this. He's sending them to hurt us. And I remember turning around and sharing it with Tim Kaine.

Marc Short, chief of staff, Vice President Pence: I don't think there was a lot of discussion about it, honestly. I mean, I think that there were a lot bigger concerns than what the president was tweeting at that moment.

As Pence waited with his family in his ceremonial office off the Senate floor, watching the violence unfold on a small television,[8] *Secret Service Agent Paul Wade called a Capitol Police official to get a report.*

Agent Paul Wade, US Secret Service: He answered the phone and at that point told me, "If you have the vice president, you need to move him now because they've—they're in the building now."

Inspector Lanelle Hawa, US Secret Service: A decision was made to relocate the vice president in order to not put ourselves in a position where we would be trapped or not have an alternate route.

Marc Short, chief of staff, Vice President Pence: It was less of a question. It was a statement of fact that "we're moving you." And the vice president had been reluctant to leave that space.

Vice President Mike Pence: I pointed my finger at his chest and said, "You're not hearing me, I'm not leaving! I'm not giving those people the sight of a sixteen-car motorcade speeding away from the Capitol."

But the rioters were closing in, and the office did not have a secure enough door. After some quick discussion, they agreed to stay in the Capitol but relocate.

Greg Jacob, counsel to Vice President Pence: At that point, the vice president and Mrs. Pence and [their daughter] Charlotte and several of us on the staff went down the stairs to the secure location.

Agent Paul Wade, US Secret Service: There were major concerns because at this point some of the agents downstairs were observing people that had broken into the building. I was closer to the Pences and the supervisors, so I did not see the rioters at that point. But other folks were interacting with them or observing them. So we knew they were getting close.

As Pence and his group evacuated down the stairwell, more rioters were swarming the first floor.

Agent Paul Wade, US Secret Service: From where we came down the staircase, when I hit the threshold, I could hear yelling and screaming from around the corner. I would say it was twenty, thirty yards.

Vice President Mike Pence: All around us was a blur of motion and chaos: security and police officers directing people to safety, staffers shouting and running for shelter. I could see the intensity in the eyes of the Secret Service detail; it was audible in the voices of the Capitol Police. I could hear the falling of footsteps and angry chanting.

Sen. Mike Lee, R-UT: Moments after the proceedings in the Senate were halted by the Capitol Police, my phone rang. The caller ID indicated that the call was coming from the White House. I thought it was Robert O'Brien, the president's national security advisor, calling to update me on a question I had asked him about a security threat from Iran. To my great surprise, it was not Robert O'Brien but President Trump on the other end of the line.

Sen. Mike Rounds, R-SD: Mike Lee, who was sitting to my right about three chairs down in the very back row, had his phone with him, and he got a phone call. And I remember him sitting there saying, "No—well, do you want me to hand him the phone?" And he turns around to Coach and he says, "Hey, Coach, I got the president on the line here. You want to talk to him?" And Tommy says, "Well, yeah, I'll talk to him."

After some back-and-forth with Trump, Sen. Lee figured out that the president was calling for new Alabama Sen. Tommy Tuberville, a loyal Trump ally and former football coach at Auburn University who had been sworn in three days earlier. Trump had mistakenly called Lee's number.

Sen. Mike Lee, R-UT: I went and found Senator Tuberville, handed him my phone, and explained that the president would like to speak to him.

Sen. Tommy Tuberville, R-AL: When he brought me the phone, it said "White House" on it. It was the president.

Sen. Mike Rounds, R-SD: And so I was sitting here, and Coach is right next to me. And the conversation—I'm only hearing one side of it, but it is "No, we're not doing much right now. No. Well, there's, you know, we can hear stuff outside. It's—no, Mike, no, they just took him out. They've taken him out. No, well, I don't know." And there is a little bit of discussion back and forth. Basically there's a lobbying effort going on. Coach wasn't answering directly back.

Sen. Mike Lee, R-UT: I stood nearby for the next five or ten minutes as they spoke, not wanting to lose my phone in the middle of a crisis. Then the Capitol Police became very nervous and ordered us to evacuate the chamber immediately. As they were forcing everyone out of the chamber, I awkwardly found myself interrupting the same telephone conversation I had just facilitated. "Excuse me, Tommy, we have to evacuate. Can I have my phone?'

Sen. Tommy Tuberville, R-AL: He said a few things. I said, "Mr. President, they've taken the vice president out. They want me to get off the phone, I gotta go." So I'm probably the only guy in the world who hung up on the president of the United States.

Sen. Mike Rounds, R-SD: And he says, "Well, Mr. President, I gotta go. I guess they're gonna get us out of here now." And I never forgot that. Because while we were in the room, and there was enough going on to where they were going to remove us, there was still a lobbying effort going on by the president of the United States to stop the ballot from moving forward.

Sen. Catherine Cortez Masto, D-NV: The Capitol Police officers then told all of us to get up and move quickly.

Officer Mark Gazelle, US Capitol Police: At this point, there were so many breaches, and the doors that we have really weren't going to—the outer doors weren't holding. We knew the inner doors weren't going to hold. So we needed to get the Senate out of there.

Andrew Taylor, congressional reporter, The Associated Press: The officers announced an evacuation. Take the elevators to the basement, then cross underneath Constitution Avenue by tunnel to a secret location in a nearby office building, they said.

Sen. Chris Murphy, D-CT: The group that I was with was not running, we were walking out. But it was pretty shocking how disorderly it was. I mean, it was pretty shocking how little police protection we had as we were leaving.

Sen. Richard Blumenthal, D-CT: I was right behind Mitch McConnell as we came from the floor. He moves a little bit more slowly because of the polio he had as a young person. I remember thinking, I am standing behind one of the most important people in the United States, and I want to get around him.

Sen. Dick Durbin, D-IL: I was behind [California Sen.] Dianne Feinstein, concerned about her physically as we were moving. But she was doing well.

Sen. Susan Collins, R-ME: I had high heels on, and they were saying, "Run! Run! Hurry! Hurry!" And I was trying to run in my high heels and trying to decide whether I should just take them off.

Sen. Mike Rounds, R-SD: Most everybody was leaving through the left-hand side, where the Democrats normally sit, but out the back doors behind the chamber. I was in the back. The thoughts that were going through my mind were number one, somebody is trying to tell us not to do our job, and it is disrupting the peaceful transfer of power. The second thing that went through my mind was—I started seeing all of the protection that we were being given and the concern that they had, and we could hear people pounding on stuff. We could hear stuff breaking. My thought was that this is going to be a very bloody day in this Capitol. And it wasn't a fear for us. It was a fear that people were going to get killed if they got anywhere close to us. Because these guys were very serious about the protection of the elected officials who had to do their duty.

As senators evacuated, quick-thinking Senate staff grabbed the mahogany ballot boxes.

Paul Kane, reporter, *The Washington Post*: In a moment of incredible historical importance, they grabbed the boxes and envelopes with all of the Electoral College votes and certificates.

Sen. Mike Rounds, R-SD: I just thought, we've got to make it clear all of us want those ballots to go with us. So [Republican Sen.] Ben Sasse and I were the last two guys in line going out. And we just walked up and we just said, "Let us help you with these things." And they said, "These are not getting out of our sight. We're responsible for them." We said, "Rest assured, they're not getting out of our sight either."

Sen. Catherine Cortez Masto, D-NV: And that's when everybody came together. All of the senators, whether you are Republican or Democrat, our floor staff that was with us, grabbing those electoral votes. And we all started going up and down stairs, through hallways until we could get to a secure location.

Sen. Bob Casey, D-PA: All of us had to file out of that one exit, and I remember lining up to go out the door. And when you come out of the door, you're in an enclosed hallway where we go in and out to vote. And for some reason when we went into that hallway, that's the first time when I had—my concern must have been building, because when I walked in that hallway I thought, someone could be shot in here. I don't know why I thought that. But at that point, I must have reached the level where I had a sense that they were in the building and that they could be armed.

Sen. Mike Rounds, R-SD: As we went down, and we were going to that secure location, I remember we could still hear the noise. We couldn't see people, but we could hear the noise. More security with long guns, with [automatic rifles] and so forth, were showing up.

Sen. Richard Burr, R-NC, a longtime member of the Senate Intelligence Committee, was furious that Vice President Mike Pence was in danger, along with Pence's military aide who was carrying the backup "nuclear football," or a briefcase that contains equipment to communicate with the office inside the Pentagon that transmits nuclear attack orders.

Sen. Richard Burr, R-NC: [Trump's] breach of office was leaving the vice president uncovered with a nuclear football. To me, that was a breach of his oath.

Sen. Mike Rounds, R-SD: I was angry. I was really angry that this was going on. I also was like, how do we explain to the next generation that we had a bloodbath here today in this building? What drove this to the point where people are going to die because they tried to stop the peaceful transfer of power?

While there was an evacuation plan for the senators, others in the building weren't sure where to go. Restaurant workers in the basement carryout where Marc Short had just ordered his lunch locked themselves into a food storage closet. Reporters in the Senate gallery had been told to go to the Capitol Visitor Center, a large underground area that is accessible from the Senate basement.

Paul Kane, reporter, *The Washington Post*: There was a lone Capitol Police officer just sort of holding the doors to the Capitol Visitor Center. And he was screaming at us something like "It's been infiltrated!" and at that point we merged in with all of the senators.

Sen. Roy Blunt, R-MO: I'm generally pretty calm, and I was pretty calm. We go out the lobby door, and the officer standing at the top of the stairs just keeps saying, "Time is not our friend. Time is not our friend." Still, nobody's running or anything like that. But you get down to the tunnel, and as I'm walking through the tunnel, I saw Schumer, who just that day knew for sure that he was going to be the majority leader. His two uniformed guys—I think they were uniformed—they had pretty good-sized weapons drawn, and they're basically whisking him down the hall. And I thought, this may be a little more serious than I thought.

Senate Democratic Leader Chuck Schumer, D-NY: A police officer in a big flak jacket and a large rifle grabbed me firmly by the collar like this. I'll never forget that grip. And said to me, "Senator, we've got to get out of here; you're in danger."

As they ran to a basement elevator that would take Schumer on a route out of the building and to a secure location, the group was surprised by rioters heading toward them. Schumer and the officers quickly turned around and ran in the opposite direction.[9]

Washington Sen. Patty Murray, the number-three Democrat, was not in the Senate chamber when her colleagues evacuated. She had been working on a speech in her Capitol office on the first floor, which is adjacent to the Upper West Terrace and the door where the first rioters broke into the building. Immediately after that initial breach, another group of people broke into the door next to Murray's office and spilled into the hallway. Murray and her husband, Rob, who had accompanied her to work, started hearing loud noises and flash-bangs outside. And then, suddenly, the rioters were immediately outside her door. Rob yelled at her to get down.

Sen. Patty Murray, D-WA: We were lying on the floor. And all of a sudden, they were in the hall. They were yelling. They were yelling that they had breached the castle. They were yelling, "Kill the infidels." And we heard somebody saying, "We saw them. They're in one of these rooms." And they were pounding on our door and trying to open it. And my husband sat with his foot against the door, praying that it would not break in.

Murray wasn't sure whether she had locked the door.

Sen. Patty Murray, D-WA: We had to be quiet. We didn't want them to know we were in there. And I'm just looking at my husband, and we're just—eye contact, and just we can see each other's eyes: "Please, please let this door be locked." And this vision of my husband just putting his foot against a door, like he might be able to hold down this incredibly loud, angry, even jubilant mob outside our door was just beyond belief. And the terror I saw in his eyes was something I have not seen, and we have been married for almost forty-nine years.

Just outside Murray's office, still on the terrace, Jason Riddle called his stepfather as he watched the other rioters break in.

Jason Riddle, former correctional officer and mail carrier, New Hampshire: I was like, "They're breaking in the windows, they're smashing doors." And he was like, "Maybe you should get out of there." That was his advice. And I was like, "I'm going to stick it out. What's the worst that could happen?"

Riddle went into the building, passing Murray's closed door. Down the hall, he found a group of people ransacking the Senate parliamentarian's office. He wasn't looking for lawmakers, but he did find a bottle of wine in a mini fridge there. Riddle took a selfie smiling with the wine, rioters still destroying the office in the background.

Back outside, Capitol Police Officer Winston Pingeon had been pushing through the crowd to try and secure the doorway that led to Murray's hallway. He could see people streaming into the building there, but he had no idea she was trapped inside. And before he could even go in, he was attacked.

Officer Winston Pingeon, US Capitol Police: Before I knew it, I was punched in the face on my left and knocked on my back. My helmet must have come down over my eyes, or somebody fell on top of me, but I couldn't see anything and they had ripped my baton from me. And I remember thinking I have to protect my gun, because I don't want them to steal my gun. And just thinking, please don't stab me, please don't shoot me. I also remember thinking, I don't want to die on the steps of the US Capitol today. But that I might. Like, this could be it.

Jason Riddle, former correctional officer and mail carrier, New Hampshire: It was euphoric, but in a weird way, like an apocalyptic way. I don't know how to explain it. I was watching my Capitol building just get destroyed, and everyone's celebrating it. It was like jubilance. And then when I saw a liquor cabinet, that's when my true nature came out and I just went and started drinking.

Sen. Patty Murray, D-WA: I was in there well over an hour. I was trying to text with my staff: What should we do? And I looked down, and my phone was running out of power, because I had been trying to text my family. I wanted them to know all of a sudden what was going on. I was trying to text my staff. I was trying to get help. And I crawled over to where the phone was on my desk, and the power had been cut. I mean, there were just so many moments like that, that it's hard to even talk about.

Jason Riddle, former correctional officer and mail carrier, New Hampshire: As I was drinking the wine, a police officer came in and started screaming at everybody to get out. He saw me with the wine, he pointed at me and he's like, "You chug that and get out of here!"

Officer Winston Pingeon, US Capitol Police: We got inside, and we saw people in the parliamentarian's office, totally ransacking it. There were papers everywhere, they found bottles of alcohol. They're like rummaging through stuff. And I remember going in and then looking to the left, and it was I think a husband and wife, middle-aged older white couple. And I kind of pushed her to the side and just grabbed him, because he was smaller than me. I grabbed him and threw him out and just kind of pushed them out.

Jason Riddle, former correctional officer and mail carrier, New Hampshire: It was just immature, silly behavior. And then other people were being violent. And then this police officer was like—this guy didn't know what to do. He was running around telling everyone to leave. Everyone was out of their element and didn't know how to act. I think I had the gall to ask someone if there was a bathroom.

Sen. Patty Murray, D-WA: I was in the Capitol on 9/11, one of the few senators that was. I was in an office looking out across the mall towards the Pentagon. We had known that the New York towers had been hit. We were talking about it. And all of a sudden, the window that I was looking out of, I could see the smoke rise from the Pentagon. Officers raced in and told us to get out of there as fast as we could. And of course, later, we learned that, but for some very brave people in a plane over Pennsylvania, we would have been hit. That's the only other time in my whole time here that I ever felt I was not safe in the Capitol, until January 6.

Two floors above, alone in his office, Chaplain Black watched the fighting begin out his window.

Senate Chaplain Barry Black: I literally watched the clash between the crowd and the Capitol Police, and it did not take very much deductive reasoning to know that the Capitol Police were outnumbered. There were people spraying whatever they had. And it was not pretty to watch. So even before they breached the Capitol, it was pretty obvious to me that they are probably going to get into the building. So here I am on the third floor. I started looking around the room—what do I do? I'm certainly not going to go back down into the chamber because of the rapidity in which this assault seems to be succeeding.

Black started looking around his office, even considering at one point whether he could remove a panel in his ceiling and hide.

Senate Chaplain Barry Black: My wife was calling and saying, "Shelter in place." That didn't seem to be the wisest option. And then I heard a knock on the door. And I said, "Oh my God, they've gotten up to the third floor already." I thought it might be a little foolish, but I opened the door, and there was Gino, who is one of the Capitol Police—big guy. He would come to our Bible studies. And he said, "We're not leaving you, man."

Gino rushed Black downstairs at the same moment that senators were evacuating. Black ran alongside them as they headed to the secure location.

Senate Chaplain Barry Black: As I was literally running for my life, I thought about a Bible verse—1 Thessalonians 5:18: "In everything give thanks, for this is the will of God concerning you in Christ Jesus." So I'm saying, "What in the world can I possibly have to be thankful for right now?" So I started thinking about the fact that I have been jogging essentially a couple of miles a day since 1970. And I was thankful for cardiovascular fitness that enabled me to run and continue without hyperventilation. And then I thought about the fact that the lawmakers were able to get out of the chamber and how catastrophic it would have been. This could have been a hostage situation. And so I was basically passing by the thorns and picking the roses of gratitude as I made my way.

Pence had made it to the secure location—a Capitol garage.

Greg Jacob, counsel to Vice President Pence: Most of us loaded into cars once we got into the secure location. That's what they asked us to do. The vice president wouldn't get in his car.

Vice President Mike Pence: As we approached, I saw that the lead police car was slowly beginning to move up the ramp, and I stopped, turned to [the lead Secret Service agent], and said, "I'm not getting in that car."

Marc Short, chief of staff, Vice President Pence: He felt like, for the world's greatest democracy, to see a motorcade, a fifteen-car motorcade fleeing the Capitol would send all the wrong signals. So he was adamant to say, I want to stay here in the Capitol.

Greg Jacob, counsel to Vice President Pence: He was determined that unless there was imminent danger to bodily safety that he was not going to abandon the Capitol and let the rioters have a victory of having made the vice president flee or made it difficult to restart the process later that day. We were down in there for several hours.

Marc Short, chief of staff, Vice President Pence: At some point, it became clear, look, just hold here, we're not going to move.

On the MPD radio, Inspector Glover was desperately calling for reinforcements. One group of rioters on the northwest side had already broken through the line and entered the building. But the police were still holding a much longer line on the lower terrace that was, for the moment at least, keeping the larger crowd at bay. Glover, who was calling many of the shots as Capitol Police leaders were quiet, had balked when a senior officer had advised pulling back.

Inspector Robert Glover, Metropolitan Police Department: I couldn't give it up. I knew if I pulled us back in, there was no defending at that point. We would lose everything, and we would have so much more to fight over. I just knew I had to get us up higher, and if I could get us up higher, we had a better chance. I knew what was inside the building. I knew what was at stake. I think every officer out there knew what we were responsible for protecting.

Officer Jesse Leasure, Metropolitan Police Department: We're just holding back the crowd at that point. There's yelling and screaming, and occasionally there's a push, and then officers are spraying pepper spray to try to keep the people back. And as I said, they'll spit it right back at you and still be screaming, and with an intensity, a wildness in their eyes. Or if they can't take it, they'll back off, and then they'll be immediately replaced by somebody fresh and just as pissed off, if not more. All the while, we're getting hit by the blowback from our own pepper spray and the blowback from their pepper spray just everywhere.

Lieutenant George Donigian, Metropolitan Police Department: It felt like the wind was blowing very east that day. And when the [chemical munitions] went off on the north side, it seemed to just affect everyone in the area.

Sergeant Aquilino Gonell, US Capitol Police: The physical violence we experienced was horrific and devastating. My fellow officers and I were punched, pushed, kicked, shoved, sprayed with chemical irritants, and even blinded with eye-damaging lasers.

Inspector Robert Glover, Metropolitan Police Department: I did see several Capitol [Police] members suffering from the effects of bear spray. You could see the dye marking out of the bear spray. You could see the orange on their faces. They suffered from lacerations from being hit in the head with items such as the flagpoles, the metal pieces of the bike rack. Sheer exhaustion, some of them just were exhausted. I remember walking through blood on the platform only to find out after the fact that one of our officers whose hand got pinched in the bike rack [had] lost a piece of his hand.

Sergeant Aquilino Gonell, US Capitol Police: Weapons included hammers, rebars, knives, batons, and police shields taken by force, as well as bear spray and pepper spray. Some rioters wore tactical gear, including bulletproof vests and gas masks.

Officer Daniel Hodges, Metropolitan Police Department: Someone grabbed my baton, and we wrestled for control and went to the ground. He kicked me in the chest, knocked me over, and the medical mask I was wearing got pulled up over my eyes. So at that point, I was on all fours and blind and surrounded by the mob. I was really afraid for my life. Fortunately, my platoon had freed themselves from their attackers and had my back while I got back on my feet.

Inspector Robert Glover, Metropolitan Police Department: A significant number of the crowd had helmets, plate carriers. I could see earpieces for the radios, high-end radios that are capable of being encrypted. I would say military grade. Gas masks. They were using pieces of bike rack. They had bear spray, which is a very strong form of cesium capsicum, which is pepper spray but at a much more robust level. They were using flagpoles, both wooden and metal. They were picking up water bottles and throwing water bottles. And later in the day, they were using heavier items, such as big fifty-pound fire extinguishers. They were using anything that was loose around them that they could use.

Officer Adam Eveland, Metropolitan Police Department: There would be moments of intense fighting the line, and then there'd be moments where they would be pleading with you, "Hey, like, join us. We're doing the right thing. You're supposed to be on our side."

President Donald Trump's supporters wait for him to speak on the Ellipse, just outside the White House, on the morning of January 6, 2021. *AP Photo/John Minchillo*

Tens of thousands of Trump supporters crowd the National Mall. *AP Photo/John Minchillo*

Sen. Josh Hawley, R-MO, pumps his fist toward protesters gathered behind barriers on the East Front of the Capitol. *Francis Chung/POLITICO via AP Images*

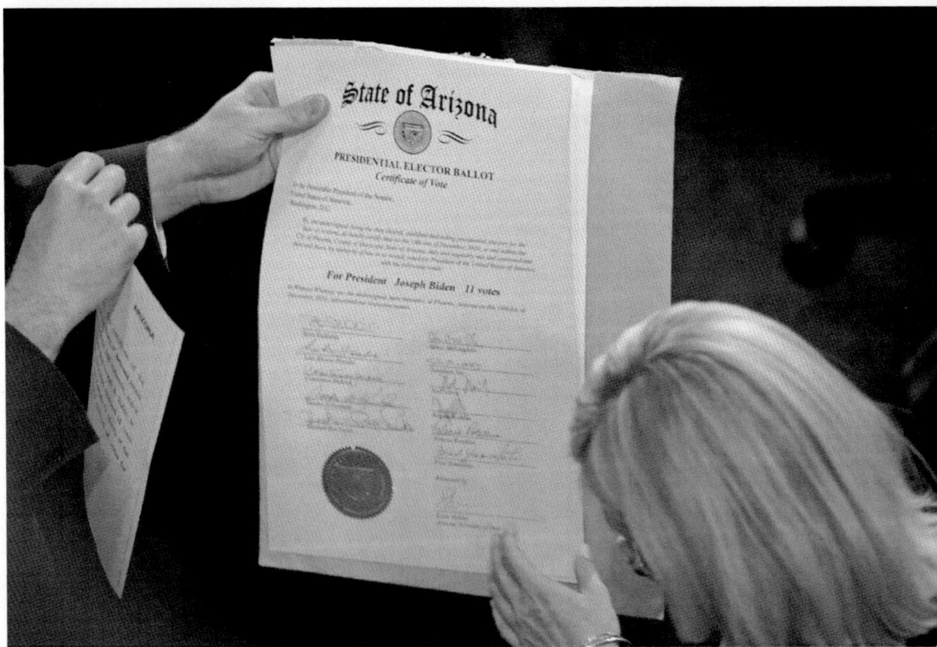

Staff open and examine Arizona's certificate of Electoral College votes as the joint session of Congress begins. *AP Photo/Andrew Harnik*

Inspector Thomas Loyd, in the police cap, fights alongside his officers as rioters quickly overwhelm Capitol Police on the West Front. *AP Photo/Julio Cortez*

Rioters are sprayed with chemicals as they try to break through a police barrier on the West Front of the Capitol. *AP Photo/Julio Cortez*

A police officer has her eyes flushed with water after a confrontation with demonstrators on the West Front. *AP Photo/John Minchillo*

Rioter Joshua Matthew Black of Alabama was shot in the face with a crowd control munition. *AP Photo/John Minchillo*

Rioters scale a West Front wall shortly after breaching the perimeter of the US Capitol grounds. *AP Photo/Jose Luis Magana*

Rioters climb to the top of a tall media tower built for President Joe Biden's inauguration. *Francis Chung/POLITICO via AP Images*

Rioters climb on vehicles and occupy the East steps of the US Capitol after breaching th security perimeter and rushing the building. *Francis Chung/POLITICO via AP Images*

Members of the Oath Keepers on the East Front steps of the Capitol. *AP Photo/Manuel Balc Ceneta*

Rioter Doug Jensen confronts Capitol Police Inspector Thomas Loyd and other officers outside the Senate chamber after breaking into the building and chasing Officer Eugene Goodman up the stairs. *AP Photo/Manuel Balce Ceneta*

acob Chansley, who called himself the "QAnon Shaman," bellows as police confront him and other rioters outside the doors of the Senate. *AP Photo/Manuel Balce Ceneta*

A protester stands with a Confederate flag in the Ohio Clock Corridor outside the Senate. *Chris Kleponis/Sipa USA/Sipa via AP Images*

Capitol Police try to hold back rioters outside the east doors to the US Capitol. *AP Photo/ Andrew Harnik*

Inspector Robert Glover, Metropolitan Police Department: The effects of the bear spray are much longer-lasting than even our law enforcement–issued OC. It's got a higher Scoville unit than what our OC does. It's meant to stop a 500- to 1,000-pound animal. So imagine what it does to a human being. And it can actually cause thermal burns as well if you don't decon quickly enough.

Sergeant Aquilino Gonell, US Capitol Police: Based on the coordinated tactics we observed and verbal commands we heard, it appeared that many of the attackers had law enforcement or military experience.

Inspector Robert Glover, Metropolitan Police Department: It almost seems like this was a War College exercise: how do I take the Capitol? It was very apparent that this had been well thought out, well planned. You could tell that this was not some willy-nilly movement. Again, they were watching what we were doing, and they were able to counter that.

Lieutenant George Donigian, Metropolitan Police Department: I didn't think we were going to be able to hold anyone back for much longer. We were being overwhelmed between—from all of the various types of assaults and just the huge crowd surge that was continuing to come towards us.

Inspector Robert Glover, Metropolitan Police Department: We again tried to maintain that line. With all the platoons coming up, I just kept assigning the platoons to strengthen the line.

Officer Chad Curtice, Metropolitan Police Department: All of a sudden, it's like they joined together and just charged the gates, so knocking us all back.

Officer Daniel Hodges, Metropolitan Police Department: We held that as long as we could. Unfortunately, they were able to break through with their superior numbers.

At 2:28 p.m., after holding for what seemed like hours, police lost their long line across the West Front. Glover frantically called out on the police radio a 10-33, code for an emergency when officers need immediate assistance:

> We lost the line! We've lost the line! All MPD, pull back! All MPD, pull back up to the upper deck! All MPD, pull back to the upper deck ASAP! All MPD, come back to the upper deck. Upper deck. Cruiser 50. We've been flanked! 10–33. I repeat, 10–33 West Front of the Capitol. We have been flanked, and we've lost the line!

Inspector Robert Glover, Metropolitan Police Department: Giving the 10-33 was my hope that anybody else that was listening would've just—whoever they would've had available would've come out and helped.

Officer Jesse Leasure, Metropolitan Police Department: The lines collapsed, and everybody's coming up the stairs, and the rioters are starting to make their way underneath the big stages that were put up there. So they're starting to make their way up and around. And somebody gets the smart idea to drop like a smoke canister down into the stairwell to prevent them from coming up. And we're trying to figure out what we're going to do, and then the general order is given to retreat inside the tunnel or go up on the upper level.

Officer Daniel Hodges, Metropolitan Police Department: The West Front devolved into a series of pitched battles. I was pushed back by several members of the mob until I hit about a waist-high wall, and a couple people held me down while one person reached underneath the visor on my helmet and tried to gouge out my eye with his thumb. You can still hear the screaming in the video from my body-worn camera when he's doing it. Thankfully, I was able to push him off before any permanent damage was done. But we couldn't get the line back.

The officers then tried to hold the upper terrace, where President-elect Biden was to take the oath of office in just two weeks. But it was quickly overrun, and orders eventually came to fall back inside. As the officers retreated, the mob kept up a close chase and continued its assault.

Before he went in, and as the rioters were closing in, Officer Leasure looked out at the huge, packed, angry crowd below. It looked like a battle scene from the Lord of the Rings *movies, he thought.*

Officer Jesse Leasure, Metropolitan Police Department: I'm just like, what the fuck is going on?

Inspector Robert Glover, Metropolitan Police Department: It was the first time in my career I didn't think we were going to go home. We were battle-tested through May and the period of unrest, and I had faith and confidence in the officers through that period. I had faith and confidence in the officers that I was working with on January 6th, but we were just outnumbered at this point. And once that line broke and they got in behind us, that's never a good thing.

Just before the line broke, Capitol Police Officers Brian Sicknick and Caroline Edwards were holding back increasingly unruly rioters on the southwest terrace when Julian Khater, a protester who lived in Somerset, New Jersey, pepper-sprayed them at close range. Khater had been sprayed himself, and he was angry. He took a spray can that his friend had brought with him and pushed to the front of the crowd.

As other rioters tried to pull away bike racks, Khater thrust his arm in the air and sprayed Sicknick.[10]

Officer Caroline Edwards, US Capitol Police: I could tell he had been sprayed with something, and his face was like white. It was pale. And if any of us here gets sprayed with something, our faces turn beet red, like that's usually the reaction. So I can remember alarm bells going off. I turned towards the crowd to see who sprayed him, what he had gotten sprayed with, and that's when I got a direct hit in the eyes with chemical spray.

Sicknick was eventually helped by other officers, and he spent the next twenty minutes on the terrace trying to wash out his eyes before returning to duty. Edwards met her husband, a fellow Capitol Police officer who was nearby, and was walking back into the building with him when she was hit with a separate round of tear gas.

Officer Caroline Edwards, US Capitol Police: So the combination of the chemicals made my throat immediately close. I couldn't take a breath at all. That was one of a few times that day where I was like, yeah, this is probably like where I'm not going to make it. But thankfully, there was a hazardous device section officer who was up there with oxygen, and they started giving me oxygen.

Edwards later went inside and threw up. But both she and Brian Sicknick returned to duty, running back into the fight that afternoon.

Just as the police line broke on the West Front, rioters were breaking into the other side of the building as well. A large group had amassed at the historic Columbus Doors, the grand East Front entrance that leads directly into the Capitol Rotunda. The heavy bronze doors, designed by the American sculptor Randolph Rogers and first brought to the Capitol in 1863, weigh twenty thousand pounds and stand seventeen feet high.[11] *But they are often kept open, leaving only a heavy glass door as the central entrance.*

The crowd had rushed the doors about thirty minutes earlier, and they were now attacking the small group of officers who were trying to keep them out. One rioter—the same man who had climbed a tree and displayed a Confederate flag at the rally earlier in the day—sprayed two officers at close range with pepper spray. Both were temporarily blinded, and one collapsed and lost consciousness as the crowd surrounded him, trying to push into the doorway.[12]

Members of the Oath Keepers and the Proud Boys were scattered throughout the crowd, and at one point, a "stack" of Oath Keepers, including Jessica Watkins, the bar owner from Ohio, approached the stairs to great fanfare. Dressed in their military gear, the group marched in a line, each with their hand on a shoulder in front of them.

Jessica Watkins, US Army veteran and bar owner, Oath Keepers, Ohio: I was getting swept up in it. It was a cool moment. Everybody was excited to see us, you know? They were just like, "Yeah, the Oath Keepers are here."

Pamela Hemphill, a retiree from Idaho, had been trampled as the crowd pushed up the steps earlier, and she was now watching as the people became violent.

Pamela Hemphill, retired drug and alcohol counselor, Idaho: They pushed again on the officers on the steps and got to the top where the door is, and that's when they started using flagpoles and pepper spray on the officers.

Hemphill had posted on social media a week earlier: "It's not going to be a FUN *Trump Rally that is planned for January 6, its a* WAR*!" In a separate post, she held a long gun and said she was headed to Washington.*[13] *She was now cut up from her fall, her glasses were broken, and she felt scared. Still, she was encouraging the crowd. "It's your House!" she yelled.*

Jessica Watkins, US Army veteran and bar owner, Oath Keepers, Ohio: So we got up to the top of the stairs, and then we turned around. We were singing the national anthem, the very, very tail end of it. And I turned around and faced out over the crowd. And we looked down the stairs. Everybody is just cheering. We were just, like, "Yeah! Woo!" And I just felt, like, really American.

As rioters broke the glass and pounded the doors, two officers stood facing the crowd with their backs to the doors, taking hits as they tried to prevent the mob from coming in.

Jessica Watkins, US Army veteran and bar owner, Oath Keepers, Ohio: People are chanting. It was definitely a protest. But it was Black Friday, when everybody wanted to get in there and get a flat-screen for two hundred bucks.

Eventually, a rioter already in the building managed to open the doors from inside. Officers pushed the crowd back at first but ultimately lost the fight. The doors were breached, and a new wave of angry, frenzied people spilled into the Capitol Rotunda.[14]

Pamela Hemphill, retired drug and alcohol counselor, Idaho: When you first walk in, it's overwhelming. It's so beautiful. The paintings—it's like in awe, like, "Oh my God, this is history." But then I sat down. The people were angry.

Watkins called into her walkie-talkie app, "We are in the mezzanine. We are in the main dome right now. We are rocking it. They are throwing grenades, they are fricking shooting people with paintballs. But we are in here." She soon headed toward the north side of the building, in the direction of the Senate chamber.

Jessica Watkins, US Army veteran and bar owner, Oath Keepers, Ohio: We were mad. We wanted them to hear us.

Metropolitan Police Officer Christopher Owens had entered the building on the Senate side with his Civil Disturbance Unit platoon and was headed toward the Rotunda when a group of rioters, including Watkins, ran right into them. They were just down the hall from the Senate, which had been evacuated minutes earlier, and close to the office of Republican Leader Mitch McConnell. When the two groups—protesters and police— clashed, it was with such force that Owens, who is six feet tall and weighs around two hundred pounds, was lifted off the ground.

Officer Christopher Owens, Metropolitan Police Department: The rioters were trying to advance; they were punching, kicking, swinging flagpoles and two-by-fours, and basically just trying to fight their way through our line.

Jessica Watkins, US Army veteran and bar owner, Oath Keepers, Ohio: They stole the election from us. They certified this election. And now I'm being crushed in the hallway, and they won't even listen to me? I got pissed off.

"This is our House!" the rioters chanted to the police. "We feed your families! You work for us! No mercy here!" And then, steps away from Mitch McConnell's office, "Bitch McConnell!" and "All for Pelosi!"

Officer Christopher Owens, Metropolitan Police Department: Rioters were grabbing for things on my vest. At one point, I had someone who was on their knees grab ahold of my sidearm and try to remove my sidearm from my holster. We had officers that had their badges ripped off, magazines for their weapons removed from their belts, their helmets pulled off, their gas masks pulled off.

The officers eventually pushed the crowd back, and the protesters dispersed into the Rotunda, away from the Senate chamber. As rioters were fighting and wandering around under the Capitol dome, sounds of clashes and shouts filled the cavernous round room in the center of the building. Officers were using tear gas, and the particles settled on the statues and paintings that surrounded them. Rioters were hunting for Nancy Pelosi and calling, "Hang Mike Pence!"[15]

Jason Dolan, former marine, Oath Keepers, Florida: It felt like Congress having certified what I saw as an illegitimate election, installing what I thought was an unelected president, was committing treason to the United States. And so I was chanting, "Treason!"

Jessica Watkins, US Army veteran and bar owner, Oath Keepers, Ohio: I wanted my voice to be heard. I did believe the election was stolen. I still have a lot of questions about the 2020 election. I'm not going to say it like I don't.

Jason Dolan, former marine, Oath Keepers, Florida: I wanted them to hear it. I wanted them to hear me. I wanted them to stop the certification of the election.

Robert Schornack, business development manager, Michigan: Well, I wasn't sure why I was going in in the first place, and then after being inside, you know, I thought there was some reason for us to be in there.

Jason Dolan, former marine, Oath Keepers, Florida: People will act out of kindness. They will act out of charity. But they'll act out of fear too, and if they weren't going to—from my perspective—do the right thing, then maybe they could be scared into doing the right thing.

Shawna Martin, missionary, Arizona: After people went in, I was [outside] for a couple hours. It got kind of quiet. I walked to the front, I walked to the back. There's people milling about, just playing, picnics, whatever. And then after a couple of hours, I left.

Alisa La, special assistant to House Speaker Nancy Pelosi: The annunciator said, "The Capitol has been breached." I knew it wasn't a drill, but I couldn't believe it. The noises were intensifying much more and more flash-bangs.

Rioters were in the building, and the remaining staff in House Speaker Nancy Pelosi's suite knew that they were in danger. The offices that make up the suite are just off the Rotunda and have a prominent sign, and Pelosi was an obvious target. The staff immediately decided to shelter in a room with reinforced doors.

Alisa La, a special assistant to Pelosi, had moved from her office to a conference room next door, and she wasn't sure whether there were people outside the doors. But she gathered her coat and her bag and shot out into the hallway and into the other room down the hall where most of the others were already waiting.

Alisa La, special assistant to House Speaker Nancy Pelosi: I got into the room and told everyone to be calm. Don't open the door for anybody.

Henry Connelly, Pelosi's communications director, was still in his office a floor below, alone and trying to decide whether he should barricade himself in the room.

Alisa La, special assistant to House Speaker Nancy Pelosi: I panic-called Henry to get up to where we were.

Henry Connelly, communications director, House Speaker Nancy Pelosi: I grabbed my coat and my laptop and my bag and ran up. When I stepped into the hallway, I could hear them in the building. The sound was loud and vivid in a way that was clearly a sign it was very bad.

Alisa La, special assistant to House Speaker Nancy Pelosi: Henry was the last to arrive. And he's like, always so cool and calm. We ensured the exterior door was locked and the interior door was locked.

Henry Connelly, communications director, House Speaker Nancy Pelosi: I realized that I had assumed that there would be Capitol Police in the room with us. And I walked into the room and I remember being like, "Oh shit, it's just us."

Alisa La, special assistant to House Speaker Nancy Pelosi: The room was a mess. It was mainly used as a storage room.

Henry Connelly, communications director, House Speaker Nancy Pelosi: It's a conference room that we hadn't used in months because of COVID. The very long table is sort of pushed into a corner, and chairs off on one side and sort of gathered around. There are bankers' boxes everywhere.

Alisa La, special assistant to House Speaker Nancy Pelosi: One of my colleagues was like, "This room is too small to be socially distanced." I'm like, "Okay, not important right now!"

Henry Connelly, communications director, House Speaker Nancy Pelosi: So we get in there and the lights are on and there's kind of a nervous energy. Fairly soon afterwards, we realized that we needed to turn out the lights.

Alisa La, special assistant to House Speaker Nancy Pelosi: I put on some lame jazz music to try to get rid of the eeriness, but that comically was off-putting. So I put on Taylor Swift's *Evermore* album, which was a little better. I tried to crack some jokes and make conversation.

Henry Connelly, communications director, House Speaker Nancy Pelosi: In the back of the room, there's like a vent or something that I think is somehow connected to the Rotunda. So you could hear, almost in surround sound, the screams as they got near us.

Alisa La, special assistant to House Speaker Nancy Pelosi: We heard yelling, hooting, hollering. Music turned off. We all stopped talking.

Henry Connelly, communications director, House Speaker Nancy Pelosi: We heard them crashing into the office. We heard them breaking down the doors, and we started thinking about our own door. We could hear them break down our outer door, and the metal part of the door-frame clanging as it popped out of the wall and hit the marble.

Alisa La, special assistant to House Speaker Nancy Pelosi: We basically went into active-shooter mode. I started a text among us in the room to communicate.

Henry Connelly, communications director, House Speaker Nancy Pelosi: Two of the guys in the room, when the sound happened, they sprang up to the door and gripped the doorknob to stop the door from being ripped open.

Alisa La, special assistant to House Speaker Nancy Pelosi: I had been texting with the Capitol Police as well, [Pelosi's] detail, and they were just like, "You are in the safest place you can be," which was not reassuring.

Henry Connelly, communications director, House Speaker Nancy Pelosi: And then we could hear a guy screaming, "Where are you, Nancy? Where are you?" And we could hear them starting to break down the doors along the hallway.

Alisa La, special assistant to House Speaker Nancy Pelosi: The noises were louder and more real, menacing, yelling, "Where's Nancy? We're going to get her. Where's that bitch? We're going to kill her." Paired with glass smashed, things being destroyed.

Henry Connelly, communications director, House Speaker Nancy Pelosi: There's just this haunting, shrill, sort of taunting, malevolent sound—somebody that's screaming, "Where are you, Nancy?" in like a serious way, and then there's, like, a whooping. Like maniacal. A little sociopathic. That voice in particular was like a horror movie.

Alisa La, special assistant to House Speaker Nancy Pelosi: The walls were so thin, we could hear everything. Then they said, "Where are you fuckers that work for her? We're going to find you and get you. We know you're in here."

Henry Connelly, communications director, House Speaker Nancy Pelosi: I made sure to tell my fiancée that I loved her, but in a way that wasn't going to raise any red flags.

Alisa La, special assistant to House Speaker Nancy Pelosi: They were at our door. I grabbed my colleague's arm. I said, "They're going to take us hostage. What do we do?" There was nothing to be done. We were trapped inside.

Henry Connelly, communications director, House Speaker Nancy Pelosi: I admitted to one guy friend of mine that things were getting pretty dicey.

Alisa La, special assistant to House Speaker Nancy Pelosi: They got to the interior door and tried opening the knob. It wouldn't open. They then started throwing their weight onto the door. I actually have a photo of my Apple Watch that day, and it shows the heartbeat. And when they're at the door, like jangling and trying to get in, like, my heart rate shot up like crazy.

The Senate had evacuated, but Capitol Police on the other side of the chamber didn't know that yet. They were still trying to push rioters out of the Ohio Clock Corridor, and what had started with the small group that chased Officer Eugene Goodman up the stairs had become a growing group of protesters and complete chaos.

Officer Brian Morgan, US Capitol Police: I was very angry. I was just trying to deescalate the situation because I knew we were extremely outnumbered. These people had broken into our building. I didn't know what weapons they had on them. They could have had anything, bombs, guns, knives. I didn't know at this point.

The rioters were now in multiple hallways surrounding the chamber, and Officer Morgan could see down the hallway, just past Mitch McConnell's office, that DC police were fighting a larger group of people who were heading toward the Senate from the Rotunda. He could tell it was a violent fight, and he heard people yelling, "Fuck McConnell!"

Officer Brian Morgan, US Capitol Police: I could see the numbers were very vast, and I knew that if they had broken through the Metropolitan officers there, that we wouldn't have the numbers to stop them. And that was of grave concern because at that time, I still didn't know if the senators had been evacuated or not.

Doug Jensen, the rioter wearing a "Q" shirt who had chased Goodman up the stairs, cheered on the rioters down the hall before he confronted another police line around the corner and was eventually escorted out of the building.[16] *But others who had been in the outer hallway, including Jacob Chansley, who had dubbed himself the "QAnon shaman," remained. Chansley was wearing a furry Viking hat with horns along with a painted American flag on his face and a bare chest. He was also carrying an American flag with a sharp tip and a bullhorn he had used to shout to the crowd.*

Officer Brian Morgan, US Capitol Police: He would yell, "Where are you hiding? Where are all the members at?" Different things like that.

With few police to hold them off and a growing number of people spilling into the building, the rioters eventually broke into the empty chamber. Josiah Colt, a rioter from Idaho, was one of the first to enter, breaching the third-floor gallery doors, climbing over the balcony, and dropping several feet down to the floor. He then helped people enter the chamber.[17]

Officer Brian Morgan, US Capitol Police: In all the chaos, I had actually seen at least ten rioters that had gone onto the Senate floor, and they had opened the doors around the chamber so others could go in.

The rioters who spilled into the Senate were able to roam freely for around ten minutes before a different Capitol police officer entered and tried to push them out. A group of rioters found Ted Cruz's desk and started to rifle through it, looking through papers. "I think Cruz would want us to do this," one of the men said. "So I think we're good."[18]

One of the rioters at Cruz's desk was Joshua Matthew Black, whose cheek had been pierced by a crowd control munition outside. Still bleeding from the face, he took a photo of Cruz's written objection to the Arizona vote, which was sitting on the desk. Black then sat down on the floor, his back resting against the dais, and talked on his cell phone for a few minutes.[19] *All around the room was evidence that senators had left quickly—papers, water bottles, and open laptops.*[20]

On the balcony, Chansley, the "shaman," loudly bellowed as a photographer took his photo. "Time's up, motherfuckers!" he screamed.[21]

Igor Bobic, reporter, HuffPost: I started to go upstairs to try to find safety, back up towards the press gallery, and I ran into maybe fifty or sixty more Trump supporters who were all up on the third floor, walking in and out of the Senate chamber. So then I kind of joined them and I went into the Senate chamber.

As Bobic followed rioters into the Senate gallery, he snapped photos and tweeted them. He posted a photo he had taken from the balcony of a man sitting in the Senate president's chair, where Pence had presided over the debate just half an hour earlier. "They're in the chamber," Bobic tweeted. "One is up on the dais yelling 'Trump won that election!' This is insane."

Igor Bobic, reporter, HuffPost: His buddy was standing there right in front of me, and he was like, "No, go back and do it again, because I have to get it on camera." It was sort of like they were doing this for mementos. So he did it again. He repeated it just for Facebook or whatever.

Chansley had made his way downstairs and also took a turn in the chair as a lone police officer stood by and calmly asked everyone to leave. "I'm gonna take a seat in this chair, because Mike Pence is a fucking traitor," he said. And then he left a note for the vice president: "It's only a matter of time, justice is coming!" Chansley then took off his fur hat and led the group in a prayer, thanking God for "filling this chamber with patriots that love you."[22]

Igor Bobic, reporter, HuffPost: It was just the surreal absurdity of it all—one woman coming up to me, thinking I worked in the building, and asking me where the restrooms were. And trying to do my best to have a disarming kind of effect and not make myself appear as though I somehow work for the government. I helped direct her to the nearest restroom. "Yes, ma'am, if you take a left and then you take a right . . . " And meanwhile, everybody's screaming around us, like people are shouting obscenities.

"Where the fuck is Nancy?" someone screamed.

In the backseat of a speeding car headed to Fort McNair, about two miles south of the Capitol, Nancy Pelosi was furious. "If they stop the proceedings, we will have totally failed!" she had said to her aides as they got into the vehicle.[23]

She was angry that the police and security officials had not been better prepared. She was accompanied by her chief of staff, Terri McCullough, and her daughter Alexandra, who was filming. "We did not have any accountability for what was going on there, and we should have," she said, adding, "I take responsibility for not having them just prepare for more."[24]

Terri McCullough, chief of staff, House Speaker Nancy Pelosi: I can't even explain the feeling—I'm still, to this day, grappling with what it felt like to be on our way to Fort McNair, trying to understand what was going on.

Around the same time, Capitol Police Chief Steven Sund and Metropolitan Police Chief Robert Contee were on the phone with the Pentagon, begging officials there to authorize National Guard troops to come to the Capitol. But the military officials didn't immediately agree to send reinforcements, and it would be three long hours before troops would arrive.[25]

Pelosi, along with Senate Democratic Leader Chuck Schumer and Senate Republican Leader Mitch McConnell, would spend the rest of the afternoon on the phone from Fort McNair, pushing military officials to send help.

As House leaders sped away from the Capitol, the rank and file were still in danger. Rioters were moving quickly through the building, but, unbelievably, the House was still in session.

Rep. Jim McGovern, D-MA: Paul Gosar was speaking, and I was told that I should suspend temporarily because there was some noise out in the hallway. I've heard disturbances in the Capitol building before, so I didn't think it was this massive crowd. But I could hear something.

McGovern slammed the gavel, suspending the debate "pursuant to clause 12(b) of Rule I"—an obscure post-9/11 rule that allows the House to recess "when notified of an imminent threat to the safety of the House." But only a few minutes later, McGovern gaveled back in again.

Rep. Jim McGovern, D-MA: I yielded to Paul Gosar, who was one of the people challenging the results in Arizona, so he could finish his speech. I remember it because listening to him was like fingernails on a chalkboard.

Jen Daulby, Republican staff director, House Administration Committee: I remember thinking, the sergeant of arms isn't in there, the chief isn't in there. None of these people I know are in the chamber right now. This has got to be really bad.

Rep. Liz Cheney, R-WY: I went over to Keith Stern on the Democratic side to say, "Look, you need to move my speaking up in this order, because we have to hear from somebody in Republican leadership who's against the objections." They agreed, and they moved me up, but then things were suspended before we were able to even begin again.

Rep. Jim McGovern, D-MA: Gosar finished his statement. And then I was told that I needed to adjourn the House again. And so that's when I adjourned the House. Meanwhile, the voices that I heard from outside the chamber just seemed to get louder.

Though they had breached the Senate side first, a steady stream of rioters was now headed toward the House, breaking through a police line that briefly held them back in the Capitol Crypt, directly underneath the Rotunda.[26] *Others walked to the House from the Rotunda after entering through the Columbus Doors on the east side. They walked through Statuary Hall and into a lobby outside the main House doors—the same doors that Pence and the Senate had walked through earlier.*

The crowd there grew quickly as more people gathered in front of a line of police trying to guard the chamber. Similar to everywhere else around the building, it was a thin line with only a handful of officers facing a large, raucous crowd. It would not be long before they would push through the police line and crowd right outside the main door.

"Well, we came this far, what do you say?" yelled one rioter. "Drag 'em out!" said another. "Tell Nancy Pelosi we're coming for her!"[27]

Inspector Thomas Loyd, US Capitol Police: There's three sets of doors. There's the ceremonial glass doors that are first. They just pushed through those. There's a second set of wooden doors. Those were breached.

And they got to the third and final set of doors made of wood and steel. There were 150-year-old original doors with the old locks, and that final set of doors actually held.

Other rioters, including Ashli Babbitt, the California pool company owner with a Trump flag cascading down her back, would walk around to the opposite side of the chamber toward an ornate hallway called the Speaker's Lobby.

Lieutenant Michael Byrd stood at the rostrum and told lawmakers that there had been a breach of the Capitol building and that both the House and the Senate were locked down:

> Capitol Police is responding to the area where the individuals have breached the building and we will advise that information once it becomes available to us. Please remain calm and remain seated. You can move around inside, but please do not try to leave at this time.

House Sergeant at Arms Paul Irving then took the microphone:

> We have folks entering the Rotunda and coming down this way. So we'll update you as soon as we can, but just be prepared. Stay calm.

Rep. Markwayne Mullin, R-OK: A lieutenant came to the mic and said they have breached the Capitol, and they are in the Capitol building.

Rep. Peter Welch, D-VT: I've never ever heard anyone other than a member or a clerk speak, and to have a Capitol Police officer was stunning.

Thomas Wickham, former House parliamentarian and senior adviser to the parliamentarian: Once the emergency recess is declared, the C-SPAN cameras and all the cameras are to stop. So, similar to any recess, that's a very important part because the proceedings are no longer televised. We're no longer in session as a legislative body, but instead just a gathering of members of Congress, staff, and press.

Lieutenant Michael Byrd, US Capitol Police, commander for House Chamber Section: I have to rely on my training. I spent over twenty years on the chamber section alone, and every exercise has prepared me for that day.

Thomas Wickham, former House parliamentarian and senior adviser to the parliamentarian: We had transitioned from a parliamentary setting into a complete security setting. We had been drilled on it many times.

Emily Cochrane, congressional reporter, *The New York Times*: There's this kind of murmuring, this anxious silence.

Rep. Hakeem Jeffries, D-NY: I stepped out of the chamber briefly and encountered a Capitol Police officer who was getting some water. And I asked him how it was going out there. He said that they were engaged in hand-to-hand combat and that they were being overwhelmed by the crowd. I asked him had the National Guard arrived? He said they had not and that there were some reinforcements from the Metropolitan Police Department, but not nearly enough.

Rep. Ronny Jackson, R-TX: The doors to the chamber are typically open, and all these doors they started shutting. You can hear the doors like, "boom, boom, boom, boom, boom"—all the doors shutting. And then you could actually hear them lock—"click, click, click, click."

Keith Stern, director of House floor operations: It was so jarring when those doors locked and you heard the "chi-chonk."

Emily Cochrane, congressional reporter, *The New York Times*: The heavy doors, as my mother would say—they don't make them like they used to. It was just one after another, these pairs of doors banging together. They just reverberated.

Keith Stern, House director of floor operations: I guess it must have been one of the East Front doors in the gallery, one of the doors was open. And so, like, I'm just screaming, "You've got to close that door!" And then they locked it, and then we were in.

Jamie Fleet, Democratic staff director, House Administration Committee: The doors closing in the gallery—there was an abruptness, and then it was silence, a stillness. Like you're just waiting for something bad to happen. It was sort of a bit of defenselessness. And I saw the members calling, and the FaceTimes. And I was talking to my former wife, who was also barricaded in her office down the hall. And we had two young kids, and we were thinking, what's going to happen? Are we going to get out of here?

Rep. Ronny Jackson, R-TX: I noticed several [police officers] were standing in front of the doors, and they had their weapons out, and I was just like, what is going on? We've already had several bomb threats in the House office buildings earlier that day—I'm in the Cannon building, and my staff had already been evacuated, resettled, and evacuated, resettled. My colleague next to me said, "Well, it's probably a bomb threat." And I said, "No, this isn't a bomb threat. If there's a bomb threat, they wouldn't be locking us inside the chamber and posting people with their weapons on the inside."

Jen Daulby, Republican staff director, House Administration Committee: The sergeant of arms protects the chamber from the inside. The police protect it from the outside. And we knew that everything was then going to go to protect the chamber.

Rep. Brian Fitzpatrick, R-PA, former FBI special agent: They were trying to maintain their composure and remain calm, cool, and collected, saying that everything's fine. But the building has been breached.

Democratic Rep. Val Demings, former chief of the Orlando Police Department: There was that word "breach"—that is probably the word that I will remember about that day for the rest of my life more than any other. I knew that that meant that the police had somehow lost the line. And I also know, having been a former police officer, that they would have done everything in their power to hold that line to protect us.

Rep. Brian Fitzpatrick, R-PA: If somebody breaches the Capitol, they're not just kind of casually strolling in. There's force involved. And if they were using force to breach the Capitol, they had a lot of people behind them.

Lieutenant Michael Byrd, US Capitol Police: One of the things is part of our training and exercises we conduct—I informed the members that they need to gather their gas masks, which we have in a specific location on the floor, and instructed them at that time to be prepared—how to use it and to be prepared to don the mask in the event that the threat escalates closer to the House chamber.

Rep. Zoe Lofgren, D-CA: The Capitol Police officer came and said that it was necessary to evacuate and that we should take the hoods—there are hoods under each seat in the chamber—take them out and be prepared to put them on. So everybody did, and when you pull the little red tag it activates.

Rep. Elise Stefanik, R-NY: The next announcement was that we had gas masks under our seats, which I didn't even know that's where the gas masks are, and we were told to take out the gas masks and that there had been tear gas released in Statuary Hall.

Emily Cochrane, congressional reporter, *The New York Times*: [Arizona Rep.] Ruben Gallego was standing on top of the chairs, jacket thrown off. He's a veteran, and he's telling lawmakers how to put the gas masks on, telling them what to do.

Rep. Hakeem Jeffries, D-NY: Now I've been in Congress at that point for about eight years. I had no idea that there were gas masks underneath everyone's seats.

Emily Cochrane, congressional reporter, *The New York Times*: That aluminum packaging was so hard to get into. I was like some sort of rodent scrambling away at this bag, just trying to rip it open.

Rep. Zoe Lofgren, D-CA: There was this tremendous kind of whirring hissing noise from all these hoods. It was the background of the moment.

Rep. Dean Phillips, D-MN: It sounded like a siren, especially when they were collectively all on together.

Rep. Adam Schiff, D-CA: The gas mask motors were buzzing like hornets.

Keith Stern, House director of floor operations: It was like this incessant whirring, which was just disconcerting, to say the least.

Drew Hammill, deputy chief of staff, House Speaker Nancy Pelosi: That sound is still ingrained in my head.

Emily Cochrane, congressional reporter, *The New York Times:* Like having a vacuum cleaner in your hands that you can't turn off. And they have these red lights on them. And so as people are opening it, I just remember seeing all of these red lights just kind of flicker on around the room.

Rep. Brian Fitzpatrick, R-PA: What was so surreal about it is, as members of Congress, we take groups of constituents on the House floor all the time. One of the first questions is, this little compartment under the seat, what is this? And you'd pull it out and show them that this is a gas mask in the event that the Capitol is ever under attack. Never in a million years ever thinking that the day would come and we would actually use it.

House Chaplain Margaret Kibben: One of the clerks looked up at me and pointed his finger at me and waved me down and put his hands together in prayer as if to say, "Chaplain, come down here and get up on the rostrum and start praying."

Lieutenant Michael Byrd, US Capitol Police: The House chaplain took my place on the podium and began to pray with the members of Congress. And I believe it was at that point in time that not only we realized this was a serious and dangerous situation. I believe the members as well started to believe that serious harm or injury could come to them.

Keith Stern, House director of floor operations: I was like, we need some sort of order here. So we get the chaplain up there to do a prayer, which just seemed weird, but I had nothing else. In hindsight, it may not have been the best thing in the world. She was three days into the job. We were like, what are we gonna do here? And I'm just like, maybe this would calm people down. The sergeant at arms was trying to figure out how to get us out.

House Chaplain Margaret Kibben: It was extemporaneous. I don't know that anybody really heard what I said.

Rep. Jim McGovern, D-MA: I don't remember all that she said. But I just thought it was somewhat surreal that here we are at this moment, still not knowing the extent of the problem outside the chamber.

Joe Novotny, House reading clerk: I compare that to the scene in *Titanic* when the ship is going down and the chaplain is praying over everybody. In the moment, I remembered that scene from the movie, and I'm thinking, this is like—the ship is going down.

House Chaplain Margaret Kibben: The two responses that have come back to me since then from members were, they thought either "Okay, it's all right, the chaplain's praying, God is in the room," or the other reaction was "Oh my God, this is like the *Titanic*, the chaplain is praying and the ship is going down."

Thomas Wickham, former House parliamentarian and senior adviser to the parliamentarian: This was an unprecedented situation, and we were in uncharted territory, so people getting up and doing things that were not in the parliamentary script or not written down anywhere—that was kind of the order of the day.

Drew Hammill, deputy chief of staff, House Speaker Nancy Pelosi: It's all surreal at that point. Members were screaming and crying and it was very messy.

Emily Cochrane, congressional reporter, *The New York Times*: You see lawmakers in one context all the time, and seeing them either revert to their past lives or show some level of fear or anger that was very human was very jarring. By nature, being politicians, they're so calculated. The humanity isn't really visible at all times. There's always this polished veneer. But it was cracking that day—cracking into all these little pieces.

Keith Stern, House director of floor operations: I was in the middle of the chamber just telling people to sit down and calm down. At one point, [Democratic Rep.] Dean Phillips started screaming at the Republicans, "This is because of YOU!" I yelled up, "Dean, at this point, that's not helpful. Let's do that later."

Rep. Dean Phillips, D-MN: I think I was representing four years of angst and anxiety and anger. Many of us saw this coming from a mile away, many in the country did. I think I represented probably millions of Americans who felt the same way. In that very moment, the entire country, including myself, recognized the fragility of our democracy. I have great appreciation for the traditions in the Congress and the decorum. I do not like to violate it. But I do not regret it, because it was what I was feeling and it was four years of pent-up anxiety about what was transpiring right in front of our eyes.

Emily Cochrane, congressional reporter, *The New York Times*: It was just that—unfiltered rage and fear, maybe a little bit of fear.

Rep. Steve Cohen, an irascible Democrat from Tennessee who was also in the gallery, chimed in, shouting to Republicans, "Call Trump! Tell him to call off his revolutionary guard! Call Trump, your friend! Call your friend and tell him to do something!"[28]

On the floor, Ohio Rep. Jim Jordan, one of Trump's closest GOP allies who was backing the president's efforts to overturn the election, approached Liz Cheney.

Rep. Liz Cheney, R-WY: I was standing on the aisle, and he said, "We need to get the ladies off the aisle. Let me help you." He used the word "ladies." And I swatted his hand away and said, "Get away from me. You fucking did this."

Rep. Rodney Davis, R-IL: At that point, I had seen what was happening on the screens. Jim Jordan was one of the objectors, and I said to Jim, "Are you aware of what's happening out there?" Because he was inside the entire time; he may not have known. And he's like, "No." And he starts looking at his phone, and I could see he was clearly visibly upset by it too.

Rep. Hakeem Jeffries, D-NY: I recall passing Jim Jordan at the time and saying to him in a somewhat animated fashion, "Is this what you wanted to happen?"

Jen Daulby, Republican staff director, House Administration Committee: My friends were all texting. I texted back, "Please just pray for us. And don't text me right now."

Rep. Bennie Thompson, D-MS: I didn't quite know exactly the seriousness of it until I got a call from my wife, who said, "Where are you?" I said, "I'm in the Capitol." She said, "Don't you know they're breaking in?" So you know, again, it doesn't register. I said, "You can't break in. I mean, there's police and barricades and a lot of things out there." She said, "But I'm watching people [on TV] climbing over the wall right now, breaking into the Capitol."

Jen Daulby, Republican staff director, House Administration Committee: I was texting my will to my uncle.

Lieutenant Michael Byrd, US Capitol Police: I could not imagine the number of people until you listen to the radio and the screams and the yells for help, and "officer down," screaming as they're being assaulted or sprayed with chemical agents. And you could hear the cheers and the loud voices escalate as they were getting closer to my area of responsibility.

It was the third day on the job for Rep. Marjorie Taylor Greene, a Georgia Republican who was close to Trump and had espoused QAnon theories.

Rep. Marjorie Taylor Greene, R-GA: We thought antifa was breaking in or BLM because of—those were the riots that had gone on and on all throughout 2020, day in and day out, just horrible riots all over the country. And that was the only thing that made sense to most of us.

Rep. Jamie Raskin had been texted a photo of Kevin Seefried, the rioter on the Senate side who was carrying a Confederate flag. He showed it to Cheney, who was sitting nearby.

Rep. Liz Cheney, R-WY: Jamie Raskin was sitting across the aisle from me, and he was looking at his phone. And he said, "My God, there's a Confederate flag inside the United States Capitol." That was obviously stunning.

Rep. Jamie Raskin, D-MD: At this point, I had no idea how serious this was. But I said to her, "It looks like we're under new management here." And she just shook her head and said, "Oh my God, what have they done?" And she was livid.

Shouts could be heard in the hallways outside, and they were getting louder. Small explosions rang out—flash-bangs used by police. It was now becoming clear to the people inside the chamber that rioters were beginning to gather at the main door on the north side of the House.

Rep. Hakeem Jeffries, D-NY: [Texas Rep.] Colin Allred was seated right behind me. [California Rep.] Pete Aguilar was in close proximity, and so was [New York Rep.] Sean Patrick Maloney as people were working through the issue of trying to open the gas masks. After someone from the sergeant at arms's staff said, "Be prepared to hit the ground," and it was clear that a mob was massing right at the front door to the House chamber, Allred says to me, "I don't know about you, but I'm not going down without a fight." Now before Colin Allred came to Congress, he was a civil rights lawyer. Before he was a civil rights lawyer, he played linebacker in the NFL for five years. And so when Colin Allred says "I ain't going down without a fight," you know he meant it. Next thing you know, his jacket came off and then my jacket came off. Sean Patrick Maloney's jacket came off. Pete Aguilar's jacket came off. Because we were literally prepared to have to fight for our lives. Because that's how perilous the situation seemed to be.

Rep. Colin Allred, D-TX: I took off my suit jacket, which I have never done on the House floor before or since. I pretty much decided, whatever happens is going to happen. And so I sent a text to my wife, saying, you know, "Whatever happens, I love you." And she wrote back, "I love you too." And for me, that text was in many ways, you know, I don't know what's gonna happen from here, but I want to make sure that I send this. Because at that point, things were really starting to deteriorate quickly.

Rep. Ronny Jackson, R-TX: All of a sudden, "boom, boom"—people just banging on the door, and then everybody just kind of freaked out who was on the floor of the House, because they were like, "Wow, they're here." And that was the first thing I thought: oh my gosh, they're here.

Rep. Markwayne Mullin, R-OK: If you're coming out of Statuary Hall, right to the House floor, there's two sets of doors. There's doors right in the hallway. And there's a small gap, like a small little foyer—I don't know if you even consider it a foyer, but it's a small little area where you walk up a couple of steps before you enter into the actual chamber. But there's a set of doors there. So the first set of doors are the ones that are actually in the hallway. And we heard them hit the doors.

Rep. Liz Cheney, R-WY: Somebody said the backs of the seats are bulletproof, and we were told that we may need to get down and seek shelter behind the seats if the mob breaks through the door.

Rep. Ronny Jackson, R-TX: We noticed that there were only three Capitol Police officers that were back there by the door, and they had their weapons drawn and they were standing there pointing their weapons at the door, expecting these people to come through the door in minutes. We realized they were going to need some help.

Rep. Markwayne Mullin, R-OK: We ran over to the Republican side corner and grabbed a desk, and we brought it over there to put it in front of the doors. And then someone else grabbed a bench and put it on top of it. So we stacked furniture in front of the door.

Rep. Elise Stefanik, R-NY: You could also start to hear very concerning sounds; they started barricading the doors. It was very, very scary.

Rep. Jim Himes, D-CT, member of the House Intelligence Committee: None of us knew that there were actually lethal hand-to-hand battles going on one hundred yards away. So we probably didn't fully appreciate how violent it had gotten until the police officers, the Capitol Police, started moving furniture in front of the main door there. In this world of massive security apparatus, it's going to be a nineteenth-century desk in front of a door that saves my life? Are you freaking kidding me? And I mean, seriously—I sat there thinking, oh my God, you know, we spend billions and billions of dollars on satellites and guns and weapons and aircraft carriers and artificial intelligence. It's going to be a freaking desk that saves my life?

Rep. Liz Cheney, R-WY: Markwayne walked over to me and said to me, "If they break through, you won't be safe in here. Do not try to take cover. You have to run." And I remember, he pointed towards the door next to a painting of Lafayette. And he said, "You need to run out that door, because you will not be safe here."

Jen Daulby looked over and saw her deputy, Tim, helping the others barricade the doors.

Jen Daulby, Republican staff director, House Administration Committee: And I was like, oh my God. This is real.

Rep. Ronny Jackson, R-TX: We started grabbing furniture and dragging the biggest, heaviest pieces of furniture we could get. We piled it in front of that door to try to stop them from coming through. And then we realized, well, if they do come through the door, we're going to need some way to defend ourselves. So we started breaking the legs off furniture, and I in particular ended up with a piece of furniture that we broke off—one of the hand sanitizer stations had a wooden post, I broke that off the base of it, and then broke the hand sanitizer off the top part. And I had that as a big stick.

Drew Hammill, deputy chief of staff, House Speaker Nancy Pelosi: There were these fancy wooden Purell dispensers, and a freshman Republican had ripped the bottom off of one and was wielding it as a club, should he need it. And I joked to him, "Did you learn that at freshman orientation?"

Rep. Jim McGovern, D-MA: I think some of the Republicans were realizing that if these people got at us, they wouldn't know the difference between a right-wing Republican or a progressive Democrat. I mean, I don't think they all studied the congressional directory.

Capitol Police Inspector Thomas Loyd had run across the Capitol after the standoff with rioters outside the Senate chamber.

Inspector Thomas Loyd, US Capitol Police: The officers in the rear of the Speaker's Lobby, both sides, they had actually locked the doors and stacked furniture on both sides to help barricade the doors because the doors are made of mostly glass. So when I got to the west side, I could see the rioters had made their way to the east side of the Speaker's Lobby and were attempting to breach that side.

With rioters trying to break in at multiple entrances to the House, it was time for the members to leave.

Inspector Thomas Loyd, US Capitol Police: I grabbed a couple of officers who were free adjacent to me. We ran a very quick evacuation route through back stairwells and hallways that are rarely used, found that the route was clear, went back to the west side of the Speaker's Lobby. I told my officers to unbarricade the west Speaker's Lobby doors. I entered the House floor and told the members of Congress, "We are leaving."

At 2:38 p.m., members of the US House evacuated the floor, streaming out into the Speaker's Lobby behind the rostrum and down a nearby set of stairs, leaving many of their belongings behind. At the other end of that corridor, more rioters were starting to pile up at the door.

Rep. Zoe Lofgren, D-CA: We were brought out to the Speaker's Gallery and down a stairway, and at that point, we could hear people at the other end of the hallway, the mob. I was down the stairs when glass was being broken.

Jamie Fleet, Democratic staff director, House Administration Committee: I could hear that pounding for weeks.

Rep. Zoe Lofgren, D-CA: We were at one end trying to escape, and they were at the other end trying to break in.

Jamie Fleet, Democratic staff director, House Administration Committee: There were so many unknowns about the building—were there more coming? How many were there? So people were moved in a pretty expeditious way.

Rep. Adam Schiff, D-CA: I waited towards the end, when you could really hear the crowd banging on the doors and breaking glass to get in. And a couple of Republicans said, "You can't let them see you. I know these people. I could talk my way through these people. You're in a whole different category." My initial instinct was to be moved by their evident concern for my safety. My next instinct was, if you guys hadn't been lying about the election, I wouldn't need to worry about my safety. None of us would.

Most House lawmakers had evacuated, but the chamber wasn't empty. About three dozen Democratic members trying to distance themselves because of COVID-19 remained in the upper galleries, along with a small group of reporters and a few staff, as police tried to determine whether the third-floor hallways were clear. The Capitol Police were moving all of the members, along with reporters in the press gallery, to the balcony on the western side of the chamber, where the first lady sits during the State of the Union. They were trying to group everyone together for a quick escape once it was safe, and the stairs just outside that area had the quickest access to the evacuation route and the secure location designated for members of the House.

Rep. Jim McGovern, D-MA: I noticed there were people up in the balcony, in the gallery, and I noticed that my Democratic colleagues had to make their way all the way across. I was told they were going to exit on the Republican side. And if anyone's ever been in the gallery before—I mean, it's really narrow and it's really hard to move around under the best of circumstances. And I was assured that they were being taken care of, that there was a plan to get them out.

Keith Stern, House director of floor operations: I remember looking up and seeing the gallery. I'm like, they're not getting evacuated. What are we doing here?

Rep. Pramila Jayapal, D-WA: Most terrifyingly, members were taken off the floor, and we were still there. And it was almost like, do you remember us?

Rep. Jason Crow, D-CO, former US Army Ranger: They evacuated the House floor first. And they forgot about those who are up in the gallery, the journalists, the members of Congress.

Rep. Brian Fitzpatrick, R-PA: My concern was for my colleagues in the gallery, because there's only one way in and out of there. That was the problem. We had multiple ways out of the chamber.

Rep. Markwayne Mullin, R-OK: They were still locked in because the only way to get out of the balcony is you actually have to go into the hallway, and it's an unsecured area.

Rep. Jason Crow, D-CO: It was at that moment where I realized we were trapped, that we weren't getting out.

Rep. Bennie Thompson, D-MS: We had to go from one side of the gallery, which is the eastern side, to the western side. So we had to go all the way around. And there's no way you can just walk around; you've either got to go over the [stair railings] or under, so it was quite a challenge. When we get to the western side, somebody says, "Get on the floor." And they said to take your pins off because if they break in, they are trying to kill members of Congress.

Rep. Pramila Jayapal, D-WA: The Capitol Police told us we had to go to the other side of the gallery, and I didn't know why. And there was no way to do that without crawling under or over the banisters between the sections of the gallery. And I didn't really know where we were going or why, but all of a sudden, I was trying to crawl under banisters with a knee that wouldn't bend and with a cane. You know, there was a lot of panic with some of the members who were there. We were having a really hard time.

Emily Cochrane, congressional reporter, *The New York Times*: There were these gold banisters divided into sections. I don't even remember who she was, but a woman tried to go under, and I remember like physically yanking her over the banister. We were just clambering as fast as you could, over the seats, over the banisters. I banged up my knees pretty badly.

Rep. Susan Wild, D-PA: I started to hear all sorts of commotion from down below. Breaking glass, huge pounding on these big heavy wooden doors. Like, a hand would not be enough to make that much of a noise through those thick doors.

Rep. Jason Crow, D-CO: Many of us went through the analysis of what are we going to do next? How are we going to get out? Are we going to have to make a stand there, or are we going to have to fight our way out?

Rep. Bennie Thompson, D-MS: I still couldn't believe this was happening at the United States Capitol.

Rep. Peter Welch, D-VT: It was so unusual that I began to do some recording of what was happening. And it was partly a way of recording it, partly a way of just giving myself something to do when I was pretty scared about what was going on and what's going to happen here.

Rep. Jason Crow, D-CO: The first thing I did was call my wife, and I talked to her and told my family that I love them and for her to tell the kids that as well. I then hung up the phone and immediately got into "Ranger mode." I just created a mental checklist of everything that I thought we could do to increase our chances of getting out and everything that we needed to prepare ourselves for.

Down on the House floor, a few Republicans were helping defend the main doors—Oklahoma Rep. Markwayne Mullin and Texas Reps. Troy Nehls, Ronny Jackson, Tony Gonzales, and Pat Fallon. All four Texans were freshmen who had just been sworn in three days earlier.

Rep. Tony Gonzales, R-TX: I distinctly remember looking at each other and knowing that however this might end, we were all in it together. We were ready for the worst—ready to fight these cowards with whatever we had to protect our chamber from their hate, evil, and violence.

Rep. Markwayne Mullin, R-OK: They broke through the first set of doors, and then they hit the second set of doors. Now they're right there. Myself and Troy Nehls, Sheriff Nehls, were the two members that were right there.

Rep. Troy Nehls, R-TX, former sheriff, Fort Bend County: It was my third day in Congress.

Rep. Markwayne Mullin, R-OK: I think it was just a second later that they broke the glass [in the door], and when they first broke it, it sounded like gunshots. Capitol Police showed great restraint by not opening fire because everybody thought shots were fired.

Rep. Pat Fallon, R-TX: The small pieces of glass went flying. "SHOTS FIRED!" Someone screamed. "Rounds fired, rounds fired!!"

Rep. Troy Nehls, R-TX: All of a sudden, the glass broke. And that was probably the most tense moment. So I see this face kind of pierced through the broken glass looking at me. And I'm eyeballing him, and I have my Texas [face] mask on. He looks at me and he says, "You're from Texas. You should be with us." And I said, "I can't support what you're doing right now."

Rep. Markwayne Mullin, R-OK: They're being very belligerent to some degree. And I started yelling, "Is it worth it? Is it worth it? You almost got killed! Is it worth it?"

Keith Stern, House director of floor operations: There were five or six members, all Republicans, that were over at the front main doors. Markwayne Mullin was like, "Look, these are our people, we can talk to them. They're conservatives, we can rationalize with them." I'm like, "You guys have got to go."

The members who were trapped in the upper gallery were peeking over the railings to watch the action down below.

Rep. Jim Himes, D-CT: They were obviously expecting a breach through the door. It was clear that they were pretty close to pulling the trigger, so they asked us all to get down.

Rep. Val Demings, D-FL: By that time, you can hear the glass breaking, and I am thinking, what in the hell is going on here? Because I have been a law enforcement officer. I have been in some dark, scary places and with some scary people. And I'm here in Congress, in the House of Representatives, which should be the safest place, I think, in the world. And they're breaking glass, trying to break the door down to do what? And I couldn't help but think, if they beat the police down—which I knew if there was a breach that they had—then they certainly weren't trying to shake our hands and tell us "Good job." Our lives were at risk.

Emily Cochrane, congressional reporter, *The New York Times*: Someone had smashed the glass to the chamber door, and they had put that huge cabinet in front of it, and their guns were drawn. And that was the moment where I sent a few "I love you" texts. Because I didn't know who was on the other side of the glass, but it was serious enough that there were guns out.

Up in the press gallery on the south side of the chamber, only one person remained after reporters had been moved. Longtime Associated Press photographer J. Scott Applewhite had refused to evacuate that side of the balcony, with its clear view of the main door.

J. Scott Applewhite, photographer, The Associated Press: The Capitol is where I work every day, and I am a familiar face to most police. When those on the chamber floor shouted up at me to get out, I told them I was fine and refused to leave. This is what we do: We stay and report. One got more belligerent until another officer, a special agent in the protection division who guards the leadership, intervened. He shouted over, "Scotty's OK!" Two words is all it took—that and the obvious; they had their hands full with a mob on the other side of the door.

Applewhite aimed his camera across the chamber as the protesters tried to beat through the door directly across from him.

J. Scott Applewhite, photographer, The Associated Press: I was pretty sure I was right where I was supposed to be. You could hear the growl of the mob just outside. In the chamber, the officers were focused, their guns aimed. And I was trained on the door as well, with a telephoto zoom. I kept my lens focused on that reinforced door. Then there was an eye trying to see inside, the face of one of the rioters wearing a Trump hat. What he did not see were the guns aiming inches from his face. I kept steady and held tight on that spot.

Immediately on the other side of the main House doors, Francis Chung, the E&E photographer who had taken the photo of Josh Hawley fist pumping the crowd, was taking photos of the rioters as they were trying to get in. Chung had come inside after watching the crowd break into the building on the East Front.

Francis Chung, staff photographer, E&E News: I followed some people going over to the House chamber and got a shot of people trying to literally break into the front door. You're not really thinking. You're just like, can I get an angle on this without getting killed?

Just down the hall from Chung, John Bresnahan of Punchbowl News was standing on a small balcony over Statuary Hall with a direct line of sight toward the doors of the House. He watched as what looked like hundreds of people streamed toward the doors and gathered outside the chamber, chanting, "Stop the steal!" and "USA!"

John Bresnahan, reporter and cofounder, Punchbowl News: There were clearly some people caught up in the moment. I saw people come in and take selfies with some of the statues. Like there was some woman who took a selfie with Rosa Parks and was laughing about that. But then there were other people who just made a beeline to the House floor. And you could see groups of guys inside the crowd, they were moving with a purpose. They looked like they were on a mission.

As the remaining members ducked down in the west gallery, Capitol Police led a few small groups into the third-floor hallway to escape, even though the area was unsecured.

Rep. Annie Kuster, D-NH: I was with a very small group, four of us, and a policeman grabbed us and said, "I'll get you to safety." And he took us across that third-floor hallway. And there was a great deal of commotion—well, it turns out, it's because the crowd had made their way up to the third floor. And they were running toward us right in the same hallway, forty or fifty feet apart from where we were. And we ducked into the elevator. And I said to this incredible policeman, I said, "Oh my God, what if the elevator doors open and they kill us?" And I will never forget this moment. He took his arms like this to block the door and he said, "Ma'am, I am here to protect you."

Kuster's group, which included newly sworn-in Rep. Sara Jacobs, D-CA, took the elevator down to a subbasement and ran through a tunnel toward the secure location.

Rep. Annie Kuster, D-NH: Honestly, we thought we were being chased. And my son called right in the middle of it as we're running through the tunnels and says, "Mom! Mom!" He's watching on television. And I said, "I'm alive, honey. I can't talk right now, we're running for our lives. I'll call you right back. But I'm gonna be okay."

Back in the gallery, at 2:44 p.m., the unmistakable sound of a gunshot rang through the House chamber, clapping loudly in the cavernous room. It had come from the Speaker's Lobby. Members ducked down below their seats, preparing for the worst.

Ashli Babbitt had been one of the first people at the Speaker's Lobby doors, steps from a House floor entrance that Pelosi had been whisked through minutes earlier. Lawmakers were still evacuating down the hall.

Lieutenant Michael Byrd, US Capitol Police: We were putting up a makeshift barricade using furniture, tables, whatever we could lift and put in front of the doorways, to barricade the doors—to give some type of separation from the members of Congress, ourselves, and the rioters.

Rep. Jim McGovern, D-MA: I walked out into the Speaker's Lobby. And there was a little bit of a bottleneck. A lot of people were still trying to work their way through this narrow doorway, to work their way down the stairwell. I turned to the opposite end of where we were exiting, and I finally realized what was happening. There was a huge crowd out there. The doors were barricaded from the inside. There were Capitol Police and other security inside the Speaker's Lobby. I remember seeing, if I remember correctly, three Capitol Police officers standing in between the crowd and the door. And these people, these rioters, were banging on the glass door.

Lieutenant Michael Byrd, US Capitol Police: If you open the doors and you're in the Speaker's Lobby—you're essentially in the chamber.

Rep. Jim McGovern, D-MA: I remember turning to somebody that was standing next to me—Keith Stern, who worked for Nancy Pelosi and used to work for me many years ago, and Don Sisson, who was the staff director of the Rules Committee, were the closest to me. I remember turning to them, and I said, "These people aren't here to make a political statement. They're not here to hand me a leaflet. I think they are here to hurt us. And they are destroying the Capitol." And I just stood there, it seemed like forever, but it really wasn't—just disbelief and with great sadness.

Keith Stern, House director of floor operations: We were talking for a second, and that's when they started screaming at him, and at me too.

Rep. Jim McGovern, D-MA: I was stunned. What's stuck with me was the viciousness that you could see in the faces of these people that were breaking the glass. I came really close to giving them the middle finger. I thank God I didn't, because I would have been accused of inciting them. I spent so much of my life here. I was an intern in the Senate. I worked for Congressman Joe Moakley of Boston. I revere this place, and you're destroying it. Like, who the hell are you people? They looked like they were manic.

Keith Stern, House director of floor operations: I knew that was a real inflection point when I saw them at the door.

Rep. Jim McGovern, D-MA: And I just looked at their faces, and the hate and the anger in their eyes was terrifying. And somebody hit the glass hard enough where it cracked, and I couldn't believe it. Like, how can this be happening?

The scene outside the Speaker's Lobby door had escalated quickly. As McGovern stood in the corridor, watching the crowd, a rioter named Zachary Alam pushed past the Capitol Police officers guarding the outside of the door and smashed his right fist into the window, hitting the glass inches from Officer Kyle Yetter's head.[29] *Alam then reached over Yetter's shoulder and broke a second window with his left fist.*[30]

Officer Kyle Yetter, US Capitol Police: There were three officers in that entire hallway. It was filled, so forty-plus rioters and protesters.

"I'm going to fuck you up!" Alam yelled at the three men guarding the doors.[31] *"Fuck the blue!" another rioter yelled. "They're leaving!" yelled another as the last lawmakers and staff evacuating the House floor disappeared down a staircase on the other end of the ornate lobby.*[32] *The members trapped in the upper gallery were still inside.*

Officer Kyle Yetter, US Capitol Police: There is no way that the three of us could hold off such a large number of people.

The officers abruptly retreated, leaving the door unprotected. Alam and the others quickly advanced, breaking much of the remaining glass.[33]

Officer Kyle Yetter, US Capitol Police: Multiple individuals began breaking the glass further and attempted to gain access to the door.

Lieutenant Michael Byrd, US Capitol Police: We were already limited in the options that we had. Once we barricaded the doors, we were essentially trapped where we were. There was no way to retreat, no other way to get out.

Byrd was behind the barricades on the other side of the door. He had heard a false report of "shots fired" on the radio just beforehand, and he didn't know the extent of the threat. He raised his gun.

Lieutenant Michael Byrd, US Capitol Police: [I was shouting,] "Get back!" "Stop!" "Get back!" "No!" "Stop!" "Get back!" Repeatedly screaming.

It's unclear whether the rioters could hear his warnings through the door and through the medical mask he was wearing.

Lieutenant Michael Byrd, US Capitol Police: I couldn't make out what they were saying, but it sounded like hundreds of people outside of that door.

"He has a gun!" one rioter yelled, followed by several others, as the tip of Byrd's weapon became visible through the cracked glass. At almost the same moment, a rioter lifted Babbitt into a broken window, where she started to try to climb through. She was just a few feet from the doorway to the chamber, and the lawmakers in the gallery were still huddled inside. Byrd fired a single shot, hitting Babbitt in the left shoulder. She fell down to the ground.[34]

Lieutenant Michael Byrd, US Capitol Police: I followed my training, and I spent countless years preparing for such a moment. You ultimately hope that moment never occurs, but you prepare as best you can, and I know I prepared myself to do the job that was required of me. I know that day I saved countless lives. I know members of Congress, as well as my fellow officers and staff, were in jeopardy and in serious danger, and that's my job.

The people surrounding Babbitt shouted in horror as she lay bleeding on the floor. A SWAT team arrived at that moment and successfully pushed the remaining rioters away from the doors.

Lieutenant Michael Byrd, US Capitol Police: I tried to wait as long as I could. I hoped and prayed no one tried to enter through those doors, but their failure to comply required me to take the appropriate action to save the lives of members of Congress and myself.

Rep. Markwayne Mullin, R-OK: He was the last person in the world that ever wanted to use force like that. He wasn't wanting to do that. I know for a fact, because after it happened, he came over. And he was physically and emotionally distraught. And I actually gave him a hug. And I said, "Sir, you did what you had to do."

Babbitt was still wearing the Trump flag around her neck and her American flag backpack when security officials picked up her limp body and ran it down the stairs.[35] *Just minutes earlier, Trump had sent another tweet:*[36]

> Please support our Capitol Police and Law Enforcement. They are truly on the side of our Country. Stay peaceful!

He did not ask the rioters to leave.

Rep. Jason Crow, D-CO: I've heard a lot of gunshots in my time, and it was very clear what that was. And it came from the Speaker's Lobby, which told me—I didn't know whether it was an officer or a member of the mob. But I knew that things had severely escalated.

Rep. Peter Welch, D-VT: There was a gunshot, but you couldn't believe it was.

Rep. Jason Crow, D-CO: We knew that the mob was on three sides of the gallery, but it wasn't until I heard the gunshot that I knew that they were on all four sides and that all of our escape routes, all of the exit routes, had been cut off at that point.

Rep. Norma Torres, D-CA: All of us were doing the same thing—asking each other, "Was that a real shot that was fired?"

Rep. Peter Welch, D-VT: I think all of us, myself included, had images of a mass shooting event, so it was terrifying in the moment. And lots of folks were making phone calls—you know, that call to your partner, your loved one.

Rep. Norma Torres, D-CA: I really thought, we're not going to be evacuated. We're going to die here.

Rep. Susan Wild was lying on her back on the floor, hand over her heart. She thought she was having a heart attack. She had just FaceTimed her family, and they could hear the sounds of the chaos in the background. Crow, who was next to her, reached over and took her hand, telling her it would be okay.

Rep. Susan Wild, D-PA: I didn't realize I was showing how upset I was. I remember thinking, how does he know how stressed out I am?

Rep. Val Demings, D-FL: I tried to remain calm and use calming words with others. And I remember saying to one of my colleagues who asked me, "What do you think is going to happen?" And I said, "I'm not sure. But if we all die today, just remember, we're on the right side of history. If we all die today, another group will come in and certify those ballots."

Rep. Lisa Blunt Rochester, D-DE: Val Demings and I grabbed each other's arms like, can you believe this is happening? And she said something like, "There's only one that can get us out of this." And I was like, "You're right. I'm going to pray." And that's how the prayer started. I just started soft and just got louder and bolder as I prayed.

Rep. Pramila Jayapal, D-WA: Lisa Blunt Rochester was praying—she was bringing God into the space to protect us and to keep us safe.

Rep. Lisa Blunt Rochester, D-DE: The scripture that was at the beginning of what I prayed was that "all things work together for the good," and that includes even the bad stuff. In that moment, I could feel from slavery to Jim Crow to women locking arms. It was almost like, instead of your life flashes before your eyes, I felt our history flash before my eyes.

Behind them, handles on the gallery doors were rattling, as rioters had made it to the third floor. Several members tried to improvise weapons in case they had to fight.

Rep. Pramila Jayapal, D-WA: I was focused on planning my escape if I had to get out. I had stretched out on the ground because I couldn't bend my knee. I'm not even sure how I got from the chair to the ground—I think I rolled—and so I was stretched out. And I had my gas mask in one hand and my cane in the other hand, and I was like, if I can't get up, I had a whole plan that I was going to whack an insurrectionist in the knee with the gas mask and then whack them in the other knee with the cane. That's what I was concerned about is, you know, were we going to get out? Were we going to survive? Were they going to come after us?

Emily Cochrane, congressional reporter, *The New York Times*: You didn't know who was on the other side of that door.

Rep. Mikie Sherrill, D-NJ, former US Navy helicopter pilot: It was so incredibly frustrating because in the Navy, we're either in a crisis or we're training for crisis. You know your position, you know who you're leading and who you're responsible for. And so to be in a situation like that and to suddenly realize, you know, I didn't even know there were gas masks.

Rep. Jason Crow, D-CO: In my time in combat, what I've learned is you never know who's able to pull that trigger until that moment comes. But I know that I can. So I actually thought for a moment about if they broke through, trying to get one of the guns from the officers to use it and try to get us out. Because I knew that I could do that if I had to.

Rep. Peter Welch, D-VT: One of my most vivid memories was a police officer, a young man standing over me with his gun drawn and an intense focus on the doors. And I could see in his eyes that the last thing he wanted to do was have to use that weapon. But his job was that he would have to protect us. And I just couldn't imagine how terrible it was for him and how it would affect his life if he actually had used that weapon.

Rep. Jim Himes, D-CT: I spend a lot of time in very high-security environments. And I've always assumed that the Capitol was one of those environments, that things that I didn't see would keep me safe. I always assumed that behind those lecterns that the Capitol Police stand behind, there's like a big red button, and you press that button and doors close and troops rappel out of the rafters and government is safe, right? Well, the opposite turned out to be the case.

Rep. Dean Phillips, D-MN: It wasn't just members of Congress. It was staff. There were journalists up in the gallery. And nobody was thinking at that moment what your job was, who you were, what side of the aisle you stood on.

Emily Cochrane, congressional reporter, *The New York Times*: It was the first time where I have felt that reporting and personal safety intersected. You go to cover a protest, you go in with the mindset that things could get complicated. But it was just unfathomable that people would ever get inside in that way.

Rep. Jason Crow, D-CO: I was talking with the officers and telling them to call whomever they could, call the command and let them know that the members and journalists were trapped and they needed to send a team in to rescue us. And then I'm trying to just get some communication with folks outside the gallery. And then also coordinating with Markwayne Mullin, who was on the floor at the barricades, about what was going down on the main floor. We were shouting to each other and going back and forth. I know him; he's a friend of mine. We actually work out together in a workout group.

Rep. Markwayne Mullin, R-OK: We still had people on top, and I saw Jason Crow, who's a congressman from Colorado, I saw him poke his head up. And Jason and I have worked out a lot together. Politically we're on different islands; we don't get along when it comes to politics. But we get along personally. And Jason and I have had a lot of workouts together because I run a workout group in the morning. He's one of them that's there quite often. I said, "Jason, get them out." He says, "The doors are locked."

Rep. Jim Himes, D-CT: It was as though you were watching water flow uphill. Something that you imagined was impossible is happening right in front of your eyes.

After fumbling with the locks—there appeared to be some confusion about the keys—the handful of Capitol Police officers protecting the gallery were finally given the all clear.

Inspector Thomas Loyd, US Capitol Police: The problem with the third floor is you have the old wooden doors with the locks. The only way to open them and lock them is with a key. There's no glass. And so when I went up to the third floor to start the evacuation, initially, my officers would not let me into the chamber because they were concerned I may have been under duress.

Andrew Harnik, photographer, The Associated Press: They started evacuating members of Congress and then the press. You really didn't have a choice. I photographed as long as I could in the room until they pushed me out the door. I made one last photograph of Scotty [Applewhite] alone in the room from his perch on the center third-floor balcony. He was the last person I saw. Scotty refused to leave.

The members, staff, and journalists were hustled out single file past a group of rioters that were lying on the floor. SWAT officers had long guns pointed at their heads.

Rep. Mikie Sherrill, D-NJ: When we did finally leave, I think we saw why—there were people face down, zip ties behind their heads, with Capitol Police guarding them. So you could see that they had been right at the doors, you know, trying to break in, and we'd heard that.

Rep. Bennie Thompson, D-MS: So after almost an hour, we were escorted out of the gallery. And it was at that point that we saw all the people spread-eagle on the floor with Capitol Police holding them with their weapons. And at that point, we knew this thing was really bad.

Andrew Harnik, photographer, The Associated Press: They were heavily armed—some sort of special unit with big submachine-gun-style weapons drawn and pointed at people on the floor. I made a couple pictures of that. I'm basically being shoved down the hall and shoved down the stairs, and I was shooting as I walked.

Rep. Bennie Thompson, D-MS: We had to go down about four flights of stairs that we had never seen before. And you know, I've been in the Capitol a long time, but these are steps that we didn't know existed.

Emily Cochrane, congressional reporter, *The New York Times*: They took us away. I didn't even know where we were.

Rep. Jason Crow, D-CO: When it was clear we had everybody out, I was the last person left. And I yelled down to Markwayne, I said, "You need to get out." And he said, "No, I'm not leaving; we need to defend the chamber." And I remember very clearly, I said, "Markwayne, these officers can't leave if you don't leave. They're vastly outnumbered. And so long as there's a member here, they've got to stay. For their protection, you need to leave so if they need to retreat, they can."

Rep. Markwayne Mullin, R-OK: As soon as they got out, then the rest of us left.

Rep. Mikie Sherrill, D-NJ: I remember the hallways were quiet. I was listening so carefully because I was so afraid that we would turn a corner and there would be the rioters. We were kind of looking around corners as we're trying to egress the building. And listening so carefully to hear—is there anybody ahead of us? Is this a safe hallway? Has this been secured?

Rep. Annie Kuster, D-NH: We could have had some type of mass casualty event with a number of members of Congress injured, wounded, or killed.

The House and Senate had evacuated, and Donald Trump's supporters had stopped the certification of Joe Biden's victory. Hundreds of rioters had already breached several entrances, but an even larger mass of people on the West Front was aimed at the center of the building.

After the police line below the inauguration stage collapsed, the mob swarmed the terrace at the top of the large scaffolding structure. They were aimed at a critical access point to the Capitol—the set of double golden doors in the middle of the West Front, set back in a small tunnel that the president walks through on inauguration day. Metropolitan Police officers were defending the area, with help from Capitol Police. But they had been ordered to retreat inside as the rioters flooded toward the building.

Lieutenant George Donigian, Metropolitan Police Department: I had recognized the futility of staying out there and how dangerous it was becoming again at that point. So I gathered all the officers I could find and told them to get inside the building.

Officer Jesse Leasure, Metropolitan Police Department: So we fall back inside, we close the double doors, and then another set of double doors. And we're like, oh, thank God. We needed the break. Then we hear a "Bang! Bang! Bang!" And then we hear someone say, "We need shields up front!" And one of the lieutenants or commanders or inspectors yells, "We're not going to lose the US Capitol today!"

In a basement hallway just inside the doors, MPD Commander Ramey Kyle had taken charge and was trying to pump up the group as they took a quick breath and prepared to go back out. "It's going to be old school CDU if they come in those doors, do you hear me?" Kyle shouted, calling out the Civil Disturbance Unit, which is trained to go toe to toe with protesters.[37]

Officer Abdulkadir Abdi, Metropolitan Police Department: The way they were breaking into the door, it looked like it was going to be a really hard fight. So they were saying pretty much, "Get ready. You're going to hit somebody or get hit."

The locked doors were not a deterrent to the angry group outside, and they were soon breaking through. After just a few minutes of rest, the officers got back into the fight, forming a thick line in the narrow space. MPD Sergeant William Bogner sprayed chemicals at the rioters through the broken glass. "We can't let you in the building!" he shouted.

Someone shouted, "They fucking stole this, and you fucking know it!"[38]

Officer Jesse Leasure, Metropolitan Police Department: The first set of double doors gets kicked open, and I see a guy come in. I'm like, "Get the fuck out of here!" And then the next thing you know, the last set of doors opens up, and it's just on. Hitting back and forth. We're just getting pounded.

The battle for the Lower West Terrace Tunnel, the iconic central entrance to the US Capitol, had begun.

Jason Riddle, the New Hampshire man who was drinking wine in the parliamentarian's office, was now back outside on the packed terrace outside the Senate, holding a leather-bound book called Senate Procedure. *When he told a fellow rioter that he had stolen it, the man offered him $40 on the spot. He took it.*

Jason Riddle, former correctional officer and mail carrier, New Hampshire: And the man was like, "You know they're shooting people, right?" I went, "No, they're not. I was just in there, and it's like a party. They're ransacking, but they're not shooting anybody." And he said, "No, they shot someone. I saw her, and she had a bullet in her, and they were carrying her away." And I've never been the same ever since.

Panicked, Riddle immediately tried to find a way to exit the grounds through the packed crowd.

Jason Riddle, former correctional officer and mail carrier, New Hampshire: I looked at the police, and I finally stopped to take a second and think about what I was doing. I'm like, they can legally shoot me right now. And I knew that I was probably in trouble.

He found an opening, and he started to run.

Jason Riddle, former correctional officer and mail carrier, New Hampshire: My phone had died, so I couldn't find [my friends]. So I ran. I ran until it looked like I was in a different town.

The House gallery was evacuated, and members had moved underground to an undisclosed location. Scotty Applewhite was still in the chamber.

J. Scott Applewhite, photographer, The Associated Press: The siege at the chamber door lasted about forty-five minutes, until tactical units moved the intruders away. I was then able to move around the balcony above the House floor to record the deserted room and the debris. The gavel used by House Speaker Nancy Pelosi sat on the dais, surrounded by discarded emergency escape hoods and debris. For another two hours, I was locked in. Then an FBI tactical team swept through and threw me out of the building.

A rioter breaks a window on the East Front, near the House chamber.
Francis Chung/POLITICO via AP Images

Thousands of protesters gather outside the West Front of the US Capitol as people break through windows and doors. *AP Photo/Jose Luis Magana*

Democratic Reps. Colin Allred, Hakeem Jeffries, and Pete Aguilar take their jackets off as rioters amass outside the doors of the US House. Republican Rep. Jim Jordan, a close ally of President Trump, holds a gas mask in the foreground. *AP Photo/Andrew Harnik*

US Capitol Police Lt. Michael Byrd orders Associated Press photographer Scotty Applewhite to evacuate the House press gallery after he refused to leave. Minutes later, Byrd fatally shot rioter Ashli Babbitt as she tried to crawl through a broken window in the Speaker's Lobby off the House floor. *AP Photo/J. Scott Applewhite*

Members duck down in the House gallery as rioters try to break down the doors below. *AP Photo/Andrew Harnik*

Rioters gather outside the House doors as lawmakers and police barricade the doors inside. *Francis Chung/POLITICO via AP Images*

Police with guns drawn face off against rioters trying to break into the House Chamber. Republican Rep. Troy Nehls, right, a former Texas sheriff, talks to the rioters through the broken glass. *AP Photo/J. Scott Applewhite*

Associated Press photographer Scotty Applewhite, who refused to leave the press gallery, keeps his camera aimed at the standoff at the main House doorway below as other reporters, photographers, and lawmakers are evacuated. *AP Photo/Andrew Harnik*

Lawmakers, staff, and reporters evacuate the House gallery after police secure an escape route. *AP Photo/Andrew Harnik*

US Capitol Police hold rioters at gunpoint on floor as lawmakers, staff, and journalists evacuate the House gallery. *AP Photo/Andrew Harnik*

Members, press gallery staff, and reporters evacuate the House after being trapped in the upper balcony. Rep. Jason Crow, D-CO, is at center. *AP Photo/Andrew Harnik*

Hundreds of people push up against the Lower West Terrace Tunnel, the main West Front entrance to the Capitol, as police officers engage in a brutal fight with rioters. *Lev Radin/Sipa USA/Sipa via AP Images*

Senate staff carry the mahogany boxes containing states' Electoral College certificates from the Senate to the House Chamber after the rioters were pushed out of the building and the joint session resumed. *AP Photo/Manuel Balce Ceneta*

Rep. Andy Kim, D-NJ, cleans up trash in the Capitol Rotunda after the building was cleared of rioters. *AP Photo/Andrew Harnik*

Marc Short, Vice President Mike Pence's chief of staff, watches the final moments of the joint session from the back of the House floor early in the morning on January 7. *AP Photo/Andrew Harnik*

Vice President Mike Pence, standing next to House Speaker Nancy Pelosi, prepares to announce that Joe Biden has won the 2020 election as the final electoral votes are counted. The four "tellers" in front are Sen. Amy Klobuchar, D-MN, Sen. Roy Blunt, R-MO, Rep. Zoe Lofgren, D-CA, and Rep. Rodney Davis, R-IL. *AP Photo/J. Scott Applewhite*

3:00 p.m.

Officer Michael Fanone, Metropolitan Police Department: When my partner Jimmy and I arrived at the Capitol around three that afternoon, it was unlike any scene I had ever witnessed. Jimmy parked our police vehicle near the intersection of South Capitol Street and D Street, SE, and we walked to the Capitol from there, passing the Longworth House Office Building. It was eerily quiet, and the sidewalks, usually filled with pedestrians, were empty. As we made our way to Independence Avenue, I could see dozens of empty police vehicles that filled the street, police barricades that had been abandoned, and hundreds of angry protesters, many of whom taunted us as we walked toward the Capitol building.

Rioters were now breaking violently into the building at multiple entrances and engaging in combat with police. They waved Trump flags and hung them on the walls, repeating the president's false claims of a stolen election.

At 3:13 p.m., as lawmakers, allies, and his own staff pushed for him to call off the rioting, Trump tweeted and again asked his supporters in the Capitol to be peaceful. He did not ask them to leave.

> I am asking for everyone at the U.S. Capitol to remain peaceful.[1] No violence! Remember, WE are the Party of Law & Order—respect the Law and our great men and women in Blue. Thank you!

Officer Michael Fanone, Metropolitan Police Department: Jimmy and I immediately began to search for an area where we could be of most assistance. We first made our way through a door on the south side of the Capitol, walking then to the Crypt and finally down to the Lower West Terrace Tunnel. It was there that I observed a police commander struggling to breathe as he dealt with the effects of CS gas that lingered in the air. Then I watched him collect himself, straighten his cap and trench coat adorned with silver eagles, and return to the line.

Officer Daniel Hodges, Metropolitan Police Department: Inside the Capitol building, officers walked through the halls briefly until they found a place to sit, decontaminate, and take a quick breather. I followed suit. Someone had managed to find a package of water bottles and was passing them out. I washed off my face as best as I could, rinsed out my mouth, and drank the rest. I took the opportunity of relative safety to don my gas mask. Not long afterward, I heard someone calling for officers to move to assist. I steeled myself for another round and descended a stairway into a long hallway filled with smoke and screams.

Senators—and the mahogany ballot boxes—had evacuated to a room in one of the Senate office buildings, the undisclosed location. They were unaware of how fierce the fighting was outside.

Sen. Bob Casey, D-PA: When I got into that room, that's when I knew that things were bad. Not the whole scale of it, but some of the scale, because it seemed like everywhere you turned, there was a heavily armed security official.

Paul Kane, reporter, *The Washington Post*: By the time we finally got to the secure location, I realized that I had a duty to file a pool report about what we had seen. And so I typed it up. That pool report got blasted out, and everybody started reporting that they saved the Electoral College certificates.

Sen. Mark Warner, D-VA: Nobody was in charge. The leadership was off sequestered elsewhere, and people are kind of milling around. There's no information. The Capitol Police don't have any information.

Sen. Roy Blunt, R-MO: I called my wife, and I said, "Abby, we had to leave the Senate floor, but we're all okay. We're all fine." And she said, "Do you have any idea what's going on outside?" And I said, "No, not really." We had no TVs.

Blunt was the chairman of the Senate Rules Committee, and Minnesota Sen. Amy Klobuchar was the panel's top Democrat. In addition to serving as tellers at the joint session, the two were in charge of figuring out logistics after leaders had evacuated to Fort McNair, a few miles away. They made periodic announcements, coordinated with law enforcement, and worked to find televisions so the senators could see what was happening outside.

Sen. Roy Blunt, R-MO: We've got all kinds of logistical concerns in the room that Amy and I are trying to take care of. The police were used to talking directly to me about things, and so we're trying to communicate all that and find everybody. At some point, I sent Capitol Police to get Senator Murray out of her office.

Sen. Amy Klobuchar, D-MN: I had talked to Chuck [Schumer], and Roy had talked to Mitch [McConnell], so we got up there and said what they said. And I remember saying that the one thing that would happen no matter what is we're going to go back to that chamber. And everyone cheered.

Sen. Susan Collins, R-ME: We turned on the televisions, and I saw the bizarre guy with the horns and I think a bare chest or something go sit in the vice president's chair. And I could see people at my desk.

Sen. Dick Durbin, D-IL: I was concerned because my grandson is a doorman in the Senate, and I didn't know where he was. I tried to reach him, and I asked my staff—take care of yourself, be safe, but if you find out where Alex is, I want to be able to tell the family. So we established that he was hiding out in a room with other pages and doormen trying to figure out what to do next.

Paul Kane, reporter, *The Washington Post*: For like the first forty minutes or so, all of the reporters and senators were in the room together. Captain Sean Patton from the Capitol Police came in and spoke. There was blood on the right side of his face. I don't know where it came from.

Capitol Police told Klobuchar that someone had posted a photo of the room on Facebook, and they were worried that more people would reveal their location online.

Sen. Amy Klobuchar, D-MN: I got up and I'm just like, "You guys, someone has posted a picture in this room on Facebook, and you know who you are." They thought I knew who they were, but I didn't know who they were.

There were microphones set up, and the Senate chaplain said a prayer to the room.

Senate Chaplain Barry Black: There were people who were coming and talking to me. There were those hyperventilating because of the trauma of it.

Sen. Roy Blunt, R-MO: There was some isolation of the two or three people who were most vigorous in protesting the vote. There was substantial tension in the room.

Sen. Ted Cruz, R-TX: In the secure location, tempers were high. Many senators were scared. Others were angry. Amid the chaos, more than one senator expressed rage at those of us who had objected to the certification of the election, blaming us explicitly for the violence that was occurring.

Sen. Mark Warner, D-VA: Some of the people who were the most forward-leaning election deniers—there were a lot of venomous looks at some of the ones who had been encouraging this.

Some members were individually reaching out to the White House.

Sen. Susan Collins, R-ME: I went to an anteroom in the secure location, and I called Ivanka [Trump], because I had a very good relationship with Ivanka. I said, "The president needs to immediately put out a tweet and talk to his supporters and tell them they've gone too far. They need to be peaceful, and they need to go home." And she said, "Well, he plans to do that." What he put out at first was totally inadequate. She was sympathetic.

Collins, a moderate Republican who was often at odds with Trump, didn't tell anyone in the room about her call.

Sen. Susan Collins, R-ME: I was trying to keep that very quiet and private. I went to the anteroom so that I wouldn't be overheard and because I was trying to make it easier for her. Probably a call from Susan Collins isn't going to have—I didn't know how that would be received by the president.

There was a debate about whether the Senate should move off campus or try to restart the session in the office building where they were waiting.

Sen. Tim Kaine, D-VA: The sergeant at arms said, "We've equipped this room so you can complete the work." Everybody said, "We're not doing it here. We're going to wait till the chamber is cleared. We don't care how long it takes, we're going back and we're doing it in the chamber." To do it back in full view of the American public was really important.

Paul Kane, reporter, *The Washington Post*: The initial plan at that moment was mass evacuation of the entire Capitol complex. Captain Patton told us that they were trying to arrange buses for a mass caravan to completely evacuate the complex because they believed that they were not going to be able to secure anything at that moment. And everybody's faces kind of went like, what the fuck? And it all sort of got pretty dour at that point.

Sen. Richard Burr, R-NC: It was the dumbest thing I'd ever heard of.

Sen. Mark Warner, D-VA: I think the overwhelming majority of senators in both parties felt that we were not going to get chased out of the Capitol of the United States by these thugs.

Sen. Roy Blunt, R-MO: My view was, and I think the general view was, that we need to do our work where we're supposed to do it, and we need to do it before we leave here today.

Almost every senator had made it to the undisclosed location, but a few were not there. Maine Sen. Angus King was trapped in his hideaway, a small one-room office in the basement just below the Senate chamber. He was there to work on a speech he was supposed to give later in the day when the rioters breached the building.

Sen. Angus King, I-ME: I just stayed put. The hideaway that I was in had a glass door, but it was frosted. So I turned the light out and locked the door and basically just sat tight, checking my phone, watching the news, watching what was going on on my monitor. I was alone.

Sen. Susan Collins, R-ME: They kept calling the roll to try to determine where all the senators were. And I remember this because Angus hadn't been on the floor, and he also did not answer the roll. So he wasn't in the secure room. Most people were there.

Sen. Angus King, I-ME: I got a fair number of texts from two people—my wife, Mary, and Chuck Schumer. And both of them essentially wanted to know where the hell I was.

Officer Mark Gazelle, US Capitol Police: I had to go back [into the Capitol] several times to do extractions of personnel that we could not locate that were not on the Senate floor during the initial evacuation. We had to go into areas that were hostile areas basically, rioters, protesters, and had to go to rooms where certain key personnel were hiding. I went on four extractions myself.

Sen. Angus King, I-ME: When somebody knocks and says, "We're the police," your first question is, are you really? But Chuck had said that they were coming, so I opened the door. And they said, "Let's go, Senator, to a safe place." So we hustled out, down through all the corridors, through the basement, through the tunnel.

Police eventually cleared the Senate chamber and the hallways around it.

Officer Brian Morgan, US Capitol Police: We didn't know if there were any weapons, anything that could hurt any senators and staff, so we did a full sweep of the chamber itself and started locking it down.

As areas were swept, officers continued to find stray members of the mob.

Officer Brian Morgan, US Capitol Police: I encountered a rioter trying to beat down a door into a back kitchen on the first floor that was occupied by a custodian, and he was trying to get to the custodian. He was yelling obscenities, saying, "Where's my mom at? Where did you take my mom?" I got him away from the custodian. I told the custodian to barricade the door and don't answer the door unless we say "Police!"

Nancy Pelosi had three main objectives while she was sequestered at Fort McNair, the secure location where police had taken congressional leaders from both parties.

House Speaker Nancy Pelosi, D-CA: One, when's the National Guard coming? Two, when is the president going to call off his thugs? And three, how soon can we get to the floor?

Pelosi didn't have her phone, so she was using her aide's phone—at first to check on the safety of her members and then to get resources to the Capitol. Pelosi and her aides were also trying to find police officers to evacuate her staff who were trapped in a room in the speaker's suite as rioters ransacked the office.

Terri McCullough, chief of staff, House Speaker Nancy Pelosi: We were trying to get information from people who were still at the Capitol, but the reception was really bad.

Emily Berret, director of operations, House Speaker Nancy Pelosi: We got the news on, so we were watching in real time what was going on. At that point, protesters completely taking over the Capitol, the smashing of the windows.

Terri McCullough, chief of staff, House Speaker Nancy Pelosi: There was a little back-and-forth with the Capitol Police, with the sergeant at arms. It felt at some point like they were telling us what we wanted to hear versus what other officers on the ground were telling us what they believed was actually happening.

House Speaker Nancy Pelosi, D-CA: Now we're starting to see on TV, because I had no phone, the violence. And that changed everything.

Terri McCullough, chief of staff, House Speaker Nancy Pelosi: We were being told different things about how soon we could get back to the Capitol, and at one point, we were being told it could take days. So we were trying to understand, how do we finish our business in a constitutional manner as soon as possible?

House Speaker Nancy Pelosi, D-CA: We just knew we had to be back. You're not going to assault the Capitol of the United States and have the response be at an undisclosed location. We needed to show the American people and the world that we were back on the floor of the House in the Congress of the United States.

As they watched the violence unfold on television, Pelosi, Senate Democratic Leader Chuck Schumer, and Senate Republican Leader Mitch McConnell made numerous calls—to the Pentagon pleading for the National Guard, to Justice

Department officials, to governors, and to Vice President Pence. Pelosi and McConnell had both authorized National Guard troops to come to the Capitol, but there were still inexplicable delays at the Pentagon.

On a particularly testy call with Acting Attorney General Jeffrey Rosen, Pelosi and Schumer sat close together on a couch and pushed him to confront Trump.

"The fact is, on any given day, they are breaking the law in many different ways, and quite frankly, much of it at the instigation of the president of the United States," Pelosi told Rosen. Schumer snapped, "Why don't you get the president to tell them to leave the Capitol, Mr. Attorney General, in your law enforcement responsibility?"[2]

As the DC National Guard was delayed, House Majority Leader Steny Hoyer called Maryland Gov. Larry Hogan, a Republican.

House Majority Leader Steny Hoyer, D-MD: I said, "Larry, all hell is breaking loose." He said, "Yeah, I know, I'm watching it." I said, "We need the National Guard here." And he said, "I know, I'm ready to send the National Guard, but I can't get authorization from the Pentagon."

The group would later call Acting Defense Secretary Chris Miller, and McConnell told him forcefully that he needed the building cleared. "We're not going to let these people keep us from finishing our business," he said.[3]

Senate Democratic Whip Dick Durbin, D-IL: I think if I had to put it on a scale, I would say McConnell may have been tops in terms of that angst, fear, concern that we get back in business that day as quickly as possible. He expressed that thought several times.

House Majority Leader Steny Hoyer, D-MD: McConnell was particularly angry. He clearly believed this president had sent down a mob to take over our institution. We were all angry, but I mean, Mitch was particularly adamant that we finish. I think he may have had a few swear words about "we're going to get this job done, and the damn mob is not going to kick us out of the Capitol." You don't hear him swear very often.

House Republican Leader Kevin McCarthy, a longtime Trump ally, did a live phone interview on Fox News, Trump's favorite channel, calling the rioting un-American. "I've already talked to the president, I called him. I think we need to make a statement, make sure we can calm individuals down," McCarthy said. "I could not be sadder or more disappointed with the way our country looks at this very moment," he told the Fox anchors. "People are getting hurt!"[4]

Back at the Capitol and in a garage underneath the chaos, Pence was making his own calls.

Greg Jacob, counsel to Vice President Pence: There had been a point at which the vice president contemplated calling the president to give him a status update, and I think the decision was made that the president hadn't called him, and so he wasn't going to make that call.

Marc Short, chief of staff, Vice President Pence: I don't recall anybody suggesting that he should be a participant in the conversation.

Greg Jacob, counsel to Vice President Pence: There was frustration that the president had not called even to check in on how he was doing.

Instead, Short called both McCarthy and McConnell on behalf of his boss, and they agreed that all of the congressional leaders should speak.

Marc Short, chief of staff, Vice President Pence: When all four leaders were on the phone together, there was a concern that the National Guard had not arrived at that point. And the vice president, I think, was, "Well, do you want me to make a call?" And, collectively, there was a "Yes, would you please?" So we hung up at that point to call over to the Pentagon, in which the vice president spoke with Secretary [Christopher] Miller and General [Mark] Milley, and they assured him that they were on top of it and the National Guard was being deployed.

Gen. Mark Milley, chairman of the Joint Chiefs of Staff: There were two or three calls with Vice President Pence. He was very animated, and he issued very explicit, very direct, unambiguous orders. There was no question about that. He was very animated, very direct, very firm to Secretary Miller: Get the military down here, get the Guard down here, put down this situation.

As the afternoon wore on in the garage, Jacob pulled out his Bible.

Greg Jacob, counsel to Vice President Pence: I read through it and just took great comfort. Daniel 6 was where I went, and in Daniel 6, Daniel has become the second in command of Babylon, a pagan nation that he completely faithfully serves. He refuses an order from the king that he cannot follow and he does his duty in—consistent with his oath to God. And I felt that that's what had played out that day.

4:00 p.m.

Ken Sicknick hadn't yet replied to his brother Brian's text from the night before that had predicted violence. So he typed a message to Brian that afternoon as he watched live reports of the clashes at the Capitol. "Good luck, man," Ken wrote. "Capitol protests are on the news."

An hour and a half later, at 4:15 p.m., Brian replied, "Tell me about it. We're fucked. Talk later. I was pepper sprayed at least twice."[1]

Ken Sicknick, brother of Capitol Police Officer Brian Sicknick: I knew it was a protest. I didn't realize how bad it was.

As afternoon approached evening, police were starting to secure some of the entrances that had been breached. But hundreds of rioters were still fighting to get into the Lower West Terrace Tunnel, the main entrance to the inaugural stage from the basement level of the Capitol. Police officers had used the space just inside as a triage area all afternoon.

Earlier, after several police lines had broken outside, the rioters had streamed into the tunnel so quickly that it created a bottleneck. The National Guard had still not arrived, and for the officers who had already been fighting for hours, it had become a ferocious last stand.

Sergeant Aquilino Gonell, US Capitol Police: The rioters were vicious and relentless. We found ourselves in a violent battle in a desperate attempt to prevent a breach of the Capitol by the entrance near the inauguration stage.

Officer Michael Fanone, Metropolitan Police Department: The fighting in the Lower West Terrace Tunnel was nothing short of brutal. Here I observed approximately thirty police officers standing shoulder to shoulder, maybe four or five abreast, using the weight of their own bodies to hold back the onslaught of violent attackers. Many of these officers were injured, bleeding, and fatigued. But they continued to hold the line.

Officer Abdulkadir Abdi, Metropolitan Police Department: A few people rushed the front of the line, and then that kind of instigated the rest of them to follow suit. At that point, it was just complete hand-to-hand combat, but very little space to maneuver.

Detective Phuson Nguyen, Metropolitan Police Department: The hallway is approximately ten feet wide. Officers shoulder to shoulder lined up by rows, and the demonstrators were trying to push in, and we were trying to push back. Initially, we're just pushing and they were yelling, "One, two, three, push." And we were doing the same thing. We were pushing back. But then it escalated into full fighting.

Officer Daniel Hodges, Metropolitan Police Department: There's a couple dozen of us in there against, you know, the thousands and thousands outside, and we just held it as long as we could. It was a brutal fight.

Officer Abdulkadir Abdi, Metropolitan Police Department: They were extremely physical. I don't think anybody was talking at that point. It was just physical, people hitting each other, punching, people with poles, metal poles.

Officer Michael Fanone, Metropolitan Police Department: The tunnel is a narrow and long hallway. It is not the sort of space where anyone would want to be pulled into hand-to-hand combat with an angry mob.

Officer Abdulkadir Abdi, Metropolitan Police Department: They had formed their own line. If you looked beyond them, there were hundreds and hundreds of people.

Officer Daniel Hodges, Metropolitan Police Department: Officers were stacked deep, but every so often one would fall back from the front line, nursing an injury or struggling to breathe, and those who remained would take a step forward.

Officer Abdulkadir Abdi, Metropolitan Police Department: Every about five to ten minutes, they would switch and then we would end up fighting a new batch of fresh bodies. That just continued on.

Officer Jesse Leasure, Metropolitan Police Department: It was guys in their fifties, guys in their thirties, guys in their twenties. Not that many really young people, but mostly just like, real adults.

Officer Daniel Hodges, Metropolitan Police Department: It was a battle of inches, with one side pushing the other a few and then the other side regaining their ground.

Sergeant Aquilino Gonell, US Capitol Police: What we were subjected to that day was like something from a medieval battlefield.

Officer Daniel Hodges, Metropolitan Police Department: Eventually it was my turn in the meat grinder that was the front line. The terrorists had a wall of shields that they had stolen from officers, as well as stolen batons and whatever other armaments they brought.

Officer Jesse Leasure, Metropolitan Police Department: Someone handed me a pitchfork at one point. It made its way all the way up the stairs. I don't remember if it was a civilian or an officer, but they said, "I don't want this being used against you guys."

Officer Michael Fanone, Metropolitan Police Department: The fighting dragged on, and I eventually joined the tactical line at the tunnel's entrance. I can remember looking around and being shocked by the sheer number of people fighting us.

Officer Daniel Hodges, Metropolitan Police Department: Even during this intense contest of wills, they continued to try to convert us to their cult. One man shouted, "We just want to make our voices heard!

And I think you feel the same! I really think you feel the same!" All while another man attempts to batter us with a stolen shield.

Officer Jesse Leasure, Metropolitan Police Department: I just heard the dumbest things ever, like "We're not here to hurt you; just let us through." While they're doing all that craziness.

Sergeant Aquilino Gonell, US Capitol Police: Many of the officers fighting alongside me were calling for shields, because their shields had been stripped from them by the rioters. I was one of the few officers left with a shield, so I spent the majority of the time at the front of the line.

Detective Phuson Nguyen, Metropolitan Police Department: At some point, one of the demonstrators was trying to pull me outside. And luckily I held on to the metal rail.

A rioter grabbed Detective Nguyen's gas mask and pulled it out, while a second rioter directly sprayed his exposed face. The first rioter then let go of the mask, snapping it back in place and trapping the gas inside.

Detective Phuson Nguyen, Metropolitan Police Department: I was choking under the mask, and I also got knocked down at the same time. And so at that point, I was choking, and I was trying to get up. I [was] panicking.

Officer Michael Fanone, Metropolitan Police Department: At some point during the fighting, I was dragged from the line of officers into the crowd. I heard someone scream, "I got one!" as I was swarmed by a violent mob.

Sergeant Aquilino Gonell, US Capitol Police: In my attempt to assist two MPD officers, I grabbed one officer by the back of the collar and pulled him back to our police line. When I tried to help the second officer, I fell on top of some police shields on the ground that were slippery because of the pepper and bear spray. Rioters started to pull me by my leg, by my shield, and by my gear straps on my left shoulder. My survival instincts kicked in and I started kicking and punching as I tried in vain to get the MPD officers' attention behind and above me. But they could not help me because they were also being attacked.

Officer Daniel Hodges, Metropolitan Police Department: The two sides were at a stalemate at a metal door frame that sat in the middle of the hallway. At the front line, I inserted myself so that the frame was at my back in an effort to give myself something to brace against and provide additional strength when pushing forward. Unfortunately, soon after I secured this position, the momentum shifted and we lost the ground that got me there. On my left was a man with a clear riot shield stolen during the assault. He slammed it against me and, with the weight of all the bodies pushing behind him, trapped me. My arms were pinned and effectively useless, trapped against either the shield on my left or the door frame on my right. With my posture granting me no functional strength or freedom of movement, I was effectively defenseless and gradually sustaining injury from the increasing pressure of the mob.

Officer Michael Fanone, Metropolitan Police Department: They ripped off my badge. They grabbed my radio. They seized the ammunition that was secured to my body. They began to beat me with their fists and with what felt like hard metal objects. At one point I came face-to-face with an attacker who repeatedly lunged for me and attempted to remove my firearm. I heard chanting from some in the crowd, "Get his gun" and "Kill him with his own gun." I was aware enough to recognize I was at risk of being stripped of, and killed with, my own firearm. I was electrocuted again and again and again with a Taser. I'm sure I was screaming, but I don't think I could even hear my own voice.

Officer Daniel Hodges, Metropolitan Police Department: Directly in front of me, a man seized the opportunity of my vulnerability. He grabbed the front of my gas mask and used it to beat my head against the door. He switched to pulling it off my head, the straps stretching against my skull and straining my neck. He never uttered any words I recognized but opted instead for guttural screams. I swear I remember him foaming at the mouth. He also put his cell phone in his mouth so that he had both hands free to assault me. Eventually he succeeded in stripping away my gas mask, and a new rush of exposure to CS gas and OC spray hit me.

Officer Michael Fanone, Metropolitan Police Department: My body camera captured the violence of the crowd directed toward me during those very frightening moments. The portions of the video I've seen remain extremely painful for me to watch. During those moments, I remember thinking that there was a very good chance that I would be torn apart or be shot to death with my own weapon. I thought of my four daughters, who might lose their dad.

Officer Daniel Hodges, Metropolitan Police Department: The mob of terrorists were coordinating their efforts now, shouting "Heave! Ho!" as they synchronized pushing their weight forward, crushing me further against the metal door frame. The man in front of me grabbed my baton that I still held in my hands, and in my current state I was unable to retain my weapon. He bashed me in the head and face with it, rupturing my lip and adding additional injury to my skull.

Officer Jesse Leasure, Metropolitan Police Department: It's just the weight of our crowd pushing against the weight of their crowd. Smoke grenades are going off—like, maybe someone lit a smoke bomb and threw it at us; I don't know what the hell happened. But I'm looking around, and I see one of my sergeants, and he's got his mask on, but I can see his eyes, and he looks like he's about ready to pass out. And I hear someone yell, "Does anybody need a break?" And I'm like, "Get him out of here!"

Sergeant Aquilino Gonell, US Capitol Police: It was a prolonged and desperate struggle. I vividly heard officers screaming in agony and pain just an arm's length from me.

Officer Daniel Hodges, Metropolitan Police Department: It hurt a great deal. Combined with everything else that was going on, it made it difficult to breathe.

Officer Jesse Leasure, Metropolitan Police Department: A bunch of bodies were pushed up right against me, and it sealed my gas mask against my cheek. And I was having a hard time breathing. So I started peeling it off, and then I was exposed, and no sooner had I done that than I was hit with a big old stream of pepper spray from one of our own super-soakers that they stole from us. I see this arc of fluid, and it hits me right in the face. I've seen my body camera from that day, and you just hear a guttural scream.

Officer Daniel Hodges, Metropolitan Police Department: At this point, I knew that I couldn't sustain much more damage and remain upright. At best I would collapse and be a liability to my colleagues, at worst be dragged out into the crowd and lynched. Unable to move or otherwise signal the officers behind me that I needed to fall back, I did the only thing I could still do and screamed for help.

Sergeant Aquilino Gonell, US Capitol Police: I too was being crushed by the rioters. I could feel myself losing oxygen and recall thinking to myself, this is how I'm going to die, trampled defending this entrance.

Detective Phuson Nguyen, Metropolitan Police Department: I thought, that's where I'm going to die. And in my head I was thinking about my family at that point before anything else.

Officer Michael Fanone, Metropolitan Police Department: During the assault, I thought about using my firearm on my attackers. But I knew that if I did that, I would quickly be overwhelmed. And that, in their minds, it would provide them with the justification for killing me. So instead, I decided to appeal to any humanity they might have. I said as loud as I could manage, "I've got kids." Thankfully, some in the crowd stepped in and assisted me. Those few individuals protected me from the crowd and inched me toward the Capitol until my fellow officers could rescue me.

Officer Jesse Leasure, Metropolitan Police Department: When you get amped up like that, sometimes it takes a slap in the face to wake you up to where the hell you are and what you've just done. And I think Fanone yelling that he had kids kind of shook some of the people out of it.

Officer Daniel Hodges, Metropolitan Police Department: Thankfully, my voice was heard over the cacophony of yells and the blaring alarm. The officer closest to me was able to extricate me from my position, and another helped me fall back to the building again.

Detective Phuson Nguyen, Metropolitan Police Department: I was telling myself, if you want to see your family again, you need to gather yourself. And luckily, you know, I gathered myself and [broke] that seal. And with the help of my colleagues behind me, they pulled me up.

Officer Jesse Leasure, Metropolitan Police Department: I'm yelling, "Hey, I'm out of service, I can't do this anymore!" Like, literally, I'm disabled. So one of my partners grabs me and just escorts me back through the crowd, and we find one of those decon stations.

Sergeant Aquilino Gonell, US Capitol Police: I finally was able to hit a rioter who was grabbing me with my baton and able to stand. I then continued to fend off new attackers as they kept rotating after attacking us.

Just steps from the tunnel, Florida Rep. Stephanie Murphy and New York Rep. Kathleen Rice, both Democrats, had locked themselves inside a Capitol hideaway that belonged to Arizona Sen. Kyrsten Sinema, a former House member who was their close friend. They thought it would be safe to be in the heart of the Capitol but instead had found themselves very close to the violence. Trapped in the small room close by, they listened to the sounds of the scuffling battle and police officers running back into the building to get help.

Rep. Stephanie Murphy, D-FL: I listened to people coughing, having difficulty breathing. I think Congresswoman Rice and I were the only members of Congress to be down there on that Lower West Terrace. We had taken refuge in that office because we thought for sure being in the basement at the heart of the Capitol was the safest place we could be, and it turned out we ended up at the center of the storm.

At 4:17 p.m., after aides had pressured him for hours, Trump tweeted a video of himself speaking outside the White House:[2]

I know your pain, I know you're hurt. We had an election that was stolen from us. It was a landslide election and everyone knows it, especially the other side. But you have to go home now. We have to have peace. We have to have law and order. We have to respect our great people in law and order. We don't want anybody hurt.

It's a very tough period of time. There's never been a time like this where such a thing happened where they could take it away from all of us—from me, from you, from our country. This was a fraudulent election, but we can't play into the hands of these people. We have to have peace. So go home. We love you. You're very special. You've seen what happens. You see the way others are treated that are so bad and so evil.

I know how you feel, but go home, and go home in peace.

Annie Howell, Pennsylvania: Somehow we all had service at one time, and I remember saying, "President Trump said go home, President Trump said go home." And it was at that point we all left.

Alisa La, special assistant to House Speaker Nancy Pelosi: We were in the conference room for about two hours. Everyone's phones were lighting up with texts from their loved ones.

Henry Connelly, communications director, House Speaker Nancy Pelosi: We could hear them rampaging through for some period of time, and then that stopped at a certain point or faded, and then we could still hear what sounded like a pitched battle going on in the Rotunda.

Terri McCullough, chief of staff, House Speaker Nancy Pelosi: I was working with the security detail to make sure somebody got to our staff in that room to ensure that they were safe and to get them out of there. It was hours until that happened.

Emily Berret, director of operations, House Speaker Nancy Pelosi: Our security team with us at the secure location were in constant communication with us about what was going on and what they were trying to do to get them out. To us, it was a very bleak situation, but I could not tell them that. They couldn't get to them. The Capitol Police just could not get through the rioters. They could not hold them back. They just—they had completely swarmed that suite, and the Capitol Police could not find a way to get to them at that time.

Alisa La, special assistant to House Speaker Nancy Pelosi: [Capitol Police Special Agent] David Lazarus, from our security detail, got to us, and we could distinctly hear his voice. I called him to make sure that it was him. So then we opened the door. I can't imagine what our faces looked like—he asked us if we were all right and told us that they were securing the Capitol. We could turn on the lights and breathe a short breath of relief. For the first time in two hours, we could look at each other and talk to each other in the light.

Henry Connelly, communications director, House Speaker Nancy Pelosi: The biggest MPD riot-geared folks lined up, maybe a dozen of them, and they were there to escort us out of the building.

Alisa La, special assistant to House Speaker Nancy Pelosi: I looked to my right, even though they were trying to pull us to the left, and I saw that the office was destroyed.

In the Senate, CNN's Manu Raju was narrating live on air as he and his producers were evacuated by police and taken to one of the office buildings. He tried to stay, but the police made everyone leave. It was the first time Raju had left his booth in hours, and he saw broken furniture everywhere and a fine gray dust covering the patterned marble floors.

Manu Raju, anchor and chief congressional correspondent, CNN: It smelled like smoke bombs, like the Fourth of July. I was talking to Jake

Tapper, who was anchoring at the time. He asked, "What are you seeing?" I said, "Jake, this looks like a war zone out here."

Police never reached the basement TV studio where Fox News's Chad Pergram had been doing live shots all day.

Chad Pergram, senior congressional correspondent, Fox News: We took TV cables and lashed them around the doors so nobody could enter, tied them to chairs. We turned the "on air" light off, covered the windows with coats. And I think it turned out that we were actually in a pretty good spot because we were able to stay on the air the entire time.

5:00 p.m.

Officer Michael Fanone, Metropolitan Police Department: I was carried back inside the Capitol Building. What happened afterwards is much less vivid to me. I had been beaten unconscious and remained so for more than four minutes. I know that [my partner] Jimmy helped evacuate me from the building and drove me to MedStar Washington Hospital Center despite suffering significant injuries himself. At the hospital, doctors told me that I suffered a heart attack, and I was later diagnosed with a concussion, traumatic brain injury, and post-traumatic stress disorder.

Officer Daniel Hodges, Metropolitan Police Department: They outnumbered us fifty-something to one, so it didn't matter how many we defeated. We just had to hold on. We couldn't let anyone through, and they always had essentially an infinite number of replacements. They'd say, you know, "We need fresh patriots up here," and there would be more. So we just had to hold until someone came to help.

Officer Jesse Leasure, Metropolitan Police Department: When enough guys are piling in behind, the advantage of being in that tunnel is that it renders their numbers useless. They can get lots of reinforcements, but in a narrow confine, they have to funnel themselves down. So that kind of makes the fight a little bit more equal.

Officer Daniel Hodges, Metropolitan Police Department: Eventually we were successful in repelling the insurgents.

Sergeant Aquilino Gonell, US Capitol Police: I was in the Lower West Terrace fighting alongside these officers, and all of them—all of them—were telling us, "Trump sent us." Nobody else. There was nobody else. It was not antifa. It was not Black Lives Matter. It was not the FBI. It was his supporters that he sent over to the Capitol that day. He could have done a lot of things; one of them was to tell them to stop.

Officer Michael Fanone, Metropolitan Police Department: I remain grateful that no member of Congress had to go through the violent assault that I experienced that day.

Detective Phuson Nguyen, Metropolitan Police Department: I made my way back to decontamination. [A worker in the Capitol] led us to a water fountain in one of the mechanical rooms. And that's where I used the water to splash my face to wash the spray and [rested] for about fifteen minutes or so. And then after I was able to see again, I went back to the line.

The Capitol HVAC shop brought eye-wash stations to police officers who had been injured by pepper spray or tear gas.

Clinton Johnson, Capitol HVAC shop: In that moment, it was kind of unbelievable what was unfolding. But as it's unfolding, you just want to make sure everybody was okay. It felt good to be able to help, but I just wanted to get through it.

Officer Daniel Hodges, Metropolitan Police Department: Without my gas mask, I was afraid I'd be a liability in the hallway, so I took the exit outside to the upper landing above the West Terrace. I found a police line being held and the terrorists encircling us, much like on the West Terrace. It was getting later in the day, however, and it appeared we weren't the only ones getting tired. It seemed most of the mob was content to yell rather than to break our line again. After some time of guarding the upper landing, I saw reinforcements arrive from the south. I'm not sure which law enforcement agency it was, but I turned to them and started clapping, as it was a sign that badly needed help was starting to finally arrive.

Sergeant Aquilino Gonell, US Capitol Police: I later found out that my wife and relatives here in the US and abroad were frantically calling and texting me from 2 p.m. onwards because they were watching the turmoil live on television.

As darkness fell, the police officers in the tunnel launched smoke bombs to clear the remaining rioters, and the fighting gradually stopped. They had held the line. With greater numbers and fewer rioters still at the Capitol, police were now able to push the rioters away from the building.[1]

Inspector Thomas Loyd, US Capitol Police: We had gotten a basic handle on the inside of the building where we could clear people out. We had enough mutual support at that point that we could retake the building and push everybody on the outside and eventually set up a perimeter on the outside.

After hours of delays, the Pentagon had finally responded to the pleas from police, congressional leadership, and the vice president and gave orders to send the DC National Guard to the Capitol. The guard began to arrive just as police got control of the situation.

William Walker, commanding general of the District of Columbia National Guard: At 5:20 p.m., the District of Columbia National Guard arrived at the Capitol. We helped to reestablish the security perimeter at the east side of the Capitol to facilitate the resumption of the joint session of Congress.

Chief Robert Contee, Metropolitan Police Department: I appreciated the help when it showed up, but I tell you, five hours into a fight, that is a long time.

Officer Winston Pingeon, US Capitol Police: I remember going out to the inauguration stage, and I could see, finally, the National Guard coming and MPD pushing them back, but there were still some people injured out there. I just remember standing out there and looking out and just being like, what the fuck just happened? How did this happen? And still being nervous, because I didn't know who was still in the building, and I'm thinking, like, what could they have done? Did they leave a bomb inside, or who knows?

Back in the Capitol, Officer Caroline Edwards helped with the arrest of a rioter who had gotten into the building.

Officer Caroline Edwards, US Capitol Police: When I was in prisoner processing, I started to notice that I was out of it. I've been in prisoner processing I can't even tell you how many times, but I started asking, like, where are the computers? And I sat down to put my password, my username and password in, and that's when I just slumped over, and I woke up in a cold sweat.

Edwards couldn't answer simple questions. She got in an ambulance and went to the hospital. She had suffered a concussion.

Officer Caroline Edwards, US Capitol Police: I was having severe ear pain and ear ringing from my jaw hitting the railing. And then with the chemical spray that day, I had burns underneath my eyes, which thankfully have gone away. The ones on my hands still kind of remain, but they're very light. I went to Johns Hopkins, and they stated that I had minor chemical burns on my vocal cords.

Sen. Amy Klobuchar, the top Democrat on the Senate Rules Committee, authorized staff to go down to a cafeteria in the Dirksen Senate Office Building and find something for senators to eat.

Sen. Amy Klobuchar, D-MN: I told them, "I give you permission for two things. One is that you can steal whatever you can out of there, I don't care, we'll work it out later. And the second thing is, you can break the glass if you need to, but don't get any of the glass in the food." And like magic, half an hour later it was all there.

Sen. Susan Collins, R-ME: They brought us water and salads and sandwiches to eat, and there were a couple of televisions on. Mainly we watched in shocked silence.

Behind the scenes, Senate Republican leaders were trying to push their colleagues to drop any planned objections to the electoral votes in the wake of the violence. But it was unclear what that group would do.

Paul Kane, reporter, *The Washington Post*: I went into a hallway there to make a phone call, and I saw some of the challengers from the Senate—Cruz, Hawley, Lankford, [Wyoming Sen. Cynthia] Lummis. They all walked out of a side door and they walked into what was basically a closet. I immediately pinged my colleagues and was like, "Guys, they're trying to get these people to stand down, and they're all huddled in a room debating what to do."

Sen. Ted Cruz, R-TX: While we waited for the Capitol to be secured, I assembled our coalition in a back room (really, a supply closet with stacked chairs) to discuss what we should do next. Several members of the group argued that in the face of the riot, we should suspend our objections and vote to certify the election. I understood the sentiment. But I vehemently disagreed with it. I urged my colleagues that the course of action we were advocating was the right and principled one. I said, "I'll be damned if I allow a handful of violent rioters to change our willingness to fulfill our constitutional responsibility." When they stormed the Capitol that day and assaulted police officers, these rioters wanted to stop the government from working; I wasn't going to let them.

At the same time, some of Trump's allies were still working the phones, encouraging senators to keep up the objections. That evening, Sen. Mike Lee, R-UT, received another mistaken call intended for Alabama Sen. Tommy Tuberville, this time from Rudy Giuliani, calling for the senator to "slow it down" when the electoral count resumed that evening.[2]

Back in the underground parking deck, Vice President Mike Pence was working with Capitol Police to ensure that the joint session could resume safely.

Marc Short, chief of staff, Vice President Pence: The vice president's interest was to reinforce how important it was to get back in that night. And he wanted to make sure that the Capitol Police were doing everything they could to ensure that inevitability.

The police had some concern that the building still had to undergo extensive sweeping in case any of the rioters had left explosive devices or other weapons. The US Secret Service sent in another canine unit to help.[3]

Rep. Zoe Lofgren, D-CA, chairwoman of the House Administration Committee: I was on the phone with Jamie Fleet, staff director for House Administration, who was over there. Jamie said it was really a mess. The mob never got into our chambers, but he said there was blood on the floor and it was really trashed. And the janitorial staff was over there cleaning it up, making sure that the Congress could reconvene as soon as it was safe and the bomb dogs had been through.

Jamie Fleet, Democratic staff director, House Administration Committee: The chamber is typically a fairly orderly place. But what you saw going into the chamber—you saw broken glass, broken furniture, bodily fluids. There was blood on the ground which wasn't cleaned up when I went in. You saw gas masks, the packaging for gas masks, you saw, like, papers strewn. It was unfortunate. It was just sort of sad to see. Clearly it looked like a place people were fleeing.

Drew Hammill, deputy chief of staff, House Speaker Nancy Pelosi: Jamie Fleet and I, escorted by three police officers, armed, went back into the Capitol before it was even secure. We surveyed the chamber to see what the extent of the damage is, what are the cleanup needs? There were people screaming out in Statuary Hall. I could hear it from the chamber. They had not fully gotten everybody out yet.

Jamie Fleet, Democratic staff director, House Administration Committee: It had a feeling of a theater of violence.

Across the Capitol, Senate Rules Committee Chairman Roy Blunt was coordinating the Senate's return.

Sen. Roy Blunt, R-MO: I said, look, we need to get over there once we're told the combination of the Guard and the Capitol Police and the DC police now feel the building is secure. So we need to get over there as quickly as we can. And I said specifically, don't worry about whether something's torn up or there's trash on the floor. If the lights work and the microphone works and the cameras work, we need to get there. Don't worry about cleaning anything up. If those things work, we need to get there.

Sen. Mike Rounds, R-SD: On the Republican side and on the Democrat side and in that room, there was no disagreement—we were going to go back and finish the job.

Sen. Richard Burr, R-NC: There was never a thought that we weren't going to finish our business and Joe Biden wasn't going to be president. I can't speak for some of my colleagues who may have still thought that they could push this to the next day or the next day or the next day. But I think the focus of the majority of folks was let's finish our business and let's get the heck out of here.

Jamie Fleet, Democratic staff director, House Administration Committee: I called the superintendent of the Capitol. He had been barricaded in his office. I asked him to come up to the House floor. He came in, and I said, "Well, can we finish the job here tonight?" And he said, "Me and my colleagues will get this done in a couple of hours." And so the cleanup effort started shortly thereafter. The women and men who left their barricaded offices to come onto that House floor that day, they had a real sense of duty and purpose. And because of them, we were able to finish the work, finish the job.

J. Brett Blanton, Architect of the Capitol: My staff undertook several amazing actions in support of Congress. Architect of the Capitol employees sheltered congressional staff in their workshops to protect them from the crowd; other members of my team raced to the roof to reverse the airflows within the building to help clear the air of chemical irritants like bear repellents and pepper spray. Additional team members rushed bottles of water and eye wash stations to the Capitol Police officers in need of assistance.

Ricardo Mitchell, Capitol labor division: We got evacuated out of the building just like everybody else. Once they got everything under control, we had to come back in the building and clean up the mess, because the members were going to return to finish voting. We had to go into the chambers and prepare them so they would be able to come back. It was a lot of masks and a lot of broken glass, some broken furniture. They had to barricade the doors.

There was also significant damage to the inaugural platform and not much time to repair it before Joe Biden was to be sworn in on January 20. Painters had been working that morning as the crowds started to form, finishing some blue detail work on the gleaming white stands. They had planned to work into that night.

J. Brett Blanton, Architect of the Capitol: Members of my team were preparing the grounds and the presidential inauguration stage. Our artists and trades teams were excited to finish painting the stands a bright white with a deep blue edging on the main stage of the platform. As crowds began to appear on the West Front at about midday, my staff was moved indoors or sent home.

Kevin Grooms, Capitol paint shop: I mean, it was completely destroyed. It was just totally demolished. The blue wet paint, they tracked it all over.

Jason McIntyre, deputy superintendent, Architect of the Capitol: There were many, many pieces of broken exterior glass and interior glass.

J. Brett Blanton, Architect of the Capitol: The platform was wrecked, there was broken glass and other debris littering the grounds, sound systems and photography equipment were damaged beyond repair or stolen, two historic Olmsted lanterns were ripped from the ground, and the blue paint was tracked all over the historic stone balustrades and Capitol Building hallways.

Kevin Grooms, Capitol paint shop: It was a real mess; it was unbelievable. You just can't imagine. We would've been right in that mess if we wouldn't have pulled out when we did. I thanked the officers many times for that, for getting us out of there and out of harm's way.

Katie Serock, Capitol grounds and arboretum team: Besides the stands having a lot of debris on them, there was a lot of broken glass. And there was a significant amount of residue from the tear gas. It was very difficult cleaning up that area.

J. Brett Blanton, Architect of the Capitol: As soon as security officials cleared the building breach, AOC employees worked tirelessly to clean up and begin repair work. Carpenters covered open windows and doors with plywood to help secure the building, laborers began sweeping up glass and broken furniture to enable Congress to continue its work, and our groundskeepers cleared a small mountain of debris left behind on the West and East Fronts. Moreover, our decorative painters carefully returned the platform to its glory.

Farar Elliott, Curator, US House of Representatives: As the Capitol was secured that evening, my curatorial colleagues and I turned our attention to potential damage to the House Collection and loans in the Capitol. During the riot, courageous staffers saved several important artifacts of the House's legislative history. Quick thinking by a journal clerk secured the House's 1819 silver inkstand, the oldest object in the chamber. Sergeant at arms staff evacuated the mace.

The four-foot silver mace is the symbol of the House's authority, and it is carried onto the House floor every day as the session begins and taken off when the proceedings end. An original mace was destroyed when the British burned the Capitol in 1814,[4] *and Joyce Hamlett, a member of the sergeant at arms's staff and the official keeper of the mace, ensured that would not happen again by rushing it off the floor when members evacuated.*[5]

Jeff Walters, Capitol carpentry shop: That night, we went around and assessed the broken windows and some of the broken doors and tried to make sure the building was secure. A lot of our job comes with unexpected challenges. There's not a whole lot that surprises us anymore, but seeing the overall condition of the building that night, that, I would have to say, was a bit shocking. I've been with the Architect of the Capitol for maybe twenty-two, twenty-three years. So I've seen a lot of the things that have gone on here, but I've never seen the building in such disarray.

Katie Serock, Capitol grounds: It's definitely disheartening to witness that. It's something that we care so much about. We are creating this vision for the entire country of having this pristine and organized US Capitol. And when you see it go into disarray, it kind of sinks your heart a bit.

Ricardo Mitchell, Capitol labor division: We put hard effort in every day to keep this building maintained. It was a lot of debris, you know? And we had a short time to clean it up. But we just got it done.

Jamie Fleet, Democratic staff director, House Administration Committee: The ability to have that proceeding commence, to endure the disruptions, the physical violence—I think we came so very close to a really terrible, terrible, terrible outcome of that day. And then to come back that night and finish the work, that was all made possible by nonpartisan institutional staff.

As the Capitol was cleared out and cleaned, Chief Sund called Pence in the underground garage with a security update. Pence asked him to come to the garage and brief him personally.[6]

Vice President Mike Pence: Sund informed me that the Capitol was being secured and we would be able to convene the joint session of Congress that night, possibly as early as 7 p.m. I thanked him and the officers who accompanied him for their efforts and then noticed that one of the officers had a cut above his eye from an altercation with rioters. I asked the White House physician with me to attend to him and placed a call to the leadership with the news that we would be able to reconvene safely that day.

Pelosi and Schumer took Pence's call together at Fort McNair. "Good news," Schumer replied.[7]

6:00 p.m.

At 6:01 p.m., Trump tweeted again:

> These are the things and events that happen when a sacred landslide election victory is so unceremoniously & viciously stripped away from great patriots who have been badly & unfairly treated for so long. Go home with love & in peace. Remember this day forever![1]

Shortly afterward, leaders on both sides of the Capitol announced publicly that they would resume the joint session that evening. The certification would begin where it had left off, with the two chambers separated and debating the Arizona objections. At the same time, the Capitol was closer to being cleared.

Robert Salesses, acting assistant defense secretary: By 6:14 p.m., the US Capitol Police and DC MPD, supported by the DC National Guard, established a perimeter on the west side of the US Capitol.

Lieutenant Tia Summers, US Capitol Police: At that time, based on what we could see on the cameras, it looked like we were starting to gain a little bit more control of the crowds.

As the tide turned and the evening started to fall, officers from the National Guard and all of the other law enforcement agencies that had arrived started pushing the rioters off the grounds together. For the first time that day, they were making rapid progress, even as some small groups of rioters were still fighting back.

Inspector Robert Glover, Metropolitan Police Department: You can see where people in the crowd—the crowd dynamics and crowd psychology started to shift, and they realized—they became cooperative, and they start listening to our members' direction, like, "Get off the platform, go."

Officer Adam Eveland, Metropolitan Police Department: We started pushing back and we started moving forward. When we did, it was a pretty intense fight. They were spraying us with chemicals, irritants and stuff like that.

Inspector Robert Glover, Metropolitan Police Department: I think it was the gravity of everything. I can't speak for them. I just think that they started to realize that this was bad, and they realized that they got in over their heads.

Officer Adam Eveland, Metropolitan Police Department: I was throwing punches and kicks and using my riot baton to defend myself, if I could, and keep the push forward. It started working. We were gaining ground. We pushed them all the way to the other side of the building, like where the Supreme Court is. And when we did that, I saw a big line of MPD, Virginia State Police, and other officers. And we just, like, charged them at that point.

Inspector Robert Glover, Metropolitan Police Department: I think they understood that this was kind of now the final line in the sand.

Officer Adam Eveland, Metropolitan Police Department: By that time, the party was over. They were thinning out a lot more because we really started to take things back. I remember after we had pushed them off the property, we were taking gates and putting them up. And we're like, "The building's fucking closed."

Throughout the building, police were still extracting lawmakers and staff who had been trapped in various offices and rooms. When they knocked on the door of Sen. Kyrsten Sinema's hideaway, where Reps. Murphy and Rice were hiding, the two lawmakers were initially wary.

Rep. Stephanie Murphy, D-FL: When Capitol Police knocked, my response to them before unlocking the door was "How do I know you are Capitol Police?" And they said, "Listen to our radios." So everybody was quiet for a minute, and we listened to the radios and confirmed that they were Capitol Police and opened the doors and then started to run. They said, "We have to move fast." And they had two teams, one team for me, one team for Rep. Rice. And we sprinted through, underground.

Murphy and Rice eventually ended up in the Senate's undisclosed location, where Sinema had told them to meet her. Standing among the senators, Murphy was still wearing yoga pants and a sweatshirt that she had put on in case she got caught in the crowd and had to blend in.

Rep. Stephanie Murphy, D-FL: I think it's important for everybody to remember that the main reason rioters didn't harm any members of Congress was because they didn't encounter any members of Congress.

7:00 p.m.

Some of the House Republicans in the secure location, a large hearing room in one of the House office buildings, refused to wear medical masks even as COVID-19 was raging that winter and most people weren't fully vaccinated. That only added to the existing tensions in the closely packed room.

Joe Novotny, House reading clerk: It ran the whole spectrum of people being emotionally just distraught and overwhelmed. There's a lot of anger. There were members dropping F bombs, and I had never heard them swear. And they were livid. They weren't afraid; they were pissed. And then there were staffers, I think, who were just kind of stunned. There was a certain degree of numbness for everybody, but I would say though a little bit of relief to be in a more controlled environment for some.

Jen Daulby and other staff were counting members to make sure they had 218 votes in case they needed to certify the election outside the chamber.

Jen Daulby, Republican staff director, House Administration Committee: We needed to control the numbers. That was my first thought—do we have a House right now? Did we have 218 members? If not, we risk not having a branch of government. We needed 218 members in a secure location, and the Capitol complex was not secure for several hours.

Thomas Wickham, former House parliamentarian and senior adviser to the parliamentarian: There were many, many objections that were in the queue. And everybody had said, the seriousness of this situation—let's try and reduce, if not eliminate, the amount of objections so we can be done with this.

There was little food or water, and people weren't sure how safe it was to venture out.

Joe Novotny, House reading clerk: Somebody found Goldfish crackers, so that was like a hot commodity. At one point, a few people had some Skittles, and that was like a thing for a moment. People were like, "Where did you get the Skittles?" It became like, you're on a desert island, a coconut falls from a palm tree, and everybody's diving for the coconut.

Because the top leaders from both parties had been whisked off campus, Democratic Rep. Hakeem Jeffries and Republican Rep. Liz Cheney realized they were the two highest-ranking members of leadership in the room. Jeffries was the chairman of the House Democratic caucus, and Cheney was the chairwoman of the House GOP conference, so both were used to leading meetings.

Rep. Liz Cheney, R-WY: We decided very early on, we're making all of our announcements jointly. This isn't partisan.

Rep. Hakeem Jeffries, D-NY: The second time we spoke together, Congresswoman Cheney and I made the determination that we were going to communicate the message that we were going to go back to the Capitol. Once the chamber had been secured, mob rule was not going to prevail, the rule of law was going to prevail. And we were going to complete our constitutional responsibilities that evening. And when I delivered that message, much to my surprise, the entire room erupted in applause both from Democrats and from Republicans. It was an American moment.

Speaker Nancy Pelosi and Majority Leader Steny Hoyer returned to the Capitol from Fort McNair around 7 p.m. and addressed the House members gathered in the secure location. Pelosi told them they would soon go back to the chamber and certify the election, and the rioters' "purpose will not be filled."[1]

Terri McCullough, chief of staff, House Speaker Nancy Pelosi: She went straight into that room and into the spot to speak without stopping.

Joe Novotny, House reading clerk: That was to me the defining moment of the day. It became this moment of us realizing, like, no, we're not going to go home. We're public servants, and we have a much bigger duty to fulfill right now. And so [Pelosi] gave a really, really powerful speech. She basically said what happened today is unacceptable, it's an atrocity, and we are in a position now where things are somewhat under control. People are cleaning up the building. People are getting everything ready that needs to be ready, and we are going back and we are going to finish our work. And we have to show the world that democracy today prevailed and that we are not going to back down.

House Majority Leader Steny Hoyer, D-MD: I essentially said, "We've had an insurrection. I know all of you have been traumatized, but we are committed to finishing our work tonight." And I said, "You are now the defenders of democracy. We are the defenders of democracy. Staying on post is very, very important."

Joe Novotny, House reading clerk: I compared [Pelosi] to your mother coming home with dad and being like, you're going to eat your vegetables, you're doing your homework, and you are finishing every chore that you have to do and then you get to go to bed, but not until then. Steny by comparison is like the father who gives you a hug and says, listen to your mother, but just remember we still love you. Because his speech was, we know you want to go home. We know you want to be with your families. We know that you want to get to your life. But we cannot do this without you. It was so powerful. In that moment I was like, let's fucking go. Let's do this. It was more than just ceremony at that point.

After Pelosi spoke, Terri McCullough spotted their staff who had been trapped in the conference room while rioters ransacked the office. They sat at a table off to the side.

Alisa La, special assistant to House Speaker Nancy Pelosi: We had an exhausted and angry energy. It was crowded, which was frustrating for COVID-19 purposes. There are a bunch of members not wearing masks. We found an open table and plopped down, reunited with our other Pelosi staff.

Henry Connelly, communications director, House Speaker Nancy Pelosi: When we arrive, the first thing that I see is [Rep.] Lisa Blunt Rochester trying to get the MAGA caucus folks to put on a damn mask. And all of them smirking at her and declining.

Alisa La, special assistant to House Speaker Nancy Pelosi: The speaker came and talked to us. I had no idea what she knew, and we're all like, just messed up. I don't really remember what she said; it's kind of a blur. But I think she asked if we were okay. And my instinct is never to worry her. We were just like, "Yes, we're all good." She could tell we were not.

House Speaker Nancy Pelosi, D-CA: They were so frightened. I've never seen any of them quite like that, or anyone quite like that. Their lives were threatened.

Terri McCullough, chief of staff, House Speaker Nancy Pelosi: I don't know that they had the capacity to even talk about it at that point.

House Speaker Nancy Pelosi, D-CA: The one thing that I've never forgiven them for is the trauma they caused for the staff—the young, idealistic people who come to work in Washington. And to have them have to hide under a table in the dark with furniture pushed up against the door, not speaking for hours.

Terri McCullough, chief of staff, House Speaker Nancy Pelosi: She knew where they had been and what they had undergone, but I'm not sure it actually hit her until she saw them.

House Speaker Nancy Pelosi, D-CA: I mean, we care about the dignity of the office and the respect for some of the old stuff that is there, but what we really cared about was the staff.

Alisa La, special assistant to House Speaker Nancy Pelosi: Our trek back to the Capitol was very eye-opening. Floors were covered with broken glass; there was a powdery film of pepper spray. In the Capitol Visitor Center, we saw MPD SWAT units completely wiped out and exhausted. These huge guys had just been to war. Sweat and water to clear the pepper spray streaming down their faces. Some of them were just laying on the ground to catch their breath. We walked by saying "Thank you." That was definitely not enough. I knew they were the ones that ultimately saved us.

Henry Connelly, communications director, House Speaker Nancy Pelosi: The thing that I remember walking back was how many different kinds of SWAT teams there were. All of these different agencies, all of these different entities represented. Just the biggest guys with the biggest weapons lying around, like, exhausted. I came back to the press office, and there were like eight huge SWAT team guys sprawled on the floor outside my office. And so I thought, well, I'm in pretty good shape.

Alisa La, special assistant to House Speaker Nancy Pelosi: We got back to the office and were greeted with a destroyed kitchen, toppled-over gifts that the speaker received over the years, a smashed mirror in her office. And on my desk was a folder with the words "you will never take this country" written on it. They stole her gavels, her Yogi Berra baseball, my notebook. We had work to do, so we pushed on.

Pelosi's suite had been completely ransacked. The rioters took the sign over the front door and stole the office laptop used for Zoom meetings. Richard "Bigo" Barnett, an Arkansas man who was holding a ten-pound flagpole and a stun device capable of delivering 950,000 volts of electricity, sat down at Emily Berret's desk and put his feet up for a photo, thinking it was Pelosi's desk. He left a note: "Hey Nancy, Bigo was here you biotch."[2]

Emily Berret, director of operations, House Speaker Nancy Pelosi: So the first thing I did was I moved my chair into the hallway and decided to have a standing desk because there was blood on the chair. There was blood on the flag on the credenza and on my desk. So I started cleaning, found some Lysol wipes and started wiping everything down.

Terri McCullough, chief of staff, House Speaker Nancy Pelosi: There was, like, just total destruction. Weirdly, I had closed the doors to my office, and they just never went in. But every other room had been looted.

Emily Berret, director of operations, House Speaker Nancy Pelosi: There were also two picture frames that had been pulled down from the wall that had some swear words written on them.

Jamie Fleet, Democratic staff director, House Administration Committee: I've seen her greet world leaders in that space. I've been there when she's made difficult phone calls of national consequence and talked to presidents. I've observed her in that room on the phone with President Trump himself. As have the staff for other speakers. You know, it's a very special place in our country. For Congress, it's the equivalent of the Oval Office. And it was violated.

Rep. Liz Cheney, R-WY: As we were leaving the secure location, one of my daughters called me. She's pretty tough. And as soon as I picked up the phone and she heard my voice, she just burst into tears. And she said, "My God, Mom, I've seen all of this coverage of the people attacking the Capitol." And that was one of the first moments of realizing, putting the pieces together, of how violent this was.

Rep. Rodney Davis, R-IL, compared the aftermath of the attack to four years earlier, when Louisiana Rep. Steve Scalise, a member of GOP leadership, had been shot along with several others at an early-morning practice for a charity baseball game. Davis was there when it happened, and the game went on the next day as Scalise lay in the hospital in critical condition.

Rep. Rodney Davis, R-IL: Our goal, just like after the baseball shooting that I experienced, was to play the game. Get this done and show the American people that we're not going to stand for this stuff. So immediately when I could, I left and went over to the Capitol.

Jen Daulby, Republican staff director, House Administration Committee: I remember there were just flags and stuff everywhere. And our officers were just downing water. And Rodney came by and shook their hands, and they were very cold towards him. I remember thinking, gosh, they are so mad at all of us. It wasn't because of Rodney, because he's so kind. And I don't think the rank and file would have known if he was a Republican or a Democrat. They just knew that they had gotten the shit beat out of them.

Rep. Rodney Davis, R-IL: I saw my good friend Harry Dunn, who'd been fighting with Capitol Police officers. I gave him a big hug and saw the tear gas residue.

Jen Daulby, Republican staff director, House Administration Committee: I think they did not feel that they were staffed correctly and had the leadership they deserved on that day. I think it was more like, you guys left us out there with this mob. And it must have been nice to have been on the inside. We all have a lot of guilt about that.

Rep. Markwayne Mullin, R-OK: I went and checked on all the Capitol Police, and I saw fifty guys at least, men and women, uniform and nonuniform, and shook their hands. There were broken noses, busted-up faces, broken arms, busted heads. I saw one guy with his eye completely gouged out, literally, and they were trying to evacuate him. I saw guys that were hyperventilating, I saw guys that got hit with pepper spray. And I thought, you know, you just think about this. They showed so much restraint. They weren't afraid to put their bodies in harm's way. They weren't cowards. They stood the line and took a beating.

Joe Novotny, House reading clerk: When we got back to the chamber, the custodians were cleaning and sweeping up glass and buffing the floors. And they had the biggest smiles on their faces when they saw us. They're heroes to me. They are true heroes.

Jen Daulby, Republican staff director, House Administration Committee: There's so many people that run that institution, and they had the whole thing cleaned up.

When it was finally time for senators to return to the chamber, they were accompanied by a massive police presence, unlike when they had evacuated.

Sen. Catherine Cortez Masto, D-NV: I walked back to the Senate floor in the evening of January 6 to finish my work. I'll remember what I saw the rest of my life. As I walked back, furniture had been thrown everywhere like matchsticks. Trash, broken glass littered the floor.

Sen. Susan Collins, R-ME: There were tactical teams and FBI agents, National Guard, all heavily armed with riot gear on. Our entire pathway was lined.

Paul Kane, reporter, *The Washington Post*: Staff and reporters went out first in the sort of walking caravan back to the Senate. We're walking, obviously the [underground] subway wasn't working at that point. Then we could hear some commotion behind us, and it was Senate parliamentarian staff carrying the electoral boxes. A couple of us yelled, like, "Clear the way"—just like, "Lead us home." And they went to the front of the line and marched over. And I remember I took a picture and tweeted out that the Electoral College certificates were being marched back to the Senate. And it's probably the most viral thing that I've ever tweeted.

Andrew Taylor, reporter, The Associated Press: Parliamentarian Elizabeth MacDonough is a beloved figure in the tight-knit Senate family. She and her colleagues had made sure the Electoral College certificates were safe—their seizure by the mob actually would have delayed the certification of the result—and she was supervising their return to the chamber. I'm not sure if MacDonough knew by then, but her office on the first floor of the Capitol was trashed.

Sen. Dick Durbin, D-IL: It was almost like coming home from vacation to find out your home has been burglarized. It just feels different.

The security of your home has been violated, and it's never going to quite be the same. The same thing with the Senate.

Sen. Susan Collins, R-ME: There were all these fingerprints and things tossed out of my desk. It was very creepy and threatening.

After returning from the loading dock, Pence was back in his office off the Senate chamber. Chaplain Black visited him there, hours after sharing his foreboding vision with him.

Senate Chaplain Barry Black: I went down to his office, and he said, "When this ends, and it shall end—and the votes are validated, I want you to give a benediction." And with the kind of relationship that we had, he said, "Whatever the Holy Spirit tells you to say, I want you to say it."

8:00 p.m.

Pence opened the Senate at 8:06 p.m., six hours after it had abruptly recessed, to resume debate over the objection to Arizona's electors. Sitting in his chair, occupied by rioters just hours before, the vice president gave opening remarks:

> Today was a dark day in the history of the United States Capitol, but thanks to the swift efforts of U.S. Capitol Police, federal, state, and local law enforcement, the violence was quelled, the Capitol is secured, and the people's work continues. We condemn the violence that took place here in the strongest possible terms. We grieve the loss of life that took place in these hallowed halls, as well as the injuries suffered by those who defended our Capitol today. And we will always be grateful to the men and women who stayed at their posts to defend this historic place. To those who wreaked havoc in our Capitol today, you did not win. Violence never wins. Freedom wins. And this is still the people's house. As we reconvene in this chamber, the world will again witness the resilience and strength of our democracy, for even in the wake of unprecedented violence and vandalism at this Capitol, the elected representatives of the people of the United States have assembled

> again on the very same day to support and defend the Constitution of the United States. So may God bless the lost, the injured, and the heroes forged on this day. May God bless all who serve here and those who protect this place. And may God bless the United States of America. Let's get back to work.

Marc Short, chief of staff, Vice President Pence: We needed permission from Leader McConnell to afford him the chance to give some remarks to the top. And Leader McConnell consented to that. So when we came back in, the vice president was able to speak to the nation from that Senate chamber.

Senators from both parties stood and clapped after Pence's remarks, which he had written with suggestions from his family. Mitch McConnell, who would serve as majority leader for a few more days before Democrats officially took the Senate, then spoke:

> I want to say to the American people, the United States Senate will not be intimidated. We will not be kept out of this chamber by thugs, mobs, or threats. We will not bow to lawlessness or intimidation. We are back at our posts. We will discharge our duty under the Constitution and for our nation, and we are going to do it tonight.

McConnell added,

> This failed attempt to obstruct the Congress, this failed insurrection, only underscores how crucial the task before us is for our republic.

As debate over Arizona's electors resumed, South Carolina Sen. Lindsey Graham, one of Trump's closest allies in Congress, gave an emotional and animated speech taking down Cruz's idea for an election audit. The 1877 commission "ain't going to work," he said. "To the conservatives who believe in the Constitution, now is your chance to stand up and be counted," Graham said.

Graham also reflected on his relationship with Trump:

> Trump and I, we've had a hell of a journey. I hate it being this way. Oh, my God, I hate it. From my point of view, he has been a consequential president. But today, the first thing you will see, all I can say is, count me out. Enough is enough. I tried to be helpful.

Sen. Lindsey Graham, R-SC: It was important for me to make sure the process was brought to a conclusion that day, to not let this effort interrupt the process and be successful. That was my main focus.

Sen. Tim Kaine, D-VA: Lindsey, who's a great lawyer, got up and gave a very effective and somewhat humorous and pithy and short but effective rebuttal to Cruz's argument.

Sen. Angus King, I-ME: Lindsey Graham famously said, "I'm through." That lasted about two weeks.

Sen. Amy Klobuchar, D-MN: It was an incredible night of speeches.

While most senators were ready to vote to reject the challenge to Arizona's results, a few were not. Missouri Sen. Josh Hawley was still planning to object later in the night to Pennsylvania's electors. "This is the lawful place where those objections and concerns should be heard," he said on the floor ahead of the vote on Arizona, previewing his objection.

Sen. Angus King, I-ME: It was tense, and it was unclear, even then, how people were going to vote on these foolish challenges.

Officer Brian Sicknick found medical help and seemed to recover after the rioter had sprayed him with chemicals on the West Front. At 8:21 p.m., he sent his brother Ken another text: "Fuck. I smell like BO, weed, OC spray and CS gas."[1]

Shortly after sending the text, as he returned to a division office in the basement of the Capitol, Sicknick started slurring his words while talking to fellow officers and collapsed. He was rushed to the hospital, where he was put on life support.

Inspector Thomas Loyd, US Capitol Police: Officer Brian Sicknick faithfully served the United States Capitol Police for thirteen years. He fought valiantly for several hours on January 6. He died suddenly at 8:30 p.m., while returning to the office in the United States Capitol Building. His body survived an additional day because his fellow officers worked so hard to keep him alive so his family could say goodbye in person on January 7.

Gladys Sicknick, mother of Capitol Police Officer Brian Sicknick: Brian's girlfriend, Sandy, called me, and I was upstairs, and she says, "Well, I have to go to the hospital, Brian is in the hospital." She had no idea how bad he was. I was shaking.

Gladys drove down from New Jersey to Washington the next morning. Ken, who thought his brother probably had just had a bad reaction to the chemicals, stayed at home, as did Brian's brother Craig. But Gladys called the rest of the family that afternoon and told them to come right away.

Craig Sicknick, brother of Capitol Police Officer Brian Sicknick: I got a call from my mother telling us to come down to DC. So myself, Kenny, and my father all hopped into one car and headed down there, not knowing what to expect at that point. Until we got halfway down the New Jersey Turnpike and we started getting calls from reporters all over the place, and we found out my brother was dead.

Ken Sicknick, brother of Capitol Police Officer Brian Sicknick: The reporter's first sentence was "My condolences," and I'm like, "Your condolences for what?"

Ken called his mother, who was already in Washington, and she had talked to staff at the hospital.

Ken Sicknick, brother of Capitol Police Officer Brian Sicknick: She called me back saying, "No, he's still alive." But I think he was already dead, and somebody leaked it to the press, and the press knew before we did.

Three months later, the Washington medical examiner's office would say that Sicknick, forty-two, had died of natural causes after suffering two strokes near the base of his brain stem.[2] *In an interview with* The Washington Post, *Medical Examiner Francisco J. Diaz said the strokes were caused by a clot in an artery.*

Inspector Thomas Loyd, US Capitol Police: Despite the official medical report, there was nothing natural about the way Officer Sicknick died.

Diaz told the Post *that Sicknick had engaged with rioters on January 6th, and "all that transpired played a role in his condition."*[3]

Inspector Thomas Loyd, US Capitol Police: Officer Howie Liebengood perished two days later when he took his own life. It is tough enough to bury any of my colleagues, but when the cause is suicide, it makes it that much more heartbreaking. Officer Liebengood faithfully served the department for sixteen years. He was fifty-one years old.

Sen. Tim Kaine, D-VA: Three days after that attack of January 6, Howie went to his home in Virginia. His wife, Serena, asked if he was doing okay. She could tell he was under enormous stress, and he said he just needed to sleep. And Howie went upstairs and, using his own service revolver, ended his life. Howie Liebengood would be alive today if President Trump hadn't urged people to gather to do something wild in Washington, DC, on January 6, 2021, and then urged those gathering to go up and raise hell at the Capitol.

Another officer who was at the Capitol on January 6th, Officer Jeffrey Smith of the MPD, also died by suicide in the days following the attack. In the months afterward, the Metropolitan Police said two more of their officers who had responded to the insurrection, Kyle DeFreytag and Gunther Hashida, had also died by suicide.[4]

Four of the rioters died, including Ashli Babbitt. Kevin Greeson and Benjamin Philips suffered medical emergencies in the crowd. Rosanne Boyland died of an overdose of amphetamines in her system, the medical examiner ruled. She collapsed outside the Lower West Terrace Tunnel amid the packed crowd that was fighting police as her friend called for help, leading many to believe she had been trampled.

At least 140 officers were injured—some seriously.[5]

Officer Jesse Leasure, Metropolitan Police Department: My platoon, CDU 42, suffered the most casualties that day. We were at less than 50 percent strength the next day. No one else got messed up as much as we did. We sent a van to the hospital filled with officers.

Officer Daniel Hodges, Metropolitan Police Department: One of my sergeants, Sergeant Brian Peake, while fighting, maintaining control over the barricades on the West Terrace, was struck by a rioter and fractured and severely lacerated his right index finger. He kept in the fight for several more hours after that and just put some tape on it, a napkin, and went back to work. He was there for several hours before finally accepting medical evac. He ended up having to have the tip of his finger removed.

Officer Jesse Leasure, Metropolitan Police Department: My sergeant, I was scared for him. He was acting kind of goofy and loopy. And I'm like, "I think he has a concussion." And he did. He was out of service for a very long time.

Officer Daniel Hodges, Metropolitan Police Department: Another officer who fought on the West Terrace and in the tunnels, instrumental to the defense, after being completely soaked with OC spray, was shocked several times by a cattle prod one of the terrorists brought with them.

Inspector Robert Glover, Metropolitan Police Department: I remember walking through the inside of the Capitol, and I just remember looking around, seeing a bunch of injured officers, both from Capitol and MPD, being treated by members of Fire and Emergency Medical Services, Office of Attending Physician, HHS [Department of Health and Human Services] doctors that are assigned to Park Police—they were there—and just the look of sheer exhaustion. You could smell that chemical munitions had been deployed inside as well. You could see the destruction.

Chief Robert Contee, Metropolitan Police Department: This was an assault on our democracy, and MPD officers held the line. Those seven hours, between the urgent call for help from the Capitol Police to MPD and the resumption of work by both houses of Congress, will be indelibly etched on the memories of every law enforcement officer who was on the scene, as it is undoubtedly in the minds of the elected officials, congressional staff, and other Capitol employees who were forced to seek safety behind locked doors. During the height of the incident, approximately 850 MPD members were at the Capitol, and by the day's end, an additional estimate of 250 had been in the area to directly support the response and aftermath.

Assistant Chief Yogananda Pittman, US Capitol Police: At the end of the day, the USCP succeeded in its mission. It protected congressional leadership. It protected members. And it protected the democratic process. At the end of a battle that lasted for hours, democracy prevailed.

Officer Jesse Leasure, Metropolitan Police Department: I was still burning from the OC, and every time I stopped moving, I started to sweat and it reactivated. So I had to keep moving, and I'm walking around, and I'm snapping pictures of everything. I walked into one of the ravaged little snack bars, and I'm like, I'm really hungry and I'm really thirsty. I want to take this, but I don't want to steal. And thankfully, there was an electronic option. It was one of those stupidly surreal moments when I saw officers come in, grab something, and pay for it. The whole world, as far as we know, has just gone fucked, and there's still officers going to snack bars that have already been ravaged. We could take whatever the hell we wanted, and they're still paying for snacks and drinks. And I still had my debit card, so I paid for it.

Officer Daniel Hodges, Metropolitan Police Department: I started feeling the effects of the day taking their toll, and I went back inside to rest. Gradually all the members of CDU 42 gathered in the room known as the Capitol Crypt. We checked on each other and convalesced, glad to see each other in one piece. Despite our exhaustion, we all would have ran out to the fight again should the need have arisen. Thankfully, as the day wore on, more and more resources arrived at the Capitol to drive off the terrorists. We stayed in the Crypt until quite late.

Officer Adam Eveland, Metropolitan Police Department: I didn't know they were in the tunnel or how bad it was. If it weren't for them in that tunnel, I'm pretty sure the whole thing would have fallen apart.

Officer Jesse Leasure, Metropolitan Police Department: I saw people from the Capitol architect doing measurements to replace everything and some people picking up the trash and whatnot. And I was in awe. I'm doing my job; that's what I'm here for. We all were a part of this. I'm in awe of the janitor who had to clean up afterwards. I'm in awe of the architects who were coming in and just fixing shit. Everybody was an important part of that day.

Officer Winston Pingeon, US Capitol Police: There was just stuff everywhere, littered—Trump signs, shoes, crutches.

Capitol Police Officer Harry Dunn had spent most of his day inside the building trying to push people out. At one point, he said, a crowd of people were screaming at him, "Boo! Fucking nigger!"

Officer Harry Dunn, US Capitol Police: Once the building was cleared, I went to the Rotunda to recover with other officers and share our experiences from that afternoon. I sat down on a bench with a friend of mine who is also a Black Capitol Police officer and told him about the racial slurs I had endured. I became very emotional and began yelling, "How the fuck can something like this happen? Is this America?" I began sobbing, and officers came over to console me.

9:00 p.m.

An hour after the Senate went into session, Speaker Nancy Pelosi opened the House:

> Today, a shameful assault was made on our democracy. It cannot, however, deter us from our responsibility to validate the election of Joe Biden and Kamala Harris. For that reason, Congress has returned to the Capitol. We always knew that this responsibility would take us into the night, and we will stay as long as it takes. Our purpose will be accomplished. We must, and we will, show to the country, and indeed to the world, that we will not be diverted from our duty, that we will respect our responsibility to the Constitution and to the American people.

Rep. Andy Kim, D-NJ: When they first gaveled back in, I was there. And I remember it was the quietest I'd ever heard the chamber. Everyone was talking in whispers. It felt like it was a funeral, where you don't raise your voice. Everyone was just somber, hugging each other. I remember seeing the broken glass still on the center doors where the guns were drawn. And that was profound, just given that those are the doors that the president walks through for the State of the Union. I sat really close to the center aisle, not for any particular reason, but that's just where I sat. And I was kind of wondering what was going to happen next. I was wondering what the tone would be. And there was actually a part of me that believed that maybe people would realize that we've gone too far. Maybe they were just going to drop these debates and we would certify and leave and just have the country move on. And the first few speeches gave me some sense that maybe we could.

In emotional remarks, Republican Leader Kevin McCarthy stood on the House floor and said that "now is the time to show America that we can work best together." He said, "Mobs don't rule America. Laws rule America." And he thanked Democratic Rep. Jason Crow, Republican Rep. Markwayne Mullin, and other members for helping keep the chamber safe earlier in the day:

> Madam Speaker, I rise to address what happened in this Chamber today and where do we go from here. The violence, destruction, and chaos we saw earlier was unacceptable, undemocratic, and un-American. It was the saddest day I have ever had serving as a member of this institution. The Capitol was in chaos. Police officers were attacked. Guns were drawn on this very floor. A woman tragically lost her life. No one wins when this building and what it stands for are destroyed. America, and this institution, is better than that. We saw the worst of America this afternoon. Yet, in the midst of violence and fear, we also saw the best of America. It starts with our law enforcement—the Capitol Police, the National Guard, the FBI, and the Secret Service—who faced the most difficult challenges but did their duty with confidence and strength. Many of them are injured right now. It also extends to this chamber, where both Democrats and Republicans showed courage, calm, and resolve.

But the appeals for unity wouldn't last. Shortly afterward, McCarthy cast a vote in favor of the objection to Arizona's votes, still siding with Trump's efforts to overturn the election.

Rep. Liz Cheney, R-WY: I was disgusted. Once it became clear a couple of minutes, or even just a minute into Kevin's remarks, what he was doing, I left the chamber. I didn't want to be sitting there. I was very angry.

Several Republicans went to the floor to echo Trump's claims of widespread fraud in the election. Others went even further, such as Florida Rep. Matt Gaetz, a fiercely loyal Trump ally, who cited an erroneous report that there was evidence that some of the rioters were antifa, or antifascists:[1]

> I don't know if the reports are true, but *The Washington Times* has just reported some pretty compelling evidence from a facial recognition company showing that some of the people who breached the Capitol today were not Trump supporters. They were masquerading as Trump supporters, and, in fact, were members of the violent terrorist group antifa. Now, we should seek to build America up, not tear her down and destroy her. And I am sure glad that, at least for one day, I didn't hear my Democrat colleagues calling to defund the police.

Gaetz also referred to the standing ovation that Rep. Jamie Raskin had received earlier in the day as members expressed condolences for the death of his son just a week earlier. For Raskin, who had hoped earlier that the momentary, bipartisan outpouring for his son could bring the chamber together, Gaetz's speech was an awful moment.

Rep. Jamie Raskin, D-MD: It just made me feel just cheap and beleaguered to be part of this process. And I thought about how ridiculous it was that I thought that somehow the sympathy that was shown could be like a bridge to a different way of relating. But it wasn't, and it just became in the hands of some people—it's just an excuse or a kind of emotional alibi. There were a lot of very honest and sincere condolences and sympathy that I got. But there was a political strategy that was being hatched and executed.

House Speaker Nancy Pelosi, D-CA: They knew right away this was a very horrible thing for our country, and they could not—they wanted to not have any tattoo of it on them, so they say "antifa," which they knew wasn't true. Not to defend antifa and what they do, but this was not anything that they did.

Republican Rep. Adam Kinzinger of Illinois felt intense rage after hearing Gaetz mention antifa. He spoke briefly on the floor:

> Here in this chamber after the events today, some speeches have been shockingly tone-deaf. I have seen people applaud cheap political lines that are embarrassing. Power and cultural fights have divided us so much that they are the ultimate goal now, and sometimes the oath we swear to uphold feels like a prop. People have been lied to by too many for too long. So here is the truth: Joe Biden won this election, the effort will fail, and everybody knows it.

Rep. Adam Kinzinger, R-IL: I just remember the dead silence when I was done. And I was surprised by that. Typically, you hear little reactions in the crowd; you could be speaking about anything. And dead silence. I turned around, and all of my colleagues in the Republican side had their heads down. And I realized this is going to be a little harder than it seems.

Alisa La, special assistant to House Speaker Nancy Pelosi: Their heads were down. It was like they were ashamed. The energy was really weird in there. When [Kinzinger] walked out, nobody said anything to him.

10:00 p.m.

After the emotional debate, the Senate rejected the challenge to Arizona's electors, 93-6.[1] *A few Republican senators, including Oklahoma Sen. Jim Lankford, abandoned their plans to call for a delay in the count and instead voted to certify Biden's win.*

Sen. James Lankford, R-OK: My decision to be able to change my vote after the riot was the obvious sense of, we are exceptionally loud and combustible as a country right now. We need to do everything we can to turn the volume down and to be able to make sure people understand we're going to be a functioning democracy that's not going to do things based on violence.

Sen. Tim Kaine, D-VA: A lot of us were really relieved, because even if we have political differences, I think a lot of us have a lot of personal regard for James Lankford as a person of principle. We always thought, as we looked at those objecting, it was like, who doesn't belong in this group?

Sen. James Lankford, R-OK: So my decision to switch was to say, okay, I'm not going to get the commission. That's not going to happen, and that's obvious. We still need to work on these issues in the days ahead, but right now is not the time to be able to do it. Right now is the time for unity as a nation.

Several other senators who had planned to bring up objections or support them also changed their minds, including Sen. Kelly Loeffler, who had been defeated the day before in Georgia's runoff election, and Indiana Sen. Mike Braun, who told reporters that night that "today changed things drastically. Whatever point you made before, that should suffice."[2] *Others, including Cruz and Hawley, still voted to reject Arizona's legitimate votes. And Hawley was still determined to object to Pennsylvania's electors later in the night—meaning that they would have to have another debate and vote.*

Sen. Bob Casey, D-PA: It was very tense. I was angry, I think we were all angry. I think people on both sides were pretty angry.

Sen. Mike Rounds, R-SD: While there were a few folks that were still doing their best to make their objection known, it was very clear that this was going to proceed, and that we understood the gravity, the seriousness of that day and how close we came to having a true successful insurrection. I remember thinking that—how close, and thinking at that point, you know, we talk about other countries and about young democracies struggling, and here we are with all these years. And somehow it would appear that we let our guard down. And when we let our guard down, it's our job to bring this back to reality again. It's our job to get this back on the straight and narrow again. And to set an example. And the historical consequences I think weighed very heavily on everybody in that room.

In statements and interviews with local news outlets, Republicans almost universally condemned the violence. On a call with South Dakota reporters, Republican Sen. John Thune said that "this kind of thuggery is not going to keep us from doing the people's work."

Asked about Trump's culpability and the falsehoods surrounding the election, Thune said that "when you sow the wind, you're going to reap the whirlwind."

"It's time for it to stop," Thune said. "It's time for the madness to stop."[3]

Igor Bobic's video of Doug Jensen chasing Capitol Police Officer Eugene Goodman up the Senate stairs quickly became one of the most shared images of the day.

Igor Bobic, reporter, HuffPost: I didn't tweet the video that went most viral until the very end, later, when I was in hiding. Because honestly, at the time, I just had no idea that it was going to be that viral. I had no idea what I had.

Doug Jensen, Iowa: I started getting messages that I'm a traitor and I'm going to jail. I was just trying to come home to go back to my normal job and my family. And next thing I know, my phone's blowing up—"You're famous."

Igor Bobic, reporter, HuffPost: People immediately started asking me, "Can we share this?" I started getting bombarded by press requests. I stayed up all night; I didn't sleep. I did *Good Morning America* the next morning. All of these foreign reporters were reaching out to me, and I just told them all to use it. Use the video, just use it. Get it out there. I still get responses to it.

Pamela Hemphill, retired drug and alcohol counselor, Idaho: I walked three hours that night because I was lost. I was a mess. My head had been stepped on. I think I was still in shock.

Annie Howell, Pennsylvania: I went back to the hotel. I was in pretty bad shape, actually, just from the crowd and everything that was going on, like I had black eyes and a fat lip, and I was tear-gassed a bunch of times; really the whole crowd was.

Alondra Propes, former parole and probation officer, Oath Keepers, Florida: I think I was in tears when I left. It was just like a sinking feeling, just kind of like, you know, what now? You know, Biden is our president now.

Annie Howell, Pennsylvania: To me, it was devastating. I never expected what happened to happen that day. So the way that I saw it at the time was like, this is it. This is the end of our country. There's not going to be a republic anymore. It's going to be a banana republic. We're going to go from capitalism to socialism, and this is it, really. I was really devastated at the time. I felt like, you know, what did I do wrong? Why was I tear-gassed? That, to me, I took really personally. But I don't know, I just—I went into a really deep depression after that.

Howell had been near the fighting in the Lower West Terrace Tunnel, briefly entering the building through a broken window.[4] *Propes, who was affiliated with the Oath Keepers, was on the Capitol grounds but never went inside. That night, she found out that the FBI had already posted a wanted list of some of the rioters, and someone in her group was on it.*

Alondra Propes, former parole and probation officer, Oath Keepers, Florida: I thought, uh-oh.

Some of the other Oath Keepers had a late-night dinner together at an Olive Garden in suburban Virginia. They were planning for the future, according to messages later released by prosecutors.[5]

"Patriots entering their own Capitol to send a message to the traitors is NOTHING compared to what's coming," wrote Stewart Rhodes, the group's founder, who had stood outside the Capitol while others in the group went inside.

"We aren't quitting!! We are reloading!!" wrote another member of the group.

In the coming days, Rhodes would try to get a message to Trump that he should not give up power. "If he's not going to do the right thing and he's just gonna let himself be removed illegally then we should have brought rifles," Rhodes said at the time. "We could have fixed it right then and there. I'd hang fucking Pelosi from the lamppost."[6]

Christopher Alberts, the rioter from Maryland who had rammed a wooden pallet into Officer Stephen Sherman, had been sidelined by the effects of the chemical spray and did not go into the Capitol. But he remained on the grounds and ranted at police. He was arrested that evening after an officer spotted his concealed gun under his clothes.[7] *Alberts hadn't tried to use his gun, but he told the police officers that the rioters would be back.*

Christopher Alberts, handyman and former National Guardsman, Maryland: I said, "Next time we come here, we're not going to be unarmed, and I can promise you that."

11:00 p.m.

The House easily rejected the Arizona challenge. But 121 Republicans, including House Republican Leader Kevin McCarthy, voted for it, even after the violence.[1] *Supporters of the objection included Oklahoma Rep. Markwayne Mullin and Texas Rep. Troy Nehls, who had defended the House doors just a few hours earlier.*

Rep. Markwayne Mullin, R-OK: I can sleep a lot better knowing that I tried.

Rep. Elise Stefanik, R-NY: Tens of millions of Americans are concerned that the 2020 election featured unconstitutional overreach by unelected state officials and judges ignoring state election laws. We can and we should peacefully and respectfully discuss these concerns.

House Speaker Nancy Pelosi, D-CA: The concern was that with all that they had seen, with all the violence that was descending upon the Capitol of the United States, all the crudeness and all the rest, that they still persisted in challenging and then overwhelmingly—led by their leadership—voted not to accept what happened.

Rep. Andy Kim, D-NJ: I just felt so disappointed. I was hoping for a defibrillator moment for our country, you know, like something that would shock us into some normal heart rhythm. And it was sad to not have that happen. I think that it was kind of this feeling of like, okay, if we can't unite after a pandemic, and after an insurrection of the Capitol—it just kind of hit home to me just how divided we are.

Frustrated with Republican votes in favor of the objection, Kim walked out of the House chamber after casting his vote. It was the first time he had come to the Capitol all day, since he had been huddled in the Rayburn House Office Building with his deputy chief of staff, Anthony DeAngelo.

He walked to the Rotunda, where he often liked to sit and take in the scenery during votes. What he found was a mess—a huge pile of trash next to a statue of Andrew Jackson, broken windows in the doors that led outside, furniture smashed and broken. He then noticed police officers holding trash bags, so he asked for one. He got down on the floor, wearing a new blue suit he had purchased for the day, and began cleaning up.

Rep. Andy Kim, D-NJ: I was just really affected emotionally. I felt this kind of heightened, kind of supercharged kind of patriotism that I just felt take over. When you see something you love that's broken, you want to fix it. I love the Capitol. I'm honored to be there. This building is extraordinary, and the Rotunda in particular is just awe-inspiring. How many countless generations have been inspired in that room?

Alongside the police officers and workers, Kim cleaned the Rotunda until there wasn't any more trash to pick up and then moved on to Statuary Hall and downstairs to the Crypt, the area immediately underneath the Rotunda. He was throwing away shattered glass, water bottles, and broken American flags. He found a small plastic eagle with the right wing broken off—probably a piece from the top of a flag—and put it in his pocket to keep.

Rep. Andy Kim, D-NJ: In the Rotunda, I actually found body armor, like a bulletproof vest. And I brought it to the officers, and I'm like, "Is this one of yours?" And they looked at it, and they said it was not something that would be issued to law enforcement. It had a serial number that actually shows you the date of purchase, and it was recent, so it was alarming that someone had bought this probably for coming here. They took that [as evidence]. I saw zip ties, that kind of stuff.

Rep. Tom Malinowski, D-NJ: There were a couple National Guardsmen, and I noticed somebody on his hands and knees leaning under a bench to pick something up. And it was Andy all by himself, just quietly removing debris and putting it in a plastic bag. He was clearly not doing it for an audience. It was for me the most poignant moment of the long night.

When Kim returned to the office, he didn't mention to his aide DeAngelo that he'd been tidying up the Rotunda. But within the hour, DeAngelo saw a photo of his boss on Twitter. Associated Press photographer Andrew Harnik had snapped a picture of him while he cleaned.

Anthony DeAngelo, deputy chief of staff for Andy Kim: It felt like a very contemplative moment. He didn't really say anything.

Andrew Harnik, photographer, The Associated Press: The images of him alone, quietly cleaning the building, were picked up by many publications in the days after and got a lot of attention. Artists and children around the country made art based on the photographs of Kim, and the Smithsonian Institution asked him to donate the suit he was wearing that day as part of its permanent collection.

Rep. Andy Kim, D-NJ: I think it was just a very tangible way for me to contribute somehow. I love this building so much, I didn't want it to be in such disrepair for one second longer than it needed to. My mom and my dad had brought me here when I was a kid, you know? They were immigrants; they were proud to take me here, show me the Capitol and show me the Rotunda. I remember as a kid thinking that it was the biggest room I'd ever seen in my life. It was just awe-inspiring, and it's just sad to me that this center point, this beautiful room where presidents lie in state, would become this battleground for hand-to-hand combat.

January 7, 2021

12:00 a.m.

After the votes on Arizona's electors failed, the tellers could finally start going through the rest of the states at a rapid clip—a process that normally takes a couple of hours. As they moved through some of the swing states that Biden had won, House Republicans stood and objected. But no senators joined until Pennsylvania.

At 12:14 a.m., almost twelve hours after the start of the session, Missouri Sen. Josh Hawley rose with Rep. Scott Perry, R-PA, and the clerk read their objection:

> We, a United States Senator and Members of the House of Representatives, object to the counting of the electoral votes of the State of Pennsylvania on the ground that they were not, under all of the known circumstances, regularly given.

Senate leaders had not been able to stop Hawley, but they did win one concession—he and others had agreed to allow the Senate to skip the two hours of debate. Senators returned to their chamber and went straight into a vote, ultimately rejecting the objection 92–7.[1]

The House would debate the objection for two more hours.

Jamie Fleet, Democratic staff director, House Administration Committee: It was really just an astonishing thing to be there. You're watching it happen with a broken window behind you, an exhausted police officer with stuff on their face, and the leadership's dignitary protection detail with their ties loosened and just beaten down—in some cases, literally beaten down.

1:00 a.m.

While the House debate continued, most senators were done for the night.

Sen. Amy Klobuchar, D-MN: The security people said everyone should go home except for me and Roy [Blunt], because we had to make that last walk with Pence.

Sen. Bob Casey, D-PA: They were offering to go from the building to your car, and they were offering rides home so that you'd have security. I chose not to because I figured I'm not the target that some people are. But I remember getting home that night, and your head is spinning from what you were just living through.

Sen. Tim Kaine, D-VA: As we're kind of getting off the floor at 1:30 or 2 a.m., everybody's adrenaline was still racing. And I have a hideaway that is often a gathering place for a lot of people. And I was just walking out, and I said to [New York Sen.] Kirsten Gillibrand, and Jess is her chief, "Why don't you just come over and have a drink." And we raised our glasses to the Constitution.

Sen. Susan Collins, R-ME: I was a bit nervous about trying to drive home. It was the wee hours of the morning, and I can never find a parking place that late. Also, I'd had so many demonstrations and abuse and threats at my house. My staff had all gone home, and I certainly was not going to ask someone to come back and drive me. So I was talking to Lisa Murkowski about it, and she invited me to spend the night at her house, which was very, very nice of her. I'll never forget walking into her house—her husband, Verne, was there, and he had two huge glasses of red wine, one for each of us, and a fire in the fireplace. We stayed up for hours just processing and talking about what had happened, because it was so incredible.

2:00 a.m.

As the House debated the Pennsylvania objection, tensions boiled over more than once. At one point, a physical fight almost broke out—Republicans and Democrats meeting in the aisle—after Pennsylvania Rep. Conor Lamb, a Democrat, said during the debate over his state's electoral votes that the violence of the day had been "inspired by lies—the same lies that you're hearing in this room tonight. And the members who are repeating those lies should be ashamed of themselves."

Members from both parties rushed to stop the altercation, Pelosi banged her gavel, and the two sides eventually backed off. But it was clear that the tragedy of the day wasn't going to bring people closer together—it would only divide them more.

At 2:30 a.m., the House started its last vote of the joint session. The objection to Pennsylvania's electoral votes was rejected, 282–138.[1]

3:00 a.m.

After the House vote on Pennsylvania, it was time for the senators, along with Pence, to return to the joint session one last time. The tellers quickly ran through the remaining states.

Sen. Amy Klobuchar, D-MN: We're walking back over, what had been this glorious walk in the morning, a celebration of democracy with a bunch of senators behind us, these pages with the mahogany boxes with all of the ballots in it. We made that walk, and this time there was no celebration, there's no glee, there's no pomp and circumstance. It was just silent. There were a few reporters around, cops obviously. We were walking over broken glass; there was spray paint on things. It was unbelievable.

With no additional challenges or votes expected, most lawmakers had gone home. But the four tellers and Pence remained, along with a handful of members, staff, and press in the upper gallery. They went through the final states very quickly, and Pence announced the final totals, including his own defeat:

> Joseph R. Biden, Jr., of the State of Delaware has received 306 votes. Donald J. Trump of the State of Florida has received 232

votes. The whole number of electors appointed to vote for Vice President of the United States is 538. Within that whole number, a majority is 270. The votes for Vice President of the United States are as follows: Kamala D. Harris of the State of California has received 306 votes. Michael R. Pence of the State of Indiana has received 232 votes.

Then he recognized Chaplain Black, who gave the benediction he had discussed with Pence earlier in the evening:

Lord of our lives and sovereign of our beloved nation, we deplore the desecration of the United States Capitol building, the shedding of innocent blood, the loss of life, and the quagmire of dysfunction that threaten our democracy. These tragedies have reminded us that words matter and that the power of life and death is in the tongue. We have been warned that eternal vigilance continues to be freedom's price. Lord, you have helped us remember that we need to see in each other a common humanity that reflects your image. You have strengthened our resolve to protect and defend the Constitution of the United States against all enemies domestic, as well as foreign. Use us to bring healing and unity to a hurting and divided nation and world. Thank you for what you have blessed our lawmakers to accomplish in spite of threats to liberty. Bless and keep us. Drive far from us all wrong desires, incline our hearts to do your will, and guide our feet on the path of peace. And God bless America.

At the conclusion of Black's prayer, Pelosi made the sign of the cross. And she reached over to "elbow bump" Pence. The House adjourned at 3:48 a.m.

House Speaker Nancy Pelosi, D-CA: I thanked him for his courage and his patriotism, because that's what it took.

Sen. Amy Klobuchar, D-MN: I thought he did the right thing. And he was solid throughout the whole disaster.

Marc Short, chief of staff, Vice President Pence: When we finally adjourned and headed our own ways, I remember texting the vice president a passage from 2 Timothy 4:7: "I fought the good fight, I finished the race, I have kept the faith."

House Speaker Nancy Pelosi, D-CA: Lincoln built this dome during the civil war. People said, "Save the steel and the manpower for the war." And Lincoln said, "No, we have to show our resilience to the world, so we're going to finish the dome." And to see that dome have Confederate flags and even Nazi imagery—all that stuff under Lincoln's dome. Well, as he finished the dome, we had to finish the mission and be on that floor that night.

Rep. Zoe Lofgren, D-CA: The tellers had to stay and sign things. I didn't get back to my residence in DC until after 3 a.m. That's when I knew that I was safe.

Rep. Adam Kinzinger, R-IL: As I'm heading home, as I'm exiting the garage, I saw my first National Guard troops. And as a National Guardsman myself, and having, you know, sat there, hoping they would show up for hours, that was a real relief. And a real sense of pride. I was very proud of the Guard at that moment.

Rep. Liz Cheney, R-WY: I got home very early the next morning, and at that moment, I was thinking, I think so many of us were—like, okay, this is it. Nobody can do what Donald Trump has just done. I just assumed, this is it; he's over.

Rep. Jamie Raskin, D-MD: Everybody had undergone this wrenching trauma, and I just remember staggering home and upstairs and into bed. And my wife asked me what happened. I said, "Well, we ended up counting the votes and Biden won, but they tried a coup."

Joe Novotny, House reading clerk: The city was locked down, and I had to walk home. I didn't see a single human being. Not a car. Nothing.

No sign of life. Anywhere. It was really bizarre. None of it felt real. It's like the end of a dream.

Emily Cochrane, congressional reporter, *The New York Times*: The Capitol is not a very tactile, emotional place. In fact, I think for some people, it's a means of surviving—the political brawling is to kind of be above it all. And I just remember that night, you're hugging people: "What happened? Are you all right?" Because I think that was the first inclination that everyone had such a different experience based on just luck of the draw, where they happened to be that day. We were all in this same kind of frozen emotional state. I couldn't bring myself to leave until it was over, and then I carpooled home with another reporter. And I just remember coming home and there was my cat, like, "Where have you been?"

Associated Press photographers Julio Cortez and John Minchillo were worried about going back to their hotel that night, as it had been packed with protesters when they left that morning and they were still shaken by the assault on Minchillo. So they slept in the AP's downtown bureau. Before he fell asleep, Cortez looked through the photos that his colleagues from the AP and other outlets had taken that day.

Julio Cortez, photographer, The Associated Press: It made me really proud to be able to be part of history. Like, okay, it was a tough day today, but we did our job. And now we're back in a safe place. And so that ultimately talked me out of quitting this job. The day shook me in many ways.

Chad Pergram, senior congressional correspondent, Fox News: As a journalist, you never want to be part of the story, but in this case, I also feel like this kind of happened to me and it happened to my workplace.

Terri McCullough, chief of staff, House Speaker Nancy Pelosi: We were there until four o'clock. I walked home. I'm not sure I slept at all.

Alisa La, special assistant to House Speaker Nancy Pelosi: I walked the speaker out to her car. She begged us not to come in tomorrow. And I told her, if she's coming in, we're all coming in.

Henry Connelly, communications director, House Speaker Nancy Pelosi: One of the people who was in the conference room with us carpooled everybody home, and she dropped me off at my apartment, and my wife—my fiancée at the time—was awake, and we took some pictures as proof of life to send off to my family.

Alisa La, special assistant to House Speaker Nancy Pelosi: I drove home and got there around 4 a.m. I was scared that someone might have followed me home, so I just sat in the car, and the coast was clear. I remember following up on memos for the next day right before sleeping.

Sergeant Aquilino Gonell, US Capitol Police: After order finally had been restored at the Capitol and after many exhausting hours, I arrived home at nearly 4 a.m. on January 7. I had to push away my wife from hugging me because of all the chemicals that covered my body. I couldn't sleep because the chemicals reactivated after I took a shower, and my skin was still burning. I finally fell asleep two hours later, completely physically and mentally exhausted.

Early Morning

After finishing the session, Klobuchar and Blunt stayed in the Capitol to survey the damage.

Sen. Amy Klobuchar, D-MN: The sun's starting to come up, and that was our goal, so that when America woke up, it was done. Can you imagine if after an insurrection we were still fighting over who won?

Sen. Roy Blunt, R-MO: She and I walked back across with a couple of staffers who were with us, and we looked around a little more closely than we had before.

Sen. Amy Klobuchar, D-MN: So then we walk out, and Roy looks at me, and the sun is coming through the window, and in that very understated Roy Blunt way, he goes, "Good job, and see you tomorrow."

Sen. Roy Blunt, R-MO: When we were over in the other building, I thought it was a terrible moment for the world as they looked at our country because the transition of power is one of the things we do best. What a needless black eye for the country. But we got our work done, where we were supposed to get our work done, with what in the fullness of time would be seen as a minor—as a fairly small interruption. At least I thought we finished about as strong as we could finish based on the hand we were dealt.

Illinois Rep. Rodney Davis, the top Republican on the House Administration Committee, had an early-morning flight home. After signing the tallies with the other tellers, he changed into more casual clothes and headed for Reagan National Airport.

Jen Daulby, Republican staff director, House Administration Committee: I remember him being like, "I want you guys to take me to the airport right now." I'm like, "Boss, don't you need a minute?" He's like, "No, I'm gonna get the bleep outta here."

Rep. Rodney Davis, R-IL: I got to the airport early. And I remember sitting at the gate, and I was like, all right, I've got time. I'm going to set my alarm on my watch and I'm going to take a nap. And I laid down, put my head back, and I fell asleep. My watch starts buzzing, probably about 6:30 a.m. And I remember looking around and there were people who were on my flight who were clearly at the protests the day before. I remember thinking, these people are so freaking clueless about what they actually want that they don't realize that one of the persons that was sitting in the well of the House reading off the electoral count that they wanted everybody to object to was sitting right by them. They didn't know who we were. They were just enraged and inspired by people who are in politics that they look at and have no idea about processes or our Constitution. And I just remember chuckling and laughing like, this is just nuts that we see this idiocy.

Officer Christopher Owens, Metropolitan Police Department: I arrived home early on the morning of January 7th. My wife of nineteen years and my teenage daughter were anxiously waiting for me in our kitchen. The look of worry, fear, and relief on their faces as I walked into our home is forever etched in my memory. I told them both that I was okay and there was no need for them to be upset, and I just wanted to grab a shower and a couple hours of sleep before I had to go back to work. They, of course, needed to talk about what happened and hear from me about my day. As I started to downplay my experiences, I'll never forget the look on my daughter's face when she hugged me with tears in her eyes and told me she loved me and immediately wrinkled her nose and said, "You stink." I smiled and told her and my wife that I was covered in sweat, bear spray, mace, OC, and who knows how many other things, which is why I smelled so bad. And we all agreed I should get a shower right away and we could continue talking about my day after.

Officer Jesse Leasure, Metropolitan Police Department: If you've ever been hit with OC spray, there's something afterwards that I call the OC hangover, because your body has been so stressed that you feel like you have a hangover the next day.

Officer Christopher Owens, Metropolitan Police Department: As I started to undress and get in the shower, I took off my long-sleeved uniform shirt and my uniform pants. I'll never forget how my wife burst into tears and sat down on the floor of our bedroom crying when she saw how bruised, battled, and bloodied my arms and legs were.

Officer Winston Pingeon, US Capitol Police: The next morning, I was just so angry and in such a blur. I blew a stop sign coming up New Jersey Avenue from the Navy Yard, and this car is honking at me, and I'm like, I just don't even care. I need to just get back to work, put my uniform on, be back with my colleagues. I had a job to do, and there was no way I could disconnect at that point because I was still running on adrenaline.

Officer Jesse Leasure, Metropolitan Police Department: While they say on the news that like one hundred–something officers were injured—more officers were injured; they just came in to work because that's what we have to do. I didn't want to come in to work the next day, but I did, because my parents beat the Puritan work ethic into me.

Terri McCullough, chief of staff, House Speaker Nancy Pelosi: I went back to work at seven o'clock in the morning to just make sure we could start to get back to normal, whatever normal was. I mean, we never really got back to normal.

Henry Connelly, communications director, House Speaker Nancy Pelosi: I probably slept for like, three hours, and then suited up and walked back into the office, and I was there at 8 a.m. or 9 a.m. the next morning.

Sen. Tim Kaine, D-VA: The next day was so beautiful. January 7, it was so beautiful and peaceful. And I was scheduled to have my first COVID-19 vaccine shot. And I'm walking down East Capitol Street to come in, and it's just like, did that happen? And yes, it did happen, because I couldn't even go in that door without a Capitol Police officer saying, "I'm a Virginia constituent, and I just want to say this to you. You've got to get to the bottom of this. As high up as it goes, you've got to get to the bottom of it."

House Democrats were already investigating, and they would impeach Trump for the second time a week later, even though he had only a few days left in office.[1] *Ten Republicans, including Cheney and Kinzinger, joined all Democrats in voting to remove him. He would be acquitted by the Senate, which didn't start its trial until after Trump left office on January 20. Fifty-seven senators, including seven Republicans, voted to convict.*[2]

My Story

I left the Capitol around 2:30 a.m., around sixteen hours after I had walked into the building that morning. I retraced my steps across the second floor, from the House chamber through Statuary Hall to the Rotunda, to the Ohio Clock Corridor, and down the same Senate steps where Doug Jensen and the mob had chased Eugene Goodman. The building was extremely quiet, and I saw no one—no police, no lawmakers, no reporters or staff. Most of the debris from the day had been cleaned up, and the only evidence of what had happened was broken glass and the thick residue on the floors, remnants of the tear gas that stuck to my shoes as I walked over the marble.

I took photos along the way, in the empty Rotunda and out the windows, where I could see flashing police lights surrounding the Capitol, and of the trash lining the stairs on the East Front as I walked out a Senate door and into the cold air. And in one of the most surreal moments of the day, I walked to my car and drove home. It seemed so routine, almost as if nothing had happened at all.

When I had walked in the same door and across the Capitol to the House press gallery that morning, our AP photographer Scotty Applewhite was already there. A legend on Capitol Hill and at the White House who has won two Pulitzer Prizes, Scotty had celebrated his fortieth anniversary at AP the day before. I was excited to be with Scotty, as I had missed the close-knit work environment we were all so used to before COVID-19 hit. The moment seemed big—we were there together, and it was an important day. I snapped a selfie of the two of us in the booth and sent it to colleagues, telling them we were ready to go.

As 1 p.m. approached, I eventually took my seat on the far left side of the press gallery in the front row, seat number 2. I had asked to sit over the Republican side since that was where the action would be. It was around that time that my mom texted me, and I told her I was in the safest possible place.

I was focused on the debate and making sure my copy got out quickly. It wasn't long, though, before it was clear something was wrong outside, and I left to take a look out a West Front window. What I saw was stunning.

There were so many people—thousands of people—and some of them were right below the window, up against the building. There was a huge, throbbing mass of protesters. I took a few videos, panning the scene, and I sent an update to my colleagues. I didn't notice it at the time, but when I zoomed in on my videos days later, I could see fighting at the thin barrier of bike racks on the House side as police helplessly tried to hold the line against a larger wave of rioters coming toward the building. Amid the mass of people, there were puffs of white tear gas in my frame. The time stamp on my videos was 1:50 p.m., one minute after law enforcement had declared the attack a riot. The building would be breached within the half hour.

I returned to an increasingly frantic scene—alerts ringing out of the overhead speakers and a warning from press gallery staff that we'd soon be locked in the chamber for safety. I rushed back to our work booth and grabbed a portable phone charger so I wouldn't lose power if we were locked in, and I ducked into the restroom. There I found New Hampshire Rep. Annie Kuster, a Democrat who had been sitting in the upper gallery in an effort to socially distance. I briefly told her what I had seen out the West Front, and we walked out together, peeking out the gallery windows to see if we could see anything. I then rushed into the chamber and sat back down in seat number 2 as the doors locked behind us.

The situation escalated within minutes. We didn't know it, but rioters were by then breaking in on the Senate side and heading toward the House chamber. I fumbled with the gas mask they gave us, and Sarah Wire, the *LA Times* reporter sitting next to me, helped me open it. The noises are still so vivid in my mind—the haunting, whining melody of my gas mask; members screaming insults at each other; police officers shouting; and eventually the loud banging sound coming from the doors below. Sarah and I exchanged looks as the new House chaplain, Margaret Kibben, said a prayer at the rostrum. And then members were suddenly flowing off the House floor, streaming en masse through the exit directly below us.

Taking video or photos from our press gallery seats is strictly forbidden and can get us kicked out of the chamber. But I quickly realized that it was far beyond a normal situation. I pulled out my phone and took video of the House members rushing out. Around the same time, it became clear that the beating sounds were rioters banging on the door directly across from us, and police and lawmakers were using furniture to barricade it.

Not too far away, my husband, George, was working out of a small press room deep in the Capitol. He left his desk to peek outside and found chaos. He watched from a balcony above as rioters were breaking through the giant doors on the East Front, and he filmed a video as others walked through Statuary Hall, headed toward the House, where I was. His video was taken at 2:33 p.m., six minutes before my video of members evacuating off the floor.

We were soon told to leave our seats in the press gallery, and we squeezed between narrow stair railings to move into another area. As I ducked to go under one of the railings, another reporter vaulted over me. We ran around the corner of the gallery, down narrow aisles, and climbed over chairs, filling in on the west side balcony as officers yelled at us to duck down and hide. I climbed down to the front row and crouched next to a C-SPAN camera, figuring I would have a marble wall to protect me and a good vantage point for the action at the main door.

My next video was at 2:42 p.m., taken by holding my phone above the balcony to capture the armed standoff below. I could hear someone loudly shouting a prayer—it turned out to be Democratic Rep. Lisa Blunt Rochester of Delaware—but I couldn't understand exactly what she was saying over the loud, buzzing din of the open gas masks, and I thought she was screaming in fear. I soon noticed that Rep. Pramila Jayapal, a Democrat from Washington state, was just down the row from where I was hiding. It was the first time I realized that we were with members of Congress, and I knew that meant there would be more police protection for all of us.

"We should not have both come in today," I texted George amid the mayhem, starting to feel a bit scared and thinking of our children. He then called me from the press room, where he was now trapped, as rioters were walking down the hallway outside and banging on the door. I told him in a low whisper about the scene down below. We quickly said we loved each other and hung up.

As the banging on the doors continued, I was alternating between taking video on my phone and trying to communicate what was happening on our office-wide messaging channels. I was typing a message at 2:44 p.m. when the loud clap of a single gunshot echoed in the large room. It was the shot that killed Ashli Babbitt, who was trying to get into the chamber directly across from where we were. But we didn't know that. "Loud band," I typed quickly into the chat. I corrected myself in the next line: "Bang."

My editors and colleagues had no idea what was going on and likely envisioned, as many in the gallery feared, a much worse scenario in which multiple shots were being fired. They told me to stay down. "Are they shooting into the chamber?" my colleague Colleen wrote. "Is that really happening?" I was now taking video again, so I never answered the question, which was probably frustrating as they tried to decipher my messages. I have second-guessed myself for this since, realizing I should have been sending clearer copy. But I was more focused on taking the video, and I am glad I was, because it is some of the only video from inside the chamber, and it is frequently used to this day.

We were soon evacuated, and the rest of the day is a haze—waiting for hours in a cafeteria, where I met up with my husband and sent in news feeds from my phone; moving back into the Capitol accompanied by police and returning to seat number 2, where my computer sat undisturbed on the balcony above the chamber. Covering the final few hours of the joint session, the unbelievable tension in the room, and surprise when Rep. Matt Gaetz, R-FL, stood up and suggested that the rioters could have been antifa. That was the beginning of a much broader effort to downplay the insurrection that I couldn't possibly have imagined in that moment.

Reporters in the Capitol are everywhere but also nowhere; we live in a strange middle world where we come to work in the same place every day but do not function as official staff. There were few security measures in place for our safety that day, but my colleagues at news organizations across the spectrum adapted and found places to work, offices to hide in, people to talk to as we reported and tried to get the news out.

At the time, I figured the violence of January 6th was most likely the end of the story that had kept us so busy every day for the last several years. But I was wrong, as were most people in the Capitol that day, and it turned out that it was only the beginning. However it all plays out, we in the press will be there to document it for history—and listen to the voices that tell us how it was lived.

Aftermath

Rep. Mike Collins, R-GA: Thousands of peaceful grandmothers gathered in Washington, DC, to take a self-guided, albeit unauthorized, tour of the U.S. Capitol building. Earlier that day, President Trump held a rally, where supporters walked to the Capitol to peacefully protest the certification of the 2020 election. During this time, some individuals entered the Capitol, took photos, and explored the building before leaving.

President Donald Trump: That was a day of love from the standpoint of the millions, it's like hundreds of thousands, it could have been the largest group I've ever spoken [to] before.

Tucker Carlson, Fox News host: If you take three steps back as historical events go, if we are being honest now, January 6th barely rates as a footnote. Really not a lot happened that day, if you think about it.

Sen. Ron Johnson, R-WI: We've seen plenty of video of people in the Capitol, and they weren't rioting.

Sen. Ted Cruz, R-TX: For the next few weeks, Washington and the country saw a level of political theater rarely experienced in public life.

Rep. Troy Nehls, R-TX: I was at the doors on January 6, face-to-face with protestors, and I know firsthand there was NO INSURRECTION.

Rep. Clay Higgins, R-LA: The whole thing was a nefarious agenda to entrap MAGA Americans.

Rep. Matt Gaetz, R-FL: We're ashamed of nothing. We're proud of the work we did on January 6 to make legitimate arguments about election integrity.

Rep. Andrew Clyde, R-GA: To call it an insurrection, in my opinion, is a boldfaced lie. Watching the TV footage of those who entered the Capitol and walked through Statuary Hall showed people in an orderly fashion staying between the stanchions and ropes taking videos and pictures. You know, if you didn't know the TV footage was a video from January the 6th, you would actually think it was a normal tourist visit.

Pamela Hemphill, retired drug and alcohol counselor, Idaho: It's like, you're five years old, you're going to go to Disneyland for the first time, you're so excited. And you go there and they blow it up.

Jason Dolan, former marine, Oath Keepers, Florida: I wanted them to be afraid of me.

Alondra Propes, former parole and probation officer, Oath Keepers, Florida: Before [Trump] ever even set foot in the office, the left was trying to destroy him with false allegations. From day one.

Pamela Hemphill, retired drug and alcohol counselor, Idaho: I was in a cult.

Annie Howell, Pennsylvania: I don't know what could have been—or what could have happened differently that day, because it seemed like to me the perfect storm, the prelude, just the rhetoric that was being shared and COVID happening and the mail-in ballots and everything, and it just made the perfect storm. So I don't know. I wish I never went, I'll tell you that.

Pamela Hemphill, retired drug and alcohol counselor, Idaho: We go to work, we come home, make dinner, take care of our kids, and turn on Fox News. And a lot of people have close friends, a spouse or a family member who may be more schooled in politics; they're more involved in it. They're watching what's happening. So you're trusting their judgment.

Lewis "Easton" Cantwell, North Carolina: Anybody who's served in the military, the president of the United States is the commander in chief, right? Like, he's the boss, you know? I mean, he's not, like, the king, but, you know, if he's out on TV telling the world that it was stolen, what else would I believe as a patriotic American who voted for him and wants to continue to see the country thrive as I thought it was?

Robert Schornack, business development manager, Michigan: I forget the exact term, but basically like confirmation bias. You know, if I would see a story that kind of promoted the way I was thinking about something, then, you know, I was more likely to click on that story and read it than something that would contradict, you know, what I was believing or feeling.

Pamela Hemphill, retired drug and alcohol counselor, Idaho: They don't know they are listening to disinformation. I didn't even know there was a disinformation war out there.

Annie Howell, Pennsylvania: I think that it's made our country stronger, personally. I think that—I don't think that DC or our country is going to allow something like that to happen again. I think that they're going to heed the warnings next time.

Pamela Hemphill, retired drug and alcohol counselor, Idaho: How did I get pulled into this? Everybody thinks they're smarter than that, but Trump was so good at his lying, and everybody around you—it's people like me that are not really paying attention, and trusting, that get pulled in real easy.

Christopher Alberts, handyman and former National Guardsman, Maryland: I wasn't expecting the size crowd that I saw, but in my mind—you know, we have been told as Trump supporters that we're not welcome. Our opinions don't matter. I felt that our right to peacefully make our voice heard was starting to be threatened. The opposite side of the political spectrum was basically telling the world that we don't have a voice, and it doesn't matter.

Sen. Mike Rounds, R-SD: Even to this day, I still have folks come up and say, "You guys let that election get stolen." And there is no evidence, no evidence that would suggest that any of it was accurate. It was propaganda. It was misinformation. It was misleading items by the people that wanted to delay the peaceful transfer of power.

Sen. Roy Blunt, R-MO: I always had a good Trump relationship. But I think I was asked at the time by a reporter, "Have you talked to Trump?" And I said, "No, I've not talked to Trump. And part of what happened today is his responsibility."

Sen. James Lankford, R-OK: There is no microphone on the planet that is louder than the microphone facing the president of the United States, no matter who they are.

Sen. Lindsey Graham, R-SC: January 6 was a dark day in the history of the country, the way people behaved. The election process worked, in spite of the efforts of some to stop it. There was definitely violence. And the people who defiled the Capitol and attacked police officers, they deserved to be held accountable.

Sen. Richard Burr, R-NC: Except for what happened, it was a normal day. The events that happened in between the getting there and the going home were historic. But we work in an institution that does historic things.

Sen. Angus King, I-ME: I'm convinced that all people have within them the capacity for good or evil. And I thought about this for many years, long before I was in politics, thinking back to Germany. And my conclusion is that which side wins depends upon how they're led. These people were misled.

Sen. Susan Collins, R-ME: I never in my life thought that would happen in our country.

Rep. Liz Cheney, R-WY: There were so many moments where the whole thing could have been stopped.

Sen. Angus King, I-ME: The rally wasn't scheduled for a Saturday, or a Friday, or the normal time that rallies are scheduled. It was scheduled for the day of the vote. It was clearly designed to impact, if not end, that vote. The battle cry that day was to "stop the steal." The word "stop" means something. It means they wanted to stop the process of voting for president of the United States.

Sen. Mike Rounds, R-SD: That day, that particular day, that crowd could have been pacified. Or it could be wound up. And the folks who organized it decided to wind them up instead. And I won't forget that.

Rep. Lisa Blunt Rochester, D-DE: It just still blows my mind, right now, that people could downplay such a horrific moment in our country's history.

House Speaker Nancy Pelosi, D-CA: We cannot let them succeed in misrepresenting what happened that day to the American people. And it's shocking in some respects that people accept their version of the story.

Rep. Dan Kildee, D-MI: As I laid on the floor of the House Gallery, and as I called my family to tell them I was safe—even though I was not sure that I was—it occurred to me I was in the same spot where I sat forty-four years earlier as I watched my uncle Dale being first sworn into Congress. A beautiful memory. And now, that memory is replaced by one of me sheltering myself from a violent mob—a violent mob whipped up by a former president pushing a cynical and dangerous lie, determined to overturn an election and to keep us—Congress—from our constitutional duty to certify the election and ensure the peaceful transfer of power.

Inspector Robert Glover, Metropolitan Police Department: I buried my dad January 5, the day before this happened. I received the flag that was on his casket as a military veteran. And to be attacked by veterans and to be attacked with the American colors—it's a challenge. It's a personal challenge to get through that.

Sergeant David Millard, US Capitol Police: I had a blue line flag, which is representative of law enforcement—the thin blue line—thrown at me and my officers when we were going through this. There is no doubt in my mind that this was a violent encounter, and just because you didn't intend to physically kill police officers that day doesn't mean that your actions weren't violent. You broke the law by entering a restricted space to disrupt a congressional process. In the same breath that you were saying, "Thank you for your service," you were also crushing me and my colleagues against the wall to get to your objective. It doesn't add up. These two things don't equal a nonviolent protest.

Officer Jesse Leasure, Metropolitan Police Department: I think the thing that fumed me the most, besides being called a traitor, and still sticks to me from that day, is the pictures of the guy with a Confederate flag. I have a bachelor's degree in history, and I understood the historical context of that situation and the historical context of somebody in the Capitol with a Confederate flag. You're carrying a flag of traitors, acting like a traitor. And fuck you if you think that it's—"oh, it's my heritage." No. You're carrying around the Nazi flag, you asshole.

Officer Caroline Edwards, US Capitol Police: It was so foreign to us that American citizens would try to destroy their own building, their own seat of the democracy, that I think that we were taken completely by surprise. I remember a lot of people told me—and myself included—the dialogue going through your head is, what happens next? What's their end goal? What are they doing?

Manu Raju, anchor and chief congressional correspondent, CNN: I still find it amazing that, how many years since, we're still learning different elements of that day. I think it's something that is going to take a long time for us to fully piece together, exactly all of the events that transpired that day. And while we were doing it in real time, we only gave a tiny little snapshot of what was going on when it was a much broader, more destructive day than what it seemed like while it was happening.

Sen. Bob Casey, D-PA: When you think about all the things that could have gone wrong, or could have gone a lot worse, the idea that the staff had the presence of mind to take the ballots—what if we ran out, and the ballots were there, and they had the ballots? They could have used the ballots as leverage. And if they had apprehended the vice president, they could have killed him or taken him hostage and put a gun to his head and said, if you don't do X, we're gonna burn the ballots. I mean, Mitt

Romney, if he had gotten another twenty yards or so, they would have known him; he's recognizable. The speaker, I mean, you don't even want to think about what could have happened. So as bad as it was, and it was horrific, it could have been a lot worse. There could have been several public officials dead. I'm certain of that.

Rep. Jim McGovern, D-MA: I think back and wonder what they would have done if they had gotten ahold of a member of Congress or staff person, or anybody for that matter. I saw what they did to the Capitol Hill police officers, and I just don't know what they would have done.

Officer Adam Eveland, Metropolitan Police Department: I was there, and I'm going to say with confidence that those people would have hurt our congressmen. Would some of the supporters there who were nonviolent have intervened? I don't know, maybe. Hopefully. But I am confident that the feeling in the crowd was one of, we need to frighten our Congress into doing what we want.

Sen. Mark Warner, D-VA: The mob wasn't going to do a sorting and say, "Okay, you're a Republican, you're a Democrat." This was a mob that I think had bloodlust.

Inspector Robert Glover, Metropolitan Police Department: I think several individual officers could have been more than justified in employing deadly force. And in their particular situations, they chose not to. They chose to go toe to toe.

Officer Christopher Owens, Metropolitan Police Department: The traumas we suffered that day were numerous.

Ken Sicknick, brother of Capitol Police Officer Brian Sicknick: We get down to DC, we get to the hospital. We're met by the Capitol Police. Brian had already passed.

At the hospital the next evening, the Sicknick family was allowed to go into a room together and see Brian one last time. Doctors eventually asked them to step out so the coroner could take him away.

Ken Sicknick, brother of Capitol Police Officer Brian Sicknick: The police led us back outside, and they said, "Just wait here in your cars." And then, while we're there waiting, we can hear motorcycles, and there must have been fifty motorcycles coming around the corner, and then a bunch of other Capitol Police cars came around. They led us in a procession behind the coroner's van past the Capitol building. And as we were going around the Capitol building, every police agency you can imagine was standing there with their lights on.

Officers from all over the city were lined up in their cars outside the Capitol to honor the fallen Capitol Police officer.

Ken Sicknick, brother of Capitol Police Officer Brian Sicknick: I was driving, so I'm all choked up and I'm trying to drive at the same time.

Craig Sicknick, brother of Capitol Police Officer Brian Sicknick: At that point, I was completely numb already.

Gladys Sicknick, mother of Capitol Police Officer Brian Sicknick: He was a very quiet person, but you did not cross him, because he wouldn't take any garbage from you. He was very caring, and he was wonderful. He was just a good, good boy growing up; I never had to yell at him.

Ken Sicknick, brother of Capitol Police Officer Brian Sicknick: He was dedicated to what he did. He loved being a police officer.

Inspector Robert Glover, Metropolitan Police Department: I think the men and women who responded knew the importance of their mission, however small it was. It's hard to understand the number of officers that got hurt that day. This was combat. This is not something that I think any police officer or first responder can understand. This was unparalleled, unprecedented. And it's the first time in my career that I didn't think I was going to go home that night. And it's left a huge impact on a number of our members to this day. I think it's left a huge impact on the Capitol Police.

Inspector Thomas Loyd, US Capitol Police: The January 6 riot changed my life forever. The legislative branch of government had not seen an attack like that since August 24, 1814, when the British broke into the United States Capitol building and burned it. I am responsible for the safety and security of the United States Capitol building on a daily basis. The people who work in the building are my colleagues, to include the 350 police officers assigned to me. The mob attacked my colleagues on January 6. The riot was an intentional, violent attack against my officers, starting at Peace Circle. We did not attack the mob; the mob attacked us.

Lieutenant Tia Summers, US Capitol Police: I worked at the Capitol a really long time. I take pride in what I do. And a lot of people that I worked next to for many years were hurt. A lot of people are still dealing with it emotionally. And it was just hard to see people that I work alongside on a regular basis have to fight for their life, essentially.

Sergeant Aquilino Gonell, US Capitol Police: I sustained multiple injuries including lacerations on both hands, contusions on my left calf, a bone fusion surgery on my right foot. On my left shoulder, I received a labrum tear and rotator cuff surgery.

Officer Winston Pingeon, US Capitol Police: There's such a culture in law enforcement of being tough and "I'm fine. Don't want to talk about it." Do not show vulnerability. Do not show weakness.

Lieutenant Michael Byrd, US Capitol Police: I was very afraid. There's nothing wrong with being afraid.

Officer Stephen Sherman, US Capitol Police: There is a common thread of emotions amongst many officers who were defending the Capitol on January 6, 2021—which is that we all thought we were going to die.

Officer Kyle Yetter, US Capitol Police: That was the worst day of my life, the most chaotic, and the most stressful.

Emily Berret, director of operations, House Speaker Nancy Pelosi: People left. We lost a lot of people in our office because of this. And January 6 was a large part of why some of our staff have completely left government service altogether.

Inspector Thomas Loyd, US Capitol Police: The ramifications of January 6 will affect all of my personnel for the rest of their lives. As a result of the riot, 20 percent of my team separated from the department. The mob leaders for January 6 should be ashamed.

Officer Winston Pingeon, US Capitol Police: When I went through the academy in 2016, my sergeant told us that we were fifteen years out from 9/11, and "if you all do your twenty-five years, it's really not a matter of if, but when—you are going to see something here that could change your life, or could change our history." He used to say too that it can be a difficult job, it can get boring, but to look up at the dome—just that reminder, this is bigger than just ourselves.

ACKNOWLEDGMENTS

A year or so after January 6th, there was a popular narrative—not just among Republicans—that the attack on the Capitol would fade into history and that people wouldn't want to read about it. I never believed that.

It's true that I may think about January 6th more than most people, thanks to working in the Capitol and working on this book. But I'm so glad that a few people agreed with me that it would continue to matter and that the details of the siege, as well as the human experiences, should be preserved and recorded.

My only regret is that there are so many more details to record, so many more people I could have talked to. I feel that I've only scratched the surface here, especially because so many people feel intimidated to talk about what they experienced that day or willingly downplay it. I hope that changes as the years go on.

My agent, Bridget Matzie, has stuck by me through this entire four-year process, even through the (many) times it seemed that the book would not happen. She is unflappable and a fantastic editor, and I feel lucky to have worked with her. At PublicAffairs, I immediately clicked with Colleen Lawrie, who had a shared vision for the book and made it happen, and later with Meagan Levinson, whose edits brought the project home and helped make it readable for people, unlike me, who don't think about January 6th every day. I am also so thankful to Julie Tate for fact-checking the manuscript and to Carrie Osgood, who brought the story more to life with maps.

At The Associated Press, I am immensely grateful to all of my very understanding bosses, Dustin Weaver, Anna Johnson, and Julie Pace, for their constant support for this project and for their friendship as well. I could not have completed this book without borrowing some of the awesome expertise—and databases!—from AP reporters Michael Kunzelman, Alanna Durkin Richer, and Lindsey Whitehurst, who spent hundreds and hundreds of hours covering the January 6th prosecutions and trials and answered so many of my questions over the years. Mike Balsamo, Colleen Long, and Eric Tucker are colleagues who have been in the thick of it with me through this story, and I have benefited in so many ways from their talent as well as that of our amazing Capitol Hill team, including current and former colleagues Andy Taylor, Alan Fram, Scotty Applewhite, Kevin Freking, Stephen Groves, and Farnoush Amiri. Their work is throughout this book. And I am grateful to my kindred work spirit, Lisa Mascaro, who has been with this project from the start and has contributed in countless and important ways.

I owe so many thanks to my family, who have been there for me through it all—my mother for her support and constant help with our kids; my children for keeping me entertained and for becoming such thoughtful citizens; and my husband, George, who was also in the Capitol on January 6th, for giving me feedback on the book and for his love and companionship every day. And also our cat, Bowie, whom my son wanted me to mention, for bringing our family so much joy even when he is being devious.

VOICES

Abdi, Abdulkadir. USA vs. McCaughey et al., Transcript of Bench Trial—Day 2, August 30, 2022, https://storage.courtlistener.com/recap/gov.uscourts.dcd.226961/gov.uscourts.dcd.226961.633.0.pdf.

Alberts, Christopher. USA vs. Alberts, Transcript of Jury Trial, April 17, 2023, morning session, https://storage.courtlistener.com/recap/gov.uscourts.dcd.226717/gov.uscourts.dcd.226717.156.0.pdf; USA vs. Alberts, Transcript of Jury Trial, April 17, 2023, afternoon session, https://storage.courtlistener.com/recap/gov.uscourts.dcd.226717/gov.uscourts.dcd.226717.157.0.pdf.

Allred, Colin. "January 6 Views from the House," C-SPAN, August 8, 2021, https://www.c-span.org/program/us-house-of-representatives/january-6-views-from-the-house-representatives-hakeem-jeffries-ronny-jackson-and-colin-allred/596354.

Applewhite, J. Scott. Interview with the author, March 12, 2025; "'We Have to Be There': AP Photographer Recalls Capitol Siege," The Associated Press, January 5, 2022, https://apnews.com/article/jan-6-capitol-siege-ap-photographer-1bd87e4d6fbe614e00fd4a5f885c2334.

Ayres, Stephen. Continued Interview of Stephen Ayres, House Select Committee to Investigate the January 6th Attack on the United States Capitol, June 22, 2022, https://www.govinfo.gov/content/pkg/GPO-J6-TRANSCRIPT-CTRL0000916062/pdf/GPO-J6-TRANSCRIPT-CTRL0000916062.pdf; Testimony of Stephen Ayres at live hearing, House Select Committee to Investigate the January 6th Attack on the United States Capitol, July 12, 2022, https://www.c-span.org/program/january-6-hearings/seventh-hearing-on-investigation-of-january-6-attack-on-the-us-capitol/614450.

Baboulis, Jessica. USA vs. Alberts, Transcript of Jury Trial, morning session, April 13, 2023, https://storage.courtlistener.com/recap/gov.uscourts.dcd.226717/gov.uscourts.dcd.226717.152.0.pdf.

Berret, Emily. USA vs. Barnett, Transcript of Jury Trial, afternoon session, January

10, 2023, https://storage.courtlistener.com/recap/gov.uscourts.dcd.226952/gov.uscourts.dcd.226952.159.0.pdf.

Black, Barry. Interview with the author, November 21, 2024.

Blanton, Brett. House Administration Committee, Statement of Brett Blanton, May 19, 2021, https://www.aoc.gov/sites/default/files/2021-05/AOC_Testimony_CHA_Hearing-2021-05-19.pdf.

Blumenthal, Richard. Interview with the author, December 3, 2024.

Blunt, Roy. Interview with the author, June 6, 2024.

Blunt Rochester, Lisa. Interview with the author, March 3, 2025.

Bobic, Igor. Interview with the author, October 11, 2024.

Bresnahan, John. Interview with the author, November 26, 2024.

Buhler, Janet. Transcribed Interview of Janet West Buhler, House Select Committee to Investigate the January 6th Attack on the United States Capitol, February 28, 2022, https://www.govinfo.gov/app/details/GPO-J6-TRANSCRIPT-CTRL0000050985/context.

Burr, Richard. Interview with the author, February 20, 2024.

Byrd, Michael. Rich Schapiro, Anna Schecter, and Chelsea Damberg, "Officer Who Shot Ashli Babbitt During Capitol Riot Breaks Silence: 'I Saved Countless Lives,'" NBC News, August 26, 2021, https://www.nbcnews.com/news/us-news/officer-who-shot-ashli-babbitt-during-capitol-riot-breaks-silence-n1277736.

Cantwell, Lewis. Transcribed Interview of Lewis Cantwell, House Select Committee to Investigate the January 6th Attack on the United States Capitol, April 26, 2022, https://www.govinfo.gov/content/pkg/GPO-J6-TRANSCRIPT-CTRL0000071092/pdf/GPO-J6-TRANSCRIPT-CTRL0000071092.pdf.

Carlson, Tucker. "Tucker: Why are our leaders obsessing over this?" Fox News, January 10, 2022, https://www.foxnews.com/transcript/tucker-why-are-our-leaders-obsessing-over-this.

Casey, Bob. Interview with the author, June 18, 2024.

Cheney, Liz. Interview with the author, February 24, 2025.

Chung, Francis. Interview with the author, October 8, 2024.

Clyde, Andrew. House Committee on Oversight and Reform, live hearing, May 12, 2021, https://www.congress.gov/117/chrg/CHRG-117hhrg44570/CHRG-117hhrg44570.pdf.

Cochrane, Emily. Interview with the author, February 19, 2025.

Collins, Mike. Post on X, January 6, 2025, https://x.com/RepMikeCollins/status/1876247374651125852?lang=en.

Collins, Susan. Interview with the author, September 23, 2024.

Connelly, Henry. Interview with the author, October 4, 2024.

Contee, Robert. Testimony of Robert Contee, House Appropriations Committee,

January 26, 2021, https://mpdc.dc.gov/sites/default/files/dc/sites/mpdc/release_content/attachments/TESTIMONY_COP_January%206_FINAL.pdf; Testimony of Robert Contee, Joint hearing by the Senate Homeland Security and Governmental Affairs Committee and Senate Rules Committee, February 23, 2021, https://www.rules.senate.gov/imo/media/doc/BA0E3F52-5056-A066-6078-13F30593703C/Testimony_Contee.pdf; Testimony of Robert Contee, House Committee on Oversight and Reform, May 12, 2021, https://mpdc.dc.gov/sites/default/files/dc/sites/mpdc/release_content/attachments/MPD%20TESTIMONY_House%20Oversight_05%2012%2021_FINAL.pdf; Transcribed Interview of Robert Contee, House Select Committee to Investigate the January 6th Attack on the United States Capitol, January 11, 2022, https://www.govinfo.gov/content/pkg/GPO-J6-TRANSCRIPT-CTRL0000036624/pdf/GPO-J6-TRANSCRIPT-CTRL0000036624.pdf.

Cooney, Shae. USA vs. Nordean et al., Transcript of Jury Trial, Day 25, morning session, February 2, 2023, https://storage.courtlistener.com/recap/gov.uscourts.dcd.228299/gov.uscourts.dcd.228299.995.0.pdf.

Cortez, Julio. Interview with the author, February 18, 2025.

Cortez Masto, Catherine. Senate floor speech, January 6, 2022, https://www.congress.gov/117/crec/2022/01/06/168/4/CREC-2022-01-06-senate.pdf.

Crow, Jason. Interview with the author, December 15, 2021.

Cruz, Ted. *Justice Corrupted: How the Left Weaponized Our Legal System.* Washington, DC: Regenery Publishing, 2022.

Curtice, Chad. USA vs. McCaughey et al., Transcript of Bench Trial—Day 2, August 30, 2022, https://storage.courtlistener.com/recap/gov.uscourts.dcd.226961/gov.uscourts.dcd.226961.633.0.pdf.

Daulby, Jen. Interview with the author, May 29, 2024.

Davis, Rodney. Interview with the author, January 25, 2024.

DeAngelo, Anthony. Interview with the author, May 28, 2024.

Demings, Val. Interview with the author, December 15, 2021.

DesCamp, Adam. USA vs. Alberts, Transcript of Jury Trial, afternoon session, April 13, 2023, https://storage.courtlistener.com/recap/gov.uscourts.dcd.226717/gov.uscourts.dcd.226717.153.0.pdf.

Dolan, Jason. USA vs. Rhodes, Transcript of Jury Trial—Day 13, October 18, 2022, afternoon session.

Donigian, George. USA vs. McCaughey et al., Transcript of Bench Trial—Day 2, August 30, 2022, https://storage.courtlistener.com/recap/gov.uscourts.dcd.226961/gov.uscourts.dcd.226961.633.0.pdf.

Dunn, Harry. Testimony of Harry Dunn at live hearing, House Select Committee to Investigate the January 6th Attack on the United States Capitol, July

27, 2021, https://www.congress.gov/117/meeting/house/113969/witnesses/HHRG-117-IJ00-Wstate-DunnO-20210727.pdf.

Durbin, Dick. Interview with the author, December 5, 2024.

Edwards, Caroline. Transcribed Interview of Caroline Edwards, House Select Committee to Investigate the January 6th Attack on the United States Capitol, April 18, 2022, https://www.govinfo.gov/content/pkg/GPO-J6-TRANSCRIPT-CTRL0000082302/pdf/GPO-J6-TRANSCRIPT-CTRL0000082302.pdf; Testimony of Caroline Edwards at live hearing, House Select Committee to Investigate the January 6th Attack on the United States Capitol, June 9, 2022, https://www.c-span.org/program/january-6-hearings/first-hearing-on-investigation-of-january-6-attack-on-the-us-capitol/612368.

Elliott, Farar. House Appropriations Subcommittee on the Legislative Branch, statement of Farar Elliott at live hearing, February 24, 2021, https://www.congress.gov/117/meeting/house/111233/witnesses/HHRG-117-AP24-Wstate-ElliottF-20210224.pdf.

Eveland, Adam. Interview with the author, November 30, 2024.

Fallon, Pat. Post on Facebook, January 6, 2021, https://www.facebook.com/fallonfortexas/posts/3658856854169672.

Fanone, Michael. Testimony of Michael Fanone at live hearing, House Select Committee to Investigate the January 6th Attack on the United States Capitol, July 27, 2021, https://www.congress.gov/117/meeting/house/113969/witnesses/HHRG-117-IJ00-Wstate-FanoneO-20210727.pdf.

Fitzpatrick, Brian. "January 6 Views from the House," C-SPAN, August 15, 2021, https://www.c-span.org/program/january-6-views-from-the-house/january-6-views-from-the-house-representatives-jamie-raskin-brian-fitzpatrick-and-dean-phillips/596355.

Fleet, Jamie. Interviews with the author, December 19, 2024, and January 15, 2025; Transcribed Interview of Jamie Fleet, House Select Committee to Investigate the January 6th Attack on the United States Capitol, March 10, 2022, https://www.govinfo.gov/app/details/GPO-J6-TRANSCRIPT-CTRL0000051200.

Gaetz, Matt. "War Room" podcast, January 6, 2022, @AccountableGOP, https://x.com/AccountableGOP/status/1479111905272745985.

Gazelle, Mark. USA vs. Jensen, Jury Trial—Day 3, September 21, 2022, https://storage.courtlistener.com/recap/gov.uscourts.dcd.225865/gov.uscourts.dcd.225865.124.0.pdf.

Glover, Robert. Transcribed Interview of Robert Glover, House Select Committee to Investigate the January 6th Attack on the United States Capitol, May 2, 2022, https://www.govinfo.gov/content/pkg/GPO-J6-TRANSCRIPT-CTRL0000082305/pdf/GPO-J6-TRANSCRIPT-CTRL0000082305

.pdf; Paul Wagner, "Retired DC Police Commander Shares Capitol Riot Experience," NBC4 Washington, July 25, 2022, https://www.youtube.com/watch?v=e6JAQp04sR0.

Gonell, Aquilino. Testimony of Aquilino Gonell at live hearing, House Select Committee to Investigate the January 6th Attack on the United States Capitol, July 27, 2021, https://docs.house.gov/meetings/IJ/IJ00/20210727/113969/HHRG-117-IJ00-Bio-GonellS-20210727.pdf; USA vs. Wilson, Transcript of a Sentencing Hearing—March 4, 2022, https://storage.courtlistener.com/recap/gov.uscourts.dcd.230999/gov.uscourts.dcd.230999.38.0.pdf.

Gonzales, Tony. "Jan. 6 Reminded Me of My Time in Combat, Not America," *El Paso Times,* January 21, 2021, https://www.elpasotimes.com/story/opinion/2021/01/21/jan-6-like-combat-not-america-district-23-us-rep-tony-gonzales/6657965002/.

Goodman, Eugene. USA vs. Seefried, Testimony of Eugene Goodman Excerpted from the Bench Trial, June 13, 2022, https://storage.courtlistener.com/recap/gov.uscourts.dcd.229853/gov.uscourts.dcd.229853.104.0.pdf; USA vs. Jensen, Jury Trial—Day 3, September 21, 2022, https://storage.courtlistener.com/recap/gov.uscourts.dcd.225865/gov.uscourts.dcd.225865.124.0.pdf.

Graham, Lindsey. Interview with the author, January 6, 2025.

Greene, Marjorie Taylor. David Rowan et al. vs. Marjorie Taylor Greene, State Court Testimony uploaded by Just Security, April 22, 2022, https://www.justsecurity.org/wp-content/uploads/2023/04/marjorie-taylor-greene-transcript-of-proceeding-before-administrative-law-judge.pdf.

Greene, Matthew. USA vs. Nordean et al., Transcript of Jury Trial—Day 20, morning session, January 24, 2023, https://storage.courtlistener.com/recap/gov.uscourts.dcd.228300/gov.uscourts.dcd.228300.991.0.pdf.

Grider, Christopher. USA vs. Grider, Transcript of Bench Trial, Day 3, December 14, 2022, https://storage.courtlistener.com/recap/gov.uscourts.dcd.226617/gov.uscourts.dcd.226617.155.0.pdf; USA vs. Grider, Transcript of Bench Trial, Day 4, December 15, 2022, https://storage.courtlistener.com/recap/gov.uscourts.dcd.226617/gov.uscourts.dcd.226617.156.0.pdf.

Grooms, Kevin. AOC Staff, "U.S. Capitol Cleanup," January 15, 2021, https://www.aoc.gov/explore-capitol-campus/blog/us-capitol-clean-up.

Hammill, Drew. Interview with the author, January 18, 2024.

Harnik, Andrew. Interview with the author, October 22, 2024; Julio Cortez and Andrew Harnik, "Images of Chaos: AP Photographers Capture Images of US Capitol Riot," January 5, 2022.

Hawa, Lanelle. USA vs. Alberts, Transcript of Jury Trial, afternoon session, April 13, 2023, https://storage.courtlistener.com/recap/gov.uscourts.dcd.226717/gov.uscourts.dcd.226717.153.0.pdf.

Hawley, Josh. Angi Gonzalez, "Hawley Sets the Record Straight on Jan. 6 Photo," Spectrum News, June 9, 2022, https://spectrumnews1.com/ca/southern-california/politics/2022/06/09/exclusive--sen--hawley-sets-record-straight-on-january-6th.

Hemphill, Pamela. Interview with the author, February 10, 2025.

Higgins, Clay. Luke Broadwater and Alan Feuer, "G.O.P. Congressman's Wild Claim: F.B.I. Entrapped Jan. 6 Rioters," *The New York Times*, April 4, 2024, https://www.nytimes.com/2024/04/04/us/politics/clay-higgins-jan-6.html.

Himes, Jim. Interviews with the author, January 6, 2021, and December 16, 2021.

Hodges, Daniel. Interview with the author, December 19, 2024; Testimony of Daniel Hodges at live hearing, House Select Committee to Investigate the January 6th Attack on the United States Capitol, July 27, 2021, https://www.congress.gov/event/117th-congress/house-event/113969/text; USA vs. McCaughey et al., "Transcript of Bench Trial—Day 2," August 30, 2022, https://storage.courtlistener.com/recap/gov.uscourts.dcd.226961/gov.uscourts.dcd.226961.633.0.pdf.

Hodgson, Chris. Deposition of Chris Hodgson, House Select Committee to Investigate the January 6th Attack on the United States Capitol, March 30, 2022, https://www.govinfo.gov/content/pkg/GPO-J6-TRANSCRIPT-CTRL0000060753/pdf/GPO-J6-TRANSCRIPT-CTRL0000060753.pdf.

Howell, Annie. Transcribed Interview of Annie Howell, House Select Committee to Investigate the January 6th Attack on the United States Capitol, December 14, 2022, https://www.govinfo.gov/content/pkg/GPO-J6-TRANSCRIPT-CTRL0000034889/pdf/GPO-J6-TRANSCRIPT-CTRL0000034889.pdf.

Hoyer, Steny. Interview with the author, December 11, 2024.

Irving, Paul. Testimony of Paul Irving, Joint Hearing by the Senate Homeland Security and Governmental Affairs Committee and Senate Rules Committee, February 23, 2021, https://www.rules.senate.gov/imo/media/doc/Testimony_Irving.pdf.

Jackson, Ronny. "January 6 Views from the House," C-SPAN, August 8, 2021, https://www.c-span.org/program/us-house-of-representatives/january-6-views-from-the-house-representatives-hakeem-jeffries-ronny-jackson-and-colin-allred/596354.

Jacob, Greg. Deposition of Greg Jacob, House Select Committee to Investigate the January 6th Attack on the United States Capitol, February 1, 2022, https://www.govinfo.gov/content/pkg/GPO-J6-TRANSCRIPT-CTRL0000040479/pdf/GPO-J6-TRANSCRIPT-CTRL0000040479.pdf; Testimony of Greg Jacob at live hearing, House Select Committee to Investigate the January 6th Attack on the United States Capitol, June 16, 2022, https://www.c-span.org/program/january-6-hearings/third-hearing-on-investigation-of-january-6-attack-on-the-us-capitol/613436.

Jayapal, Pramila. Interview with the author, December 10, 2021.

Jeffries, Hakeem. "January 6 Views from the House," C-SPAN, August 8, 2021, https://www.c-span.org/program/us-house-of-representatives/january-6-views-from-the-house-representatives-hakeem-jeffries-ronny-jackson-and-colin-allred/596354.

Jensen, Doug. FBI Interview, January 8, 2021, https://storage.courtlistener.com/recap/gov.uscourts.dcd.225865/gov.uscourts.dcd.225865.69.1_2.pdf.

Johnson, Clinton. AOC Staff, "U.S. Capitol Cleanup," January 15, 2021, https://www.aoc.gov/explore-capitol-campus/blog/us-capitol-clean-up.

Johnson, Ron. "'Life, Liberty & Levin' Questions How Justice Is Being Served to Capitol Hill Rioters," Fox News, June 13, 2021, https://www.foxnews.com/transcript/life-liberty-levin-questions-how-justice-is-being-served-to-capitol-hill-rioters.

Kaine, Tim. Interview with the author, September 17, 2024; Senate floor speech, January 28, 2025, https://www.congress.gov/119/crec/2025/01/28/171/18/modified/CREC-2025-01-28-pt1-PgS410.htm.

Kane, Paul. Interview with the author, October 10, 2024.

Kerkhoff, Shauni. USA vs. Alberts, Transcript of Jury Trial, morning session, April 13, 2023, https://storage.courtlistener.com/recap/gov.uscourts.dcd.226717/gov.uscourts.dcd.226717.152.0.pdf; USA vs. Alberts, Transcript of Jury Trial, afternoon session, April 13, 2023, https://storage.courtlistener.com/recap/gov.uscourts.dcd.226717/gov.uscourts.dcd.226717.153.0.pdf.

Kibben, Margaret. "Prayers in the Storm: U.S. House Chaplain Reflects on Division and Hope," Interview with Rev. Dr. Katie Givens, Day 1, November 5, 2024, https://day1.org/articles/672a51aa6615fb3ef0001031/prayers-in-the-storm-us-house-chaplain-reflects-on-division-and-hope.

Kildee, Dan. "Congressman Kildee's Remarks on First Anniversary of January 6th Attack," Legistorm, January 6, 2022, https://www.legistorm.com/stormfeed/view_rss/2003135/member/2921/title/transcript-congressman-kildees-remarks-on-first-anniversary-of-january-6th-attack.html.

Kim, Andy. Interview with the author, June 25, 2024; Mike Catalini, "'What Else Could I Do?' NJ Rep. Kim Helps Clean Up Capitol," The Associated Press, January 7, 2021, https://apnews.com/article/andy-kim-cleans-capitol-siege-c5a303337cd63e4312ef7e1a17509371.

King, Angus. Interview with the author, September 18, 2024; "Angus King: An Independent in the Senate," *60 Minutes*, January 10, 2021.

Kinzinger, Adam. Interview with the author, December 16, 2021.

Klobuchar, Amy. Interview with the author, December 19, 2024.

Kuster, Annie. Interview with the author, December 15, 2021.

La, Alisa. Interview with the author, October 4, 2024.

Lankford, James. "Lankford Speaks with KWGS About Insurrection and Impeachment," Public Radio Tulsa, January 13, 2021, https://www.publicradiotulsa.org/local-regional/2021-01-13/full-interview-lankford-speaks-with-kwgs-about-insurrection-and-impeachment.

Leasure, Jesse. Interview with the author, October 1, 2024.

Lee, Mike. Bryan Schott, "What Sen. Mike Lee Told Me About Trump's Call the Day of the Capitol Riot," *The Salt Lake Tribune*, February 10, 2021.

Lofgren, Zoe. Interviews with the author, December 16, 2021, and December 18, 2024; "January 6 Views from the House," C-SPAN, August 8, 2021, https://www.c-span.org/program/january-6-views-from-the-house/january-6-views-from-the-house-representatives-zoe-lofgren-rodney-davis-and-madeleine-dean/596353.

Loyd, Thomas. USA vs. Jensen, Government's Sentencing Supplement, December 13, 2022, https://storage.courtlistener.com/recap/gov.uscourts.dcd.225865/gov.uscourts.dcd.225865.113.0_1.pdf; USA vs. Jensen, Jury Trial—Day 3, September 21, 2022, https://storage.courtlistener.com/recap/gov.uscourts.dcd.225865/gov.uscourts.dcd.225865.124.0.pdf; USA vs. Nordean et al., Transcript of Jury Trial—Day 14, January 13, 2023, https://storage.courtlistener.com/recap/gov.uscourts.dcd.228300/gov.uscourts.dcd.228300.943.0.pdf; USA vs. Nordean et al., Transcript of Jury Trial—Day 15, morning session, January 17, 2023, https://storage.courtlistener.com/recap/gov.uscourts.dcd.228300/gov.uscourts.dcd.228300.943.0.pdf; USA vs. Seefried, "Transcript of Bench Trial—Day 1," June 13, 2022, https://storage.courtlistener.com/recap/gov.uscourts.dcd.229853/gov.uscourts.dcd.229853.105.0.pdf.

Malinowski, Tom. Mike Catalini, "'What Else Could I Do?' NJ Rep. Kim Helps Clean Up Capitol," The Associated Press, January 7, 2021, https://apnews.com/article/andy-kim-cleans-capitol-siege-c5a303337cd63e4312ef7e1a17509371.

Martin, Shawna. Transcribed Interview of Shawna Martin, House Select Committee to Investigate the January 6th Attack on the United States Capitol, April 19, 2022, https://www.govinfo.gov/content/pkg/GPO-J6-TRANSCRIPT-CTRL0000082292/pdf/GPO-J6-TRANSCRIPT-CTRL0000082292.pdf.

McCullough, Terri. Interview with the author, January 17, 2025.

McGovern, Jim. Interview with the author, December 17, 2024; "January 6 Views from the House," C-SPAN, August 22, 2021, https://www.c-span.org/program/january-6-views-from-the-house/january-6-views-from-the-house-representatives-jim-mcgovern-and-susan-wild/596356.

McIntyre, Jason. USA vs. Nordean et al., Transcript of Jury Trial—Day 41, March 1, 2023, https://storage.courtlistener.com/recap/gov.uscourts.dcd.228300/gov.uscourts.dcd.228300.1009.0.pdf.

Mendoza, Carneysha. Statement by Captain Mendoza, Joint Hearing by the Senate Homeland Security and Governmental Affairs Committee and Senate Rules Committee, February 23, 2021, https://www.rules.senate.gov/download/statement-of-captain-mendoza.

Millard, David. Transcribed Interview of David Millard, House Select Committee to Investigate the January 6th Attack on the United States Capitol, April 18, 2022, https://www.govinfo.gov/content/pkg/GPO-J6-TRANSCRIPT-CTRL0000071084/pdf/GPO-J6-TRANSCRIPT-CTRL0000071084.pdf.

Milley, Mark. Transcribed Interview of Mark Milley, House Select Committee to Investigate the January 6th Attack on the United States Capitol, November 17, 2021, https://www.govinfo.gov/content/pkg/GPO-J6-TRANSCRIPT-CTRL0000034620/pdf/GPO-J6-TRANSCRIPT-CTRL0000034620.pdf.

Minchillo, John. Interview with the author, February 25, 2025; "2021 Notebook: On Jan. 6, Chaos Inside the Capitol and Out," The Associated Press, December 15, 2021, https://apnews.com/article/joe-biden-crime-riots-donald-trump-capitol-siege-f7f8dead93998991cfc728e83ea31602.

Mitchell, Ricardo. AOC Staff, "U.S. Capitol Cleanup," January 15, 2021, https://www.aoc.gov/explore-capitol-campus/blog/us-capitol-clean-up.

Morgan, Brian. USA vs. Seefried, Transcript of Bench Trial—Day One, June 13, 2022, https://storage.courtlistener.com/recap/gov.uscourts.dcd.229854/gov.uscourts.dcd.229854.110.0.pdf; USA vs. Jensen, Jury Trial—Day 4, September 22, 2022, https://storage.courtlistener.com/recap/gov.uscourts.dcd.225865/gov.uscourts.dcd.225865.125.0.pdf.

Mullin, Markwayne. "January 6 Views from the House," C-SPAN, July 25, 2021, https://www.c-span.org/program/january-6-views-from-the-house/january-6-views-from-the-house-representatives-markwayne-mullin-jason-crow-and-tom-malinowski/596352; Allison Herrera, "Despite Capitol Violence, Markwayne Mullin Holds Firm in Objecting to Electoral College Results," KOSU, January 8, 2021, https://www.kosu.org/politics/2021-01-08/despite-capitol-violence-markwayne-mullin-holds-firm-in-objecting-to-electoral-college-results.

Murphy, Chris. Interview with the author, February 1, 2023.

Murphy, Stephanie. Interview with the author, December 7, 2021; Comments at live hearing, House Select Committee to Investigate the January 6th Attack on the United States Capitol, July 27, 2021, https://www.congress.gov/event/117th-congress/house-event/113969/text.

Murray, Patty. "Sen. Patty Murray Recounts Her Narrow Escape from a Violent Mob Inside the U.S. Capitol," PBS NewsHour, February 12, 2021, https://www.pbs.org/newshour/show/sen-patty-murray-recounts-her-narrow-escape-from-a-violent-mob-inside-the-u-s-capitol.

Nehls, Troy. "U.S. Rep. Troy Nehls Shares Memories of What He Witnessed in the House Chamber on Jan. 6, 2021," Interview with Robert Arnold, KPRC Houston, January 6, 2022, https://www.click2houston.com/news/investigates/2022/01/07/former-fort-bend-co-sheriff-us-rep-troy-nehls-who-was-in-the-capitol-building-on-jan-6-shares-his-experience; Troy Nehls, post on X, October 31, 2023, https://x.com/RepTroyNehls/status/1719355014060060834.

Nguyen, Phuson. USA vs. Fitzsimons, Transcript of Bench Trial, August 16, 2022, https://storage.courtlistener.com/recap/gov.uscourts.dcd.228113/gov.uscourts.dcd.228113.136.0.pdf.

Novotny, Joe. Interview with the author, June 24, 2024.

Ode, Mark. USA vs. Nordean et al., Transcript of Jury Trial, Day 27, morning session, February 7, 2023, https://storage.courtlistener.com/recap/gov.uscourts.dcd.228300/gov.uscourts.dcd.228300.997.0.pdf.

Ortega, Ronald. USA vs. Rhodes, Transcript of Jury Trial—Day 13, October 18, 2022, morning session, p. 84.

Owens, Christopher. USA vs. Rhodes, Transcript of Jury Trial, October 26, 2022, https://storage.courtlistener.com/recap/gov.uscourts.dcd.239207/gov.uscourts.dcd.239207.740.0.pdf; USA vs. Rhodes, Transcript of Omnibus Motion Hearing Proceedings, May 24, 2023.

Pelosi, Nancy. Interview with the author, December 9, 2024.

Pence, Mike. *So Help Me God.* New York: Simon and Schuster, 2022.

Pergram, Chad. Interview with the author, March 18, 2025.

Pezzola, Dominic. USA vs. Nordean et al., Transcript of Jury Trial, Day 67, morning session, April 19, 2023, https://storage.courtlistener.com/recap/gov.uscourts.dcd.228300/gov.uscourts.dcd.228300.1036.0.pdf.

Phillips, Dean. "January 6 Views from the House," C-SPAN, August 15, 2021, https://www.c-span.org/program/january-6-views-from-the-house/january-6-views-from-the-house-representatives-jamie-raskin-brian-fitzpatrick-and-dean-phillips/596355.

Pingeon, Winston. Interview with the author, October 1, 2024.

Pittman, Yogananda. Testimony of Yogananda Pittman, House Appropriations Committee, February 25, 2021, https://docs.house.gov/meetings/AP/AP24/20210225/111235/HHRG-117-AP24-Wstate-PittmanY-20210225.pdf; Transcribed Interview of Yogananda Pittman, House Select Committee to Investigate the January 6th Attack on the United States Capitol, January 13, 2022, https://www.govinfo.gov/content/pkg/GPO-J6-TRANSCRIPT-CTRL0000034888/pdf/GPO-J6-TRANSCRIPT-CTRL0000034888.pdf.

Propes, Alondra. Transcribed Interview of Alondra Propes, House Select Committee to Investigate the January 6th Attack on the United States Capitol, January 31, 2022, https://www.govinfo.gov/content/pkg/GPO

-J6-TRANSCRIPT-CTRL0000039559/pdf/GPO-J6-TRANSCRIPT-CTRL0000039559.pdf.

Quested, Nick. Testimony of Nick Quested at live hearing, House Select Committee to Investigate the January 6th Attack on the United States Capitol, June 9, 2022, https://www.c-span.org/program/january-6-hearings/first-hearing-on-investigation-of-january-6-attack-on-the-us-capitol/612368.

Quigley, Mike. Interview with the author, December 14, 2021.

Raju, Manu. Interview with the author, March 18, 2025.

Raskin, Jamie. Interview with the author, May 30, 2024.

Riddle, Jason. Interview with the author, February 11, 2025.

Rodriguez, Daniel. USA vs. Rodriguez, Exhibit A, FBI interview from March 31, 2021, https://storage.courtlistener.com/recap/gov.uscourts.dcd.229256/gov.uscourts.dcd.229256.38.1.pdf.

Rounds, Mike. Interview with the author, January 26, 2024.

Salesses, Robert. Testimony of Robert Salesses, Senate Homeland Security and Governmental Affairs Committee and Senate Rules Committee, March 3, 2021, https://www.hsgac.senate.gov/wp-content/uploads/imo/media/doc/Testimony-Salesses-2021-03-03.pdf.

Schiff, Adam. Interviews with the author, January 13, 2021, December 10, 2021, and December 4, 2024.

Schornack, Robert. Transcribed Interview of Robert Schornack, House Select Committee to Investigate the January 6th Attack on the United States Capitol, February 1, 2022, https://www.govinfo.gov/content/pkg/GPO-J6-TRANSCRIPT-CTRL0000040480/pdf/GPO-J6-TRANSCRIPT-CTRL0000040480.pdf.

Schumer, Chuck. "Majority Leader Schumer Floor Remarks on the First Anniversary of the January 6th Insurrection of the US Capitol," January 6, 2022, https://www.democrats.senate.gov/newsroom/press-releases/majority-leader-schumer-floor-remarks-on-the-first-anniversary-of-the-january-6th-insurrection-of-the-us-capitol.

Serock, Katie. AOC Staff, "U.S. Capitol Cleanup," January 15, 2021, https://www.aoc.gov/explore-capitol-campus/blog/us-capitol-clean-up.

Sherman, Stephen. USA vs. Alberts, Victim Impact Statement, July 19, 2023, https://storage.courtlistener.com/recap/gov.uscourts.dcd.226717/gov.uscourts.dcd.226717.179.0.pdf.

Sherrill, Mikie. Interview with the author, December 22, 2021.

Short, Marc. Deposition of Marc Short, House Select Committee to Investigate the January 6th Attack on the United States Capitol, January 26, 2022, https://www.govinfo.gov/content/pkg/GPO-J6-TRANSCRIPT-CTRL0000038861/pdf/GPO-J6-TRANSCRIPT-CTRL0000038861.pdf.

Sicknick, Craig. Interview with the author, February 12, 2025.

Sicknick, Gladys. Interview with the author, February 12, 2025.

Sicknick, Ken. Interview with the author, February 12, 2025.

Stefanik, Elise. Alex Gault, "Stefanik Tells of Hiding During Mob Attack on Capitol: 'It Was Very, Very Scary,'" *Watertown Daily Times*, January 8, 2021, https://www.adirondackdailyenterprise.com/news/local-news/2021/01/stefanik-tells-of-hiding-during-mob-attack-on-capitol-it-was-very-very-scary/.

Stern, Keith. Interview with the author, October 8, 2024.

Summers, Tia. USA vs. Fitzsimons, Transcript of Bench Trial, August 16, 2022, https://storage.courtlistener.com/recap/gov.uscourts.dcd.228113/gov.uscourts.dcd.228113.136.0.pdf.

Sund, Steven. Testimony by Steven Sund, Senate Homeland Security and Governmental Affairs Committee and Senate Rules Committee, February 23, 2021, https://www.rules.senate.gov/imo/media/doc/BA0E3F52-5056-A066-6078-13F30593703C/Testimony_Sund.pdf; Transcribed Interview of Steven Sund, House Select Committee to Investigate the January 6th Attack on the United States Capitol, April 20, 2022, https://www.govinfo.gov/app/details/GPO-J6-TRANSCRIPT-CTRL0000071087.

Taylor, Andrew. "The Day My 'Second Home,' the Capitol, Was Overtaken by Mob," The Associated Press, January 7, 2021, https://apnews.com/article/mitch-mcconnell-electoral-college-0dae4e82df7392d1aff053d5a80c06cf.

Thompson, Bennie. Interview with the author, July 9, 2021.

Thompson, Dustin. USA vs. Thompson, Transcript of Jury Trial—Volume 3 of 4, April 13, 2022, https://storage.courtlistener.com/recap/gov.uscourts.dcd.228115/gov.uscourts.dcd.228115.108.0.pdf.

Torres, Norma. Interview with the author, December 16, 2021.

Trump, Donald. Colleen Long, "Harris Is Speaking at the Same Spot Where Trump Fanned Anger on Jan. 6, 2021. Here's What Happened," The Associated Press, October 24, 2024, https://apnews.com/article/kamala-harris-donald-trump-2024-election-599719041f7d51b541f4f024936ad8d8.

Tuberville, Tommy. Interview with reporters, February 12, 2021, sent to Capitol Hill pool by Trish Turner, ABC News.

Wade, Paul. USA vs. Fitzsimons, Transcript of Bench Trial, August 16, 2022, https://storage.courtlistener.com/recap/gov.uscourts.dcd.228113/gov.uscourts.dcd.228113.136.0.pdf.

Walker, William. Testimony of William Walker, Senate Homeland Security and Governmental Affairs Committee and Senate Rules Committee, March 3, 2021, https://www.hsgac.senate.gov/wp-content/uploads/imo/media/doc/Testimony-Walker-2021-03-03.pdf.

Walters, Jeff. AOC Staff, "U.S. Capitol Cleanup," January 15, 2021, https://www.aoc.gov/explore-capitol-campus/blog/us-capitol-clean-up.

Warner, Mark. Interview with the author, September 16, 2024.

Watkins, Jessica. USA vs. Rhodes, Transcript of Jury Trial, afternoon session, November 16, 2022, https://storage.courtlistener.com/recap/gov.uscourts.dcd.239207/gov.uscourts.dcd.239207.764.0.pdf.

Welch, Peter. Interview with the author, December 14, 2021.

Wickham, Thomas. Interview with the author, February 13, 2025.

Wild, Susan. "January 6 Views from the House," C-SPAN, August 22, 2021, https://www.c-span.org/program/january-6-views-from-the-house/january-6-views-from-the-house-representatives-jim-mcgovern-and-susan-wild/596356.

Yetter, Kyle. USA vs. Grider, Transcript of Bench Trial, December 13, 2022, https://storage.courtlistener.com/recap/gov.uscourts.dcd.226617/gov.uscourts.dcd.226617.154.0.pdf.

NOTES

Prologue

1. Senate Committee on Homeland Security and Governmental Affairs and Senate Rules and Administration Committee, Joint Report, "Examining the U.S. Capitol Attack: A Review of the Security, Planning and Response Failures on January 6," June 8, 2021, https://www.rules.senate.gov/imo/media/doc/Jan%206%20HSGAC%20Rules%20Report.pdf (hereafter cited as Senate Joint Report).

2. Devlin Barrett, Matt Zapotosky, Carole D. Leonnig, and Julie Tate, "FBI Report Warned of 'War' at Capitol, Contradicting Claims There Was No Indication of Looming Violence," *The Washington Post*, January 12, 2021, https://www.washingtonpost.com/national-security/capitol-riot-fbi-intelligence/2021/01/12/30d12748-546b-11eb-a817-e5e7f8a406d6_story.html.

3. Senate Joint Report.

4. Kevin Liptak, "A List of the Times Trump Has Said He Won't Accept the Election Results or Leave Office If He Loses," CNN, September 24, 2020, https://www.cnn.com/2020/09/24/politics/trump-election-warnings-leaving-office.

5. USA vs. Rhodes, Transcript of Jury Trial, US District Court for the District of Columbia, October 7, 2022, https://storage.courtlistener.com/recap/gov.uscourts.dcd.239207/gov.uscourts.dcd.239207.719.0.pdf.

6. The American Presidency Project, Tweets of December 19, 2020, https://www.presidency.ucsb.edu/documents/tweets-december-19-2020.

7. Senate Joint Report.

8. Michael Balsamo, "Disputing Trump, Barr Says No Widespread Election Fraud," The Associated Press, December 1, 2020, https://apnews.com/article/barr-no-widespread-election-fraud-b1f1488796c9a98c4b1a9061a6c7f49d.

9. Mark Sherman, "Electoral College Makes It Official: Biden Won, Trump Lost," The Associated Press, December 14, 2020, https://apnews.com/article/electoral-college-confirm-joe-biden-win-2d4fd7368d8fd6cb47ff0b2cc206271a.

10. Kevin Freking and Lisa Mascaro, "Trump, House Lawmakers Plot Futile Effort to Block Biden Win," The Associated Press, December 21, 2020, https://apnews.com

/article/election-2020-joe-biden-donald-trump-mo-brooks-elections-927d23e741ff72ca73afe734ffe278d.

11. Congressional Research Service, "Joint Session of Congress for Counting Electoral Votes for President," December 10, 2024, https://www.congress.gov/crs-product/R48309#:~:text=On%20January%206%2C%20or%20another,the%20election%20is%20formally%20announced.

12. C-SPAN, "Electoral College Ballot Count," January 6, 2005, https://www.c-span.org/program/joint-session-of-congress/electoral-college-ballot-count/139350.

13. C-SPAN, "Counting of Electoral College Votes," January 6, 2017, https://www.c-span.org/program/campaign-2016/counting-of-electoral-college-votes/465852.

14. Freking and Mascaro, "Trump, House Lawmakers Plot Futile Effort to Block Biden Win."

15. Mike Pence, *So Help Me God* (New York: Simon and Schuster, 2022).

16. Farnoush Amiri, "How the Trump Fake Electors Scheme Became a 'Corrupt Plan,' According to the Indictment," The Associated Press, December 18, 2023, https://apnews.com/article/donald-trump-jan-6-investigation-fake-electors-608932d4771f6e2e3c5efb3fdcd8fcce.

17. Pence, *So Help Me God.*

18. Senate Joint Report.

19. Senate Joint Report.

20. Senate Joint Report.

21. Senate Joint Report.

22. Senate Joint Report.

23. Senate Joint Report.

24. Senate Joint Report.

25. Senate Joint Report.

26. "Subject: Administrative: Security Information—Wednesday, January 6 Joint Session," email to House staff from House Sergeant at Arms Paul Irving, January 4, 2021.

27. Donald Trump, @realDonaldTrump, Twitter, January 5, 2021, 5:05 p.m., https://x.com/realDonaldTrump/status/1346578706437963777.

28. Interview with Sicknick family, February 12, 2025.

9:00 a.m.

1. *Pelosi in the House*, directed by Alexandra Pelosi, HBO, 2022, https://www.hbo.com/movies/pelosi-in-the-house.

2. Author interviews.

3. *Pelosi in the House.*

4. Mike Pence, *So Help Me God* (New York: Simon and Schuster, 2022).

5. Kevin Freking and Lisa Mascaro, "Trump, House Lawmakers Plot Futile Effort to Block Biden Win," The Associated Press, December 21, 2020, https://apnews.com/article/election-2020-joe-biden-donald-trump-mo-brooks-elections-927d23e741ff7b2ca73afe734ffe278d.

6. Michael Tackett, *The Price of Power* (New York: Simon and Schuster, 2024).

7. Lisa Mascaro and Mary Clare Jalonick, "McConnell Warns GOP Off Electoral College Brawl in Congress," The Associated Press, December 15, 2020, https://apnews.com/article/mitch-mcconnell-congratulates-joe-biden-2ed09a34fbbc3342fe45c733ee0dd725.

8. "Trump Lashes Out at Thune: 'He Will Be Primaried in 2022,'" The Associated Press, December 23, 2020, https://apnews.com/article/joe-biden-donald-trump-media-south-dakota-social-media-f184932e1dddde9ace5374f1d059164a.

9. "Sen. Hawley Will Object During Electoral College Certification Process on Jan 6," office of Sen. Josh Hawley, December 30, 2020.

10. Lisa Mascaro and Mary Clare Jalonick, "More GOP Lawmakers Enlist in Trump Effort to Undo Biden Win," The Associated Press, January 2, 2021, https://apnews.com/article/election-2020-joe-biden-donald-trump-michael-brown-mitch-mcconnell-7ff6b30f2e2f25c0cc7e1d7420a0f058.

11. "Joint Statement from Senators Cruz, Johnson, Lankford, Daines, Kennedy, Blackburn, Braun, Senators-Elect Lummis, Marshall, Hagerty, Tuberville," office of Sen. Ted Cruz, January 2, 2021, https://www.cruz.senate.gov/newsroom/press-releases/joint-statement-from-senators-cruz-johnson-lankford-daines-kennedy-blackburn-braun-senators-elect-lummis-marshall-hagerty-tuberville.

11:00 a.m.

1. USA vs. Alberts, Transcript of Jury Trial, US District Court for the District of Columbia, April 17, 2023, https://storage.courtlistener.com/recap/gov.uscourts.dcd.226717/gov.uscourts.dcd.226717.156.0.pdf.

2. FBI Interview of Doug Jensen, January 8, 2021, https://storage.courtlistener.com/recap/gov.uscourts.dcd.225865/gov.uscourts.dcd.225865.69.1_2.pdf.

3. "Final Report," House Select Committee to Investigate the January 6th Attack on the United States Capitol, December 22, 2022, p. 585, https://www.govinfo.gov/content/pkg/GPO-J6-REPORT/pdf/GPO-J6-REPORT.pdf.

4. "Review of the U.S. Department of the Interior's Actions Related to January 6, 2021," Office of the Inspector General, US Department of the Interior, December 18, 2023, https://www.doioig.gov/sites/default/files/2021-migration/SpecialReview_Review%20of%20the%20U.S.%20Department%20of%20the%20Interior%E2%80%99s%20Actions%20Related%20to%20January%206%2C%202021.pdf.

5. C-SPAN, "President Trump's January 6 Rally Speech," January 6, 2021, https://www.c-span.org/program/campaign-2020/president-trumps-january-6-rally-speech/587224.

12:00 p.m.

1. "Transcript of Trump's Speech at Rally Before Capitol Riot," The Associated Press, January 13, 2021, https://apnews.com/article/election-2020-joe-biden-donald-trump-capitol-siege-media-e79eb5164613d6718e9f4502eb471f27.

2. Videos of the House floor proceedings on January 6, 2021, along with remarks excerpted from the debate, can be found on C-SPAN, "Breach of U.S. Capitol January 6, 2021," January 6, 2021, https://www.c-span.org/program/us-house-of-representatives/breach-of-us-capitol-january-6-2021/607039; written transcripts of floor action and floor debate are found in the Congressional Record, https://www.congress.gov/117/crec/2021/01/06/167/4/CREC-2021-01-06-house.pdf.

3. Videos of the Senate floor proceedings on January 6, 2021, along with remarks excerpted from debate, can be found on C-SPAN, "Senate Session," January 6, 2021, https://www.c-span.org/program/us-senate/senate-session/587150; written transcripts of

floor action and floor debate are found in the Congressional Record, https://www.congress.gov/117/crec/2021/01/06/167/4/CREC-2021-01-06-senate.pdf.

4. Mike Pence, *So Help Me God* (New York: Simon and Schuster, 2022).

5. *Pelosi in the House*, directed by Alexandra Pelosi, HBO, 2022, https://www.hbo.com/movies/pelosi-in-the-house.

6. Chris Cameron and Michael Gold, "Trump Acknowledges He Wanted to Go to the Capitol on Jan. 6," *The New York Times*, May 1, 2024, https://www.nytimes.com/2024/05/01/us/politics/trump-capitol-jan-6.html.

7. "United States Capitol Police Timeline for January 6, 2021 Attack," https://www.govinfo.gov/content/pkg/GPO-J6-DOC-CTRL0000000056/pdf/GPO-J6-DOC-CTRL0000000056.pdf.

8. "United States Capitol Police Timeline for January 6, 2021 Attack."

9. Deposition of Henry Tarrio, House Select Committee to Investigate the January 6th Attack on the United States Capitol, February 4, 2022, https://www.govinfo.gov/content/pkg/GPO-J6-TRANSCRIPT-CTRL0000042157/pdf/GPO-J6-TRANSCRIPT-CTRL0000042157.pdf.

10. Kathleen Ronayne and Michael Kunzelman, "Trump to Far-Right Extremists: 'Stand Back and Stand By,'" The Associated Press, September 30, 2020, https://apnews.com/article/election-2020-joe-biden-race-and-ethnicity-donald-trump-chris-wallace-0b32339da25fbc9e8b7c7c7066a1db0f.

11. District of Columbia vs. Proud Boys International, "Amended Complaint," US District Court for the District of Columbia, April 1, 2022, https://storage.courtlistener.com/recap/gov.uscourts.dcd.238425/gov.uscourts.dcd.238425.94.0.pdf.

12. District of Columbia vs. Proud Boys International, "Amended Complaint."

13. House Select Committee to Investigate the January 6th Attack on the United States Capitol, video at live hearing, June 9, 2021, https://www.c-span.org/program/january-6-hearings/first-hearing-on-investigation-of-january-6-attack-on-the-us-capitol/612368.

14. Transcribed Interview of Caroline Edwards, House Select Committee to Investigate the January 6th Attack on the United States Capitol, April 18, 2022, https://www.govinfo.gov/content/pkg/GPO-J6-TRANSCRIPT-CTRL0000082302/pdf/GPO-J6-TRANSCRIPT-CTRL0000082302.pdf.

15. Transcribed Interview of Caroline Edwards, House Select Committee to Investigate the January 6th Attack on the United States Capitol, April 18, 2022, https://www.govinfo.gov/content/pkg/GPO-J6-TRANSCRIPT-CTRL0000082302/pdf/GPO-J6-TRANSCRIPT-CTRL0000082302.pdf.

16. House Select Committee to Investigate the January 6th Attack on the United States Capitol, live hearing, June 9, 2021.

17. House Select Committee to Investigate the January 6th Attack on the United States Capitol, live hearing, June 9, 2021.

18. "United States Capitol Police Timeline for January 6, 2021 Attack."

1:00 p.m.

1. Mike Pence, *So Help Me God* (New York: Simon and Schuster, 2022), 449.

2. District of Columbia vs. Proud Boys International, "Amended Complaint," April 1, 2022, https://storage.courtlistener.com/recap/gov.uscourts.dcd.238425/gov.uscourts.dcd.238425.94.0.pdf.

3. "United States Capitol Police Timeline for January 6, 2021 Attack," https://www.govinfo.gov/content/pkg/GPO-J6-DOC-CTRL0000000056/pdf/GPO-J6-DOC-CTRL0000000056.pdf.

4. Testimony of Thomas Loyd, USA vs. Nordean et al., Transcript of Jury Trial—Day 14, January 13, 2023, https://storage.courtlistener.com/recap/gov.uscourts.dcd.228300/gov.uscourts.dcd.228300.943.0.pdf.

5. USA vs. Jensen, "Government's Sentencing Memorandum," December 6, 2022, https://storage.courtlistener.com/recap/gov.uscourts.dcd.225865/gov.uscourts.dcd.225865.107.0.pdf.

6. USA vs. Jensen, "Government's Sentencing Memorandum."

7. Eliot Spagat and Amy Taxin, "Woman Fatally Shot at Capitol Echoed Trump on Social Media," The Associated Press, January 7, 2021, https://apnews.com/article/donald-trump-us-news-shootings-san-diego-veterans-e8c7563ff4cce671a2b52a8e7645945c.

8. "Our Mission," 113th Wing, https://www.113wg.ang.af.mil/Mission-Organization.

9. "Ashli Babbitt, Enthusiastic Video Marching to Capitol," TMZ, January 7, 2021, https://www.tmz.com/2021/01/07/ashli-babbitt-final-video-marching-us-capitol-before-fatally-shot.

10. Spagat and Taxin, "Woman Fatally Shot at Capitol Echoed Trump on Social Media."

11. Martha Mendoza and Juliet Linderman, "Officers Maced, Trampled: Docs Expose Depth of Jan. 6 Chaos," The Associated Press, March 10, 2021, https://apnews.com/article/docs-expose-depth-january-6-capitol-siege-chaos-fd3204574c11e453be8fb4e3c81258c3.

12. USA vs. Rhodes et al., Indictment, January 13, 2022, https://www.justice.gov/archives/opa/press-release/file/1462481/dl.

13. USA vs. Rhodes et al., Indictment.

14. USA vs. Rhodes et al., Indictment.

15. USA vs. Nordean et al., "Dominic Pezzola Additional Sentencing Arguments," August 17, 2023, https://storage.courtlistener.com/recap/gov.uscourts.dcd.228300/gov.uscourts.dcd.228300.855.5.pdf.

16. Mary Clare Jalonick, "Stinging Report Raises New Questions About Capitol Security," The Associated Press, April 14, 2021, https://apnews.com/article/capitol-police-riot-security-failures-3309c46a9e0bc21c2b6f3287a2e3b831.

17. Nomaan Merchant and Colleen Long, "Police Command Structure Crumbled Fast During Capitol Riot," The Associated Press, January 18, 2021, https://apnews.com/article/police-command-structure-us-capitol-riot-a27921d08ca949c0b1e64c33628dd80e.

18. Metropolitan Police Department radio recordings from (1) "Senate Impeachment Trial Day 2, Part 3," C-SPAN, February 10, 2021, https://www.c-span.org/program/us-senate/senate-impeachment-trial-day-2-part-3/589124; (2) House Select Committee to Investigate the January 6th Attack on the United States Capitol, live hearing, June 9, 2021, https://www.c-span.org/program/january-6-hearings/first-hearing-on-investigation-of-january-6-attack-on-the-us-capitol/612368; (3) *The New York Times* visual investigation, "'We've Lost the Line!' Radio Traffic Reveals Police Under Siege at Capitol," https://www.nytimes.com/video/us/100000007655234/weve-lost-the-line-radio-traffic-reveals-police

-under-siege-at-capitol.html; (4) Dalton Bennett et al., "17 Requests for Backup in 78 Minutes," *The Washington Post*, https://www.washingtonpost.com/investigations/interactive/2021/dc-police-records-capitol-riot (hereafter cited as MPD radio recordings).

19. MPD radio recordings.

20. Michael Kunzelman, "Wounded Man Who Invaded Senate with Knife Sentenced to Prison for Capitol Riot," The Associated Press, May 16, 2023, https://apnews.com/article/capitol-riot-joshua-black-sentencing-alabama-knife-de16d97c5efc2e7f4c000d683ff73df4.

21. MPD radio recordings.

22. Michael Tackett, *The Price of Power* (New York: Simon and Schuster, 2024).

2:00 p.m.

1. USA vs. Jensen, "Government's Sentencing Memorandum," December 6, 2022, https://storage.courtlistener.com/recap/gov.uscourts.dcd.225865/gov.uscourts.dcd.225865.107.0.pdf.

2. Roger Parloff (@rparloff), post on X of video court exhibit in USA vs. Nordean et al., March 13, 2023, https://x.com/rparloff/status/1635259149423607808.

3. USA vs. Nordean et al., "Third Superseding Indictment," June 6, 2022, https://storage.courtlistener.com/recap/gov.uscourts.dcd.228300/gov.uscourts.dcd.228300.380.0_5.pdf.

4. Elena Schor, "Sen. Lankford Criticizes Trump's False Voter Fraud Allegations," Politico, November 28, 2016, https://www.politico.com/story/2016/11/trump-voter-fraud-james-lankford-231878.

5. Nomaan Merchant, "New Riot Video Shows Officer Goodman Point Romney to Safety," The Associated Press, February 10, 2021, https://apnews.com/article/donald-trump-riots-impeachments-trump-impeachment-mitt-romney-6e43d3b499a30d9a77891d76ea923b6f.

6. Jack Gillum, Lucas Waldron, and Maya Eliahou, "'Where They Countin' the Votes?!': New Video Details Tense Moments as Capitol Mob Sought Out Lawmakers," ProPublica, January 15, 2021, https://www.propublica.org/article/capitol-eugene-goodman.

7. "Day of Rage: How Trump Supporters Took the U.S. Capitol," *The New York Times*, June 30, 2021, 21:10, https://www.nytimes.com/video/us/politics/100000007606996/capitol-riot-trump-supporters.html.

8. Mike Pence, *So Help Me God* (New York: Simon and Schuster, 2022), 463.

9. "Senate Impeachment Trial Day 2, Part 3," C-SPAN, February 10, 2021, 1:15:00, https://www.c-span.org/program/us-senate/senate-impeachment-trial-day-2-part-3/589124.

10. Michael Kunzelman, "Man Gets Prison for Attacking Capitol Officer Who Later Died," The Associated Press, January 27, 2023, https://apnews.com/article/politics-crime-legal-proceedings-capitol-siege-new-jersey-fe8477543a228ef7e3319363d967a075.

11. "Columbus Doors," Architect of the Capitol, https://www.aoc.gov/explore-capitol-campus/art/columbus-doors.

12. USA vs. Easterday, "Government's Sentencing Memorandum," April 16, 2024, https://storage.courtlistener.com/recap/gov.uscourts.dcd.250276/gov.uscourts.dcd.250276.115.0.pdf.

13. USA vs. Hemphill, "Government's Sentencing Memorandum," May 11, 2022, https://storage.courtlistener.com/recap/gov.uscourts.dcd.235161/gov.uscourts.dcd.235161.32.0_1.pdf.

14. Scott MacFarlane (@MacFarlaneNews), post on Twitter of government video exhibit, January 25, 2022, https://x.com/MacFarlaneNews/status/1486088649087332358.

15. "Third Hearing on Investigation of January 6 Attack on U.S. Capitol," video clip, House Select Committee to Investigate the January 6th Attack on the United States Capitol, June 16, 2022, https://www.c-span.org/clip/january-6-hearings/user-clip-january-6th-2021-riots-hang-mike-pence/5020172.

16. USA vs. Jensen, "Government's Sentencing Memorandum," December 6, 2022, https://storage.courtlistener.com/recap/gov.uscourts.dcd.225865/gov.uscourts.dcd.225865.107.0.pdf.

17. USA vs. Colt, "Government's Sentencing Memorandum," May 3, 2023, https://storage.courtlistener.com/recap/gov.uscourts.dcd.227088/gov.uscourts.dcd.227088.41.0.pdf.

18. Luke Mogelson, "A Reporter's Video from Inside the Capitol Siege," *The New Yorker*, January 16, 2021, https://www.newyorker.com/video/watch/a-reporters-footage-from-inside-the-capitol-siege.

19. USA vs. Black, "Government's Sentencing Memorandum," April 28, 2023, https://storage.courtlistener.com/recap/gov.uscourts.dcd.227700/gov.uscourts.dcd.227700.89.0_1.pdf.

20. Mogelson, "A Reporter's Video from Inside the Capitol Siege."

21. Mogelson, "A Reporter's Video from Inside the Capitol Siege."

22. Mogelson, "A Reporter's Video from Inside the Capitol Siege."

23. *Pelosi in the House*, directed by Alexandra Pelosi, HBO, 2022, https://www.hbo.com/movies/pelosi-in-the-house.

24. U.S. Committee on House Administration, "Obtained HBO Footage Shows Pelosi Again Taking Responsibility for Capitol Security on Jan. 6," August 28, 2024, https://cha.house.gov/2024/8/new-obtained-hbo-footage-shows-pelosi-again-taking-responsibility-for-capitol-security-on-january-6.

25. *Pelosi in the House.*

26. "Final Report," House Select Committee to Investigate the January 6th Attack on the United States Capitol, December 22, 2022, https://www.govinfo.gov/content/pkg/GPO-J6-REPORT/pdf/GPO-J6-REPORT.pdf.

27. "Day of Rage," 21:40.

28. Steve Cohen (@RepCohen), post of audio on Twitter, July 29, 2021, https://x.com/RepCohen/status/1420762277817556995.

29. USA vs. Alam, "Government's Sentencing Memorandum," April 5, 2024, https://storage.courtlistener.com/recap/gov.uscourts.dcd.228477/gov.uscourts.dcd.228477.123.0.pdf.

30. Jon Swaine et al., "Video Shows Fatal Shooting of Ashli Babbitt in the Capitol," *The Washington Post*, January 9, 2021, https://www.washingtonpost.com/investigations/2021/01/08/ashli-babbitt-shooting-video-capitol/.

31. USA vs. Alam, "Government's Sentencing Memorandum."

32. Swaine et al., "Video Shows Fatal Shooting of Ashli Babbitt in the Capitol."

33. Swaine et al., "Video Shows Fatal Shooting of Ashli Babbitt in the Capitol."

34. Swaine et al., "Video Shows Fatal Shooting of Ashli Babbitt in the Capitol."

35. Video provided to author by Nick Quested.

36. Donald Trump, @realDonaldTrump, Twitter, January 6, 2021, 2:38 p.m., https://x.com/realDonaldTrump/status/1346904110969315332?lang=en.

37. Zoe Tillman, "What an Hour Looked Like for Police on Jan. 6," Buzzfeed News, June 24, 2021, 2:41, https://www.buzzfeednews.com/article/zoetillmancapitol-riot-police-body-cam-footage.

38. USA vs. McCaughey et al., Transcript of Bench Trial—Day 2, August 30, 2022, https://storage.courtlistener.com/recap/gov.uscourts.dcd.226961/gov.uscourts.dcd.226961.633.0.pdf.

3:00 p.m.

1. Donald Trump, @realDonaldTrump, Twitter, January 6, 2021, 3:13 p.m., https://x.com/realDonaldTrump/status/1346912780700577792?lang=en.

2. *Pelosi in the House*, directed by Alexandra Pelosi, HBO, 2022, https://www.hbo.com/movies/pelosi-in-the-house.

3. Video shown at live hearing, House Select Committee to Investigate the January 6th Attack on the United States Capitol, July 21, 2022, https://www.c-span.org/program/january-6-hearings/eighth-hearing-on-investigation-of-january-6-attack-on-the-us-capitol/614883.

4. "Rep. Kevin McCarthy on Protesters Storming Capitol," Fox News, January 6, 2021, https://www.facebook.com/watch/?v=232725075039919.

4:00 p.m.

1. Sicknick family, interview with the author, February 12, 2025.

2. "President Donald Trump Video Statement on Capitol Protesters," C-SPAN, January 6, 2021, https://www.c-span.org/program/white-house-event/president-trump-video-statement-on-capitol-protesters/587285.

5:00 p.m.

1. "Final Report," House Select Committee to Investigate the January 6th Attack on the United States Capitol, December 22, 2022, p. 668, https://www.govinfo.gov/content/pkg/GPO-J6-REPORT/pdf/GPO-J6-REPORT.pdf.

2. "Final Report," House Select Committee to Investigate the January 6th Attack on the United States Capitol, December 22, 2022, https://www.govinfo.gov/content/pkg/GPO-J6-REPORT/pdf/GPO-J6-REPORT.pdf; Transcribed Interview of Rudy Giuliani, House Select Committee to Investigate the January 6th Attack on the United States Capitol, May 20, 2022, https://www.govinfo.gov/content/pkg/GPO-J6-TRANSCRIPT-CTRL0000083774/pdf/GPO-J6-TRANSCRIPT-CTRL0000083774.pdf.

3. Deposition of Marc Short, House Select Committee to Investigate the January 6th Attack on the United States Capitol, January 26, 2022, https://www.govinfo.gov/content/pkg/GPO-J6-TRANSCRIPT-CTRL0000038861/pdf/GPO-J6-TRANSCRIPT-CTRL0000038861.pdf.

4. Office of the Historian, U.S. House, "Mace of the U.S. House of Representatives," https://history.house.gov/Collection/Listing/2006/2006-162-000/.

5. "Tribute to Joyce Hamlett," remarks by Democratic Leader Hakeem Jeffries, *Congressional Record*, July 25, 2023, https://www.congress.gov/congressional-record/volume-169/issue-128/house-section/article/H3934-3.

6. Mike Pence, *So Help Me God* (New York: Simon and Schuster, 2022), 449.

7. *Pelosi in the House*, directed by Alexandra Pelosi, HBO, 2022, https://www.hbo.com/movies/pelosi-in-the-house.

6:00 p.m.

1. "Tweets of January 6, 2021," The American Presidency Project, https://www.presidency.ucsb.edu/documents/tweets-january-6-2021.

7:00 p.m.

1. *Pelosi in the House*, directed by Alexandra Pelosi, HBO, 2022, https://www.hbo.com/movies/pelosi-in-the-house.

2. USA vs. Barnett, "Government's Sentencing Memorandum," May 23, 2023, https://storage.courtlistener.com/recap/gov.uscourts.dcd.226952/gov.uscourts.dcd.226952.199.0_1.pdf.

8:00 p.m.

1. Sicknick family, interview with the author, February 12, 2025.

2. Michael Balsamo and Colleen Long, "Medical Ruling: Capitol Cop Sicknick Died of Natural Causes," The Associated Press, April 19, 2021, https://apnews.com/article/politics-government-and-politics-b497800805aedae48b72bc4837b90042.

3. Peter Hermann and Spencer S. Hsu, "Capitol Police Officer Brian Sicknick, Who Engaged Rioters, Suffered Two Strokes and Died of Natural Causes, Officials Say," *The Washington Post*, April 19, 2021, https://www.washingtonpost.com/local/public-safety/brian-sicknick-death-strokes/2021/04/19/36d2d310-617e-11eb-afbe-9a11a127d146_story.html.

4. Chris Cameron, "These Are the People Who Died in Connection with the Capitol Riot," *The New York Times*, January 5, 2022, https://www.nytimes.com/2022/01/05/us/politics/jan-6-capitol-deaths.html.

5. Colleen Long and Michael Balsamo, "Capitol Police Officers Sue Trump, Allies over Insurrection," The Associated Press, August 26, 2021, https://apnews.com/article/capitol-siege-michael-pence-4cd64aab06e0f943ca8f83fd0b65037d.

9:00 p.m.

1. Rowan Scarborough, "Facial Recognition Identifies Extremists Storming the Capitol," January 6, 2021, *The Washington Times*, https://www.washingtontimes.com/news/2021/jan/6/xrvision-firm-claims-antifa-infiltrated-protesters. A story correction reads, "An earlier version of this story incorrectly stated that XRVision facial recognition software identified Antifa members among rioters who stormed the Capitol Wednesday. XRVision did not identify any Antifa members. The Washington Times apologizes to XRVision for the error."

10:00 p.m.

1. Senate Votes, Vote No. 1, 117th Cong., 1st Sess., January 6, 2021, https://www.senate.gov/legislative/LIS/roll_call_votes/vote1171/vote_117_1_00001.htm.

2. Sen. Mike Braun to Capitol Hill pool, January 6, 2021, sent by Frank Thorp, NBC News.

3. Sen. John Thune call with South Dakota reporters, evening of January 6, 2021, notes from Stephen Groves, Associated Press reporter in Sioux Falls, SD.

4. USA vs. Howell, "Government's Sentencing Memorandum," February 23, 2022, https://storage.courtlistener.com/recap/gov.uscourts.dcd.228846/gov.uscourts.dcd.228846.35.0.pdf.

5. Alanna Durkin Richer, "'Fighting Fit': Trial to Show Oath Keepers' Road to Jan. 6," The Associated Press, September 24, 2022, https://apnews.com/article/capitol-siege-biden-presidential-elections-donald-trump-election-2020-e81901ad99b8ddc5c8f23280e67fa63e.

6. Lindsay Whitehurst, "Witness: Oath Keepers Head Tried to Reach Trump After Jan. 6," The Associated Press, November 2, 2022, https://apnews.com/article/capitol-siege-texas-donald-trump-veterans-conspiracy-d159e7b101fd7fc63f7821a0bc7daa9d.

7. USA vs. Alberts, "Government's Sentencing Memorandum," July 12, 2023, https://storage.courtlistener.com/recap/gov.uscourts.dcd.226717/gov.uscourts.dcd.226717.168.0.pdf.

11:00 p.m.

1. House Roll Call Votes, Roll Call No. 10, 117th Cong., 1st Sess., January 6, 2021, https://clerk.house.gov/Votes?CongressNum=117&Session=1st&Date=01/06/2021.

12:00 a.m.

1. Senate votes, Vote No. 2, 117th Cong., 1st Sess., January 7, 2021, https://www.senate.gov/legislative/LIS/roll_call_votes/vote1171/vote_117_1_00002.htm.

2:00 a.m.

1. House Roll Call Votes, Roll Call No. 11, 117th Cong., 1st Sess., January 7, 2021, https://clerk.house.gov/Votes/202111.

Early Morning

1. Lisa Mascaro et al., "Trump Impeached After Capitol Riot in Historic Second Charge," The Associated Press, January 13, 2021, https://apnews.com/article/trump-impeachment-vote-capitol-siege-0a6f2a348a6e43f27d5e1dc486027860.

2. Lisa Mascaro, Eric Tucker, and Mary Clare Jalonick, "Trump Acquitted, Denounced in Historic Impeachment Trial," The Associated Press, February 13, 2021, https://apnews.com/article/donald-trump-capitol-siege-riots-trials-impeachments-b245b52fd7d4a079ae199c954baba452.

INDEX

Credit: David Baratz

Mary Clare Jalonick covers Congress for the Associated Press, where she has worked for two decades. She has covered politics and policy under five presidents and reported from inside the Capitol on January 6th. She lives in the Washington, DC, area.